Strangers Either Way

European Anthropology in Translation
Published in Association with the Society for the Anthropology of
Europe (AAA)
Editor: **Susan Mazur-Stommen**, Research Anthropologist, University
of California, Riverside

This new series introduces research from a new generation of scholars working as Europeans and producing ethnographies of Europe. All these works
were originally published in their native languages and were only selected
for translation after a rigorous review process. This series gives an opportunity for fresh voices to be heard and gives an indication of what is to come
in the field of European Anthropology.

Strangers Either Way

The Lives of Croatian Refugees in Their New Home

Jasna Čapo Žmegač

translated by

Nina H. Antoljak
Mateusz M. Stanojević

Berghahn Books
New York • Oxford

First published in 2007 by
Berghahn Books
www.berghahnbooks.com

© 2007, 2011 Jasna Čapo Žmegač
First paperback edition published in 2011

© of the English-language edition Berghahn Books,
New York/Oxford.
Originally published as Srijemski Hrvati.
Etnološka studija migracije, identifikacije i interakcije
by Durieux in 2002.

Library of Congress Cataloging-in-Publication Data

Capo, Jasna.
  Strangers either way: the lives of Croatian refugees in their new home /
Jasna Capo Zmegac; translated by Nina H. Antoljak.
    p. cm. — (European anthropology in translation; vol. 2)
  Includes bibliographical references and index.
  ISBN 978-1-84545-317-6 (hbk) -- ISBN 978-0-85745-149-1 (pbk)
  1. Yugoslav War, 1991–1995—Refugees—Croatia. 2. Croats—Srem
(Serbia and Croatia)—History—20th century. 3. Srem (Serbia and Croa-
tia)—History—20th century. 4. Srem (Serbia and Croatia)—Ethnic rela-
tions. 5. Croats—Migrations—History—20th century. I. Title.

DR1313.7.R43C37
305.9'06914094972—dc22   2007007087

British Library Cataloguing in Publication Data

A catalogue record for this book is available from the British Library

Printed in the United States on acid-free paper

ISBN 978-1-84545-317-6 (hardback)
ISBN 978-0-85745-149-1 (paperback)

For my late mother,
who cherished her Srijem homeland above all

Contents

Acknowledgements

The list of those who have supported me in this long-lasting endeavor includes many of my close relatives and friends. Thank you all for your love, understanding, criticism, and last but not least, material support for the Croatian edition of the book.

It also includes several people who have in some way contributed to the English edition of the book. Foremost, my thanks should go to Nina H. Antoljak, whose fine translations and editing have accompanied me in this and in many other projects. I am also grateful to Mateusz Milan Stanojević for the translation of chapters 3 and 4, Ivo Žanić for his painstaking teachings in the matters of Croatian linguistics, and Mladen Klemenčić and Darko Sekeli for kindly supplying detailed maps for this edition. I thank the Croatian Ministry of Science, Technology and Sports and the Croatian Ministry of Culture for financially supporting the translation of the book, and my Croatian publisher, Durieux, for transferring copyright to me for all foreign publications of the book.

This book is dedicated to the memory of my dear mother, a loving and knowledgeable woman, who did not live to see its publication.

List of Maps

Map 1. Southeast Europe

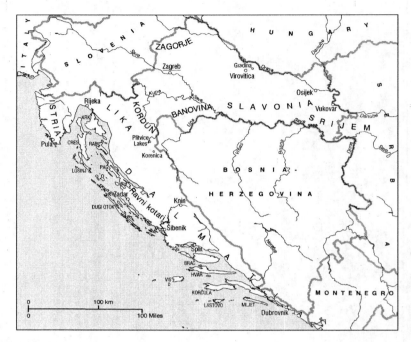

Map 2. Croatia

Map 3. Srijem at present

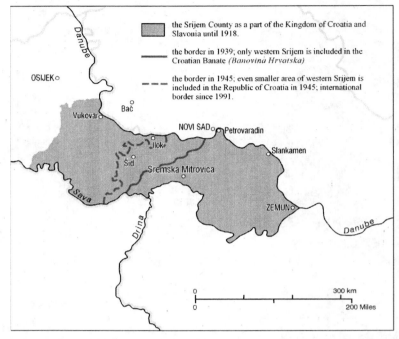

the Srijem County as a part of the Kingdom of Croatia and Slavonia until 1918.

the border in 1939; only western Srijem is included in the Croatian Banate *(Banovina Hrvatska)*

the border in 1945; even smaller area of western Srijem is included in the Republic of Croatia in 1945; international border since 1991.

Map 4. Changes of administrative borders in the region of Srijem 1986–1945

Introduction

Massive population displacements occurred in the former Yugoslavia, particularly in Croatia, Bosnia-Herzegovina, Kosovo and Vojvodina, during the 1990s (see map 1). The migrations took place within and outside of the former Yugoslav republics and provinces and ranged over various ethnic groups, particularly among the Croats, Serbs, and Muslims in the initial period, and later also the Albanians. Migration across the borders of the former Yugoslav republics resulted in ethnic homogenization of previously heterogenous populations.

Two types of migration can be differentiated in regard to the permanency of resettlement. The majority of the people were forced out of or fled from their homes in Croatia and Bosnia-Herzegovina during the hostilities in those states in 1991, 1992, and 1995 and in Kosovo in 1999, and were temporarily accommodated either in some other part of the former Yugoslavia or in European countries. Along with them, groups of migrants from Vojvodina, Kosovo, and Bosnia settled permanently in Croatia. This book will speak of the latter group, largely Croats, who moved from the Vojvodina part of Srijem to settle permanently in Croatia (see maps 1, 2, and 3).

The unsuccessful attempts at a solution of the Yugoslav "crisis" through political negotiations, which lead to war in Croatia in 1991 and 1992, caused endless problems for ethnic Croats living outside Croatia, particularly those in Vojvodina and Kosovo. Right up until the 1980s, these provinces in the former Yugoslav Republic of Serbia enjoyed considerable autonomy and, for all practical purposes, had equal standing with the six Yugoslav republics. However, in 1988, Serbia rescinded their independence and both provinces became Serbia's satellites. After Croatia's secession from the Yugoslav Federation in 1991, those provinces remained parts of Serbia, which, as the crisis intensified, initiated military attacks against Croatia. Spurred on by the hostilities and the troubles to which they were exposed in Serbia as an enemy ethnic group, numerous Croats started moving out of those regions at the end of 1991. This migration to Croatia took place either in an organized way as, for example, from the Kosovo village of Letnica (Duijzings 1995, 2000), or was disorganized and individual, as in the case of Vojvodina. In 1992, it became migration on a massive scale and, according to some estimates, some ten thousand people (Bičanić 1999: 197) moved out of Vojvodina between June and August 1992. It is estimated that a total of between thirty and forty-five thousand Croats left the province to resettle in Croatia (Bićanić 1994, 1999; Černelić 1994: 73), of whom twenty-two thousand were settlers from Srijem and the remainder largely from Bačka, another province in Vojvodina.

The exodus of the Croatian population from Vojvodina, largely from Srijem, bears the characteristics of forced migration, and, since this was migration to Croatia—their "ethnic homeland" (Heleniak 1997)—we may also refer to it as being "ethnically privileged" (Münz and Ohliger 1997: 7) or "coethnic migration." According to Rogers Brubaker (1995, 1998), such population displacements are engendered by transitions from multinational empires or states to incipient nation states. Under certain conditions, the reconfiguration of political space along national lines and the concomitant ethnic homogenization entail the migration of ethnic/national groups which, in the aftermath of the multinational state, are transformed into national minorities in new nation states. These minorities move to their "ethnic homeland," that is, to nation states in which they become part of the national majority.

The new settlers were largely Croats, although there were members of other ethnic groups among them: Serbs, Hungarians, Slovaks, Roma, Ruthenians, etc. The majority came from villages and had a secure economic base in Croatia, since they had exchanged their holdings—houses, vegetable gardens, land and farm implements—with Serbs from Croatia who moved to Serbia. As well as providing existential security, the exchange of holdings also gave social security and offered a foundation for integration in the new environment. More or less compact immigration of the main body of Srijem Croats into homeland communities in various areas of Croatia lead to confrontation of the diverse life styles of the immigrants and the homeland inhabitants. Even though their displacement increased ethnic homogenization in some hitherto ethnically heterogenous regions—regions with both Croatian and Serbian populations—at the same time it resulted in the cultural diversification of Croatia. The consequences of heightened cultural heterogeneity on Croatian ethnicity and the nation have not been given specific attention in scholarly studies in Croatia. It can be assumed that the underlying reason for this has been the expectation that the coethnic population would integrate speedily and easily, and contribute to the creation of an unproblematic and monolithic national identity that was part of the political agenda in the mid 1990s.

However, as shown by this anthropological study of the processes of identification of the newly settled Srijem migrants in a village in northern Croatia, the common national belonging of the new and old inhabitants did not play a substantial integrating role. The support given to the Srijem Croats at the state level, and also at the regional and local government level as well as the initially pronounced homogeneity of the nation caused by the war in Croatia, were not strongly echoed in the concrete migration situation.

According to Georg Simmel, the immigrant position is constituted by a synthesis of nearness and distance. Immigrants share with the local people in the place of resettlement only some general similarities. Being too general, the similarities bind the immigrants to the locals only to the extent that they draw them nearer, on the whole, to all other people. Therefore, distance wins out over nearness and the immigrant is perceived as a stranger (Simmel 1984). The reverse also holds in the case under observation: the immigrants perceive the homeland population as strangers. To paraphrase Wolfgang Kaschuba (1996), the German ethnologist, who speaks of the attitude of Germans from former West and East Germany toward each other after unification, or, for her part Regina Römhild (1999), who speaks of the stance of the homeland population of Germany toward the newly settled ethnic Germans from the former USSR: homeland inhabitants and new settlers became foreigners to one another. As a result of the perception of mutual cultural diversities, the characteristic common to both groups—their belonging to the same nation—shows itself to be too general and too abstract to bind the two groups. The reality of these perceptions is not decisive in the relations between the two groups. The perceptions are based on a selection of characteristics to which features of diversity are ascribed in order to prove the "foreign character" and "otherness" of the other group. Although they are only representations about the Other, they act as social facts.

It is not the intention of this study to establish the "accuracy" or "reality" of the images and perceptions that the migrants and the homeland population harbor about each other, but to research the emergence of the symbolic boundaries between the two groups and their function in social interaction, at the micro- and macro-level. The focus of the study is dislocated from establishing the "essence" of the groups to analysis of the manner of representation of their own and the other group, and to interpretation of the individual and collective strategies of self-identification and identification of others in the specific situation of a coethnic encounter.

My hope is that this book will contribute to a better understanding of the dynamics of identity and multicultural interaction within the national community. Analysis of the settlers' identity building in the processes of adaptation and integration into the local community, and of their construct of the homeland inhabitants as Others (and vice versa—perceptions of and attribution of differences to the migrants on the part of the homeland inhabitants), followed by analysis of the role of stereotypes and national rhetoric in the processes of attribution of identity, will enable an insight into the particular migration and resettlement circumstances as well as into the misunderstandings that arose between the homeland population and the new settlers.

Let us look here at the themes of the chapters in this book. Epistemological, theoretical, and methodological premises of the study, as well as the information on the migrants and the area of resettlement are presented in chapter 1. In chapter 2, the Srijem Croats lead us into the theme with their narrations about exchanging their homes and land, with comments on the irreplaceability of things they left behind in Srijem. In chapter 3, an analysis is given of the settlers' individual strategies of identification in the researched location. Attention is paid in chapter 4 to the elderly settlers and the changes they experienced as a result of the caesura imposed upon their lives by the forced migration. Attributing superior identity to their own group at the local level is the subject of analysis in chapter 5, while in chapter 6, the process of ethnic community formation is observed from the aspect of the organized activities of the migrants in Croatian society.[1] Chapter 7 summarizes the foregoing chapters and interprets the encounter between the migrants and the homeland population as a paradigmatic social configuration resulting from the process of migration in the course of which two formerly independent groups become interdependent as neighbors. The last chapter—the Epilogue—has been added to the English edition. It is a reflection on the reception experienced by the Croatian edition of the book (Čapo Žmegač 2002b).

Notes

1. Some material presented in chapters 3, 5, and 6 has been used in other publications (Čapo Žmegač 1999, 2000a, 2002a).

Chapter 1

The Ethnology of Individuals

European ethnology deals with so-called "ordinary" people and directs its attention at their cultural expression: material possessions, utilitarian objects, oral and written tradition, habits, particular activities, and modes of behavior. All of these types of cultural phenomena rely on the corresponding images and conceptions. Therefore, everyday reality consists of two layers and can be studied on two levels: at the level of observation and at the level of representations.

At the end of the 1980s, the respected German ethnologist, Helge Gerndt (1988: 9) claimed that European ethnology up to that time had dealt more with the external cultural world, the world of cultural phenomena, and less with the internal world of thought and representations: worldviews, mentalities, style of life, class awareness, and the like. The author interpreted that shortcoming by the greater demands placed on researchers in analysis of collective representations in comparison with descriptions, for example, of village economies.

However, just that collection of papers on stereotypes, which contained Gerndt's cited article, was one in a series of books and articles which amply made up for the shortcoming from the second half of the 1980s. In any case, it is doubtful whether this was a characteristic of European ethnology as a whole.[1] There is no doubt, however, that Gerndt's evaluation can be applied to a major part of Croatian ethnology. Although research was done on cultural values as early as the 1970s (Rihtman-Auguštin 1970), only over the last ten years or so can one speak to any greater extent about research into collective representations, largely within the framework of thematic research into identity building and research into mentality (Čapo Žmegač 1994, Grbić 1994, 1996, 1997; Povrzanović

1995, 1997; Povrzanović and Jambrešić Kirin 1996; Rihtman-Auguštin 1991, 1996, 1997, 2000; Zebec 1998, 2005; Žanić 1998).

The Individual and Her/His Culture

Identity is the notion that has characterized recent European ethnological practice and since the 1980s, has displaced the key term until then–culture (Frykman 1999: 18). With the transfer of focus to identity research, research into objective cultural content has been neglected at the expense of analysis of the subjective internal world of people: the representations of persons about themselves and about others, and about the cultural world in which they live. That process is in direct relation to the abandonment of the structural-functional paradigm, to the redefinition of the subject matter of research and criticism of objectivistic epistemologies in ethnological and anthropological research in the second half of the twentieth century, and to an orientation toward symbolic analyses that treat subjective meaning as an ethnological/anthropological issue. Expounding those processes would be outside the scope of interest and theme of this book. Therefore, I shall limit myself to indicating those that are relevant to it: shifts in research and the conception of culture and the role of the individual in creating and using culture.

Right up until today, the reified comprehension of culture as a coherent, integrated, homogenous, and static system of thought, belief, behavior patterns, products, and the like, which characterize a particular group, has prevailed in everyday speech and use. As the result of such understanding, culture is utilized in identifying social entities (ethnic groups, nations, and other groups), which, analogously to the assumed characteristics of culture, are given the attributes of homogeneity, fundamental diversity, and incommensurability with other such entities (Abu-Lughod 1991; Baumann 1996; Stolcke 1996).

Reexamining the discipline, anthropologists see a threat in the notion of culture, since it essentializes the differences between human groups (Rihtman-Auguštin 1994; Wolf 1994). Some contemporary theoreticians have therefore supported the idea of "writing against culture," that is, that this concept be replaced in ethnological and anthropological disciplines by the concepts of discourse and practice (Abu-Lughod 1991: 147–148). Others emphasize that culture is primarily an analytical and heuristic concept, and not a reified given. The following definition of culture derives from Geertz's semiotic concept of culture as an interactive symbolic system, whose meanings are not given in advance but are the subject of constant negotiation between social actors:

> [C]ulture is not a real thing, but an abstract and purely analytical notion. It does not cause behaviour, but summarizes an abstraction from it, and is thus neither normative nor predictive. As a deliberate abstraction it is there to help anthropologists conceptualize that ever-changing "complex whole" . . . through which people engage in the continual process of accounting, in a mutually meaningful manner, for what they do, say, and might think. Culture thus exists only insofar as it is performed, and even then its ontological status is that of a pointedly analytical abstraction (Baumann 1996: 11).

Thus, culture is not a closed, once-and-forever defined list of elements characteristic to a particular group and possessed by an individual, but rather an open system of meanings that people constantly reinterpret, utilizing its resources for defining their own position in society. Such understanding casts aside cultural logic (Stolcke 1996) that attributes a particular culture to a community as a fixed given, which, within an altered context, as for example in the migratory situation, is nurtured and, indeed, retraditionalized with the intensification of certain protoforms (Schuladen 1994: 54–55), or abandoned, usually with its being pushed aside into the private sphere.

If culture is not a reified whole with certain fixed content, if it is not a thing that people possess and which defines their behavior, but is the result of negotiations and agreement between social actors, then it is necessary to revisit the role of the individual in culture. In that case, we can no longer call individuals "culture-bearers."[2] They are not victims of imposed external structures, that is, culture and society; they are not passive recipients of the culture into which they have been enculturated; and they are not the replicas or reflections of the social structures within which they find themselves. According to psychosocial, ethnological, and other theories, largely of modernistic provenance, the claim is that the individual in the process of self-realization is her/himself a "culture-builder."[3] Neither culture nor identity are imposed on the individual from outside: in interpreting in her/his own specific manner the meaning of the system in which s/he lives, the individual places her/himself in an active relationship with culture and society in the process of self-identification, while the subject matter of ethnological and anthropological analysis are the processes of creating culture and strategies and discourses of identification of the individual and the group in the dynamic corelationship with culture.

Modernistic theories explain the recent boom in identity research with the characteristics of contemporary society. In other words, it is believed that the identity of the individual in premodern societies would be shaped by the social and cultural context in which s/he lived and that the representations and values common to groups would define to a considerable extent the question of who the individual is.[4] Contrary to that, argue theoreticians of the modern age, the capability of giving a priori sense to social subjects has been lost in the context of modernity. In other words, tradition is not imposed on the individual, but rather s/he is relatively free to define her/his own cultural heritage her/himself, in keeping with her/his own needs and wishes, but also with the pressures to which s/he is exposed. The theory of modernity leaves individuals broad room for self-building and self-definition, while it regards the construction of identity to be the project of the individual aimed at the development of one's own, "authentic" self (Frykman 1999: 18; Siebers 2000: 233ff.). In the equally fragmented and globalized modern world, in which "culture appears as something discordant and pluralistic, characterized by non-sharing and difference" (Siebers 2000: 235), according to Giddens' variant of modernistic theory, the individual manages to build her/his own coherent identity by its constant revision with the aid of autobiographic narrations, the constant reflexive inscription of her/his history in the light of new knowledge attained and the new juncture in which s/he lives, and by actively relating to the social environment and configurations of values that it offers (Giddens, according to Siebers 2000; see also Camilleri 1998; Frykman 1999).

Socio-psychological, psychological, psychoanalytical, and anthropological theories describe the process of identity building in almost the same way, emphasizing the active role of the individual in that process (Lipiansky 1998: 143–147). They argue that individual identity with its dual dimensions—personal and social—is the result of the interaction between the mental mechanisms of the individual and social factors (institutions). The concept of "inter-structuring of subjects and institutions" (Tap, according to Lipiansky 1998) explains the mechanisms of identification of the individual and the interiorization of social models, stressing that identity is not the result of the mechanical and one way influences of society on the individual. In the process of identification, the individual is socialized into the social environment but also differentiates and individualizes from it. Therefore, the social identity of the individual is not a reflection of her/his social roles: it is a dynamic totality in which diverse social components are mutually active, while the individual interprets them in an effort to establish the continuity of her/his experience and the definition of who she or he is. The identity of the individual is the result of tensions between the maintenance of one's own coherence, one's own ontological identity, and the values of the culture in which one lives, which confers the characteristics to another dimension of identity. Carmel Camilleri, the French cultural psychologist, calls that other dimension of identity pragmatic or instrumental (Camilleri 1998: 254). The tensions between personal and social values are solved by identity strategies.

The Relational Notion of Identity

Collective identities are no less changeable cultural constructs and dynamic social processes than individual identities. The dynamic of collective identity rests on both its alteration in order to reconcile with the current juncture, and on its relational, interactive characteristic. The mechanism of self-definition, that is, formation of conceptions about one's own group, does not derive from a certain substance or from some reified and unchangeable characteristic of the group. At the foundation of creating representations about one's own group is the relation toward the other group(s). Definition of the we-group is thus interactive and reflexive, the concept of the group about itself is a reflection of the concept of other groups with which it comes into contact, and with which it compares itself. The definition of the we-group contains the image of self that is often formed in contrast with the image of others:

> The identity of the group then has less features of objective reality, and more features of the constructed social representation, which rests on myth and ideology. The representation by which a collective demonstrates its unity as a difference from other collectives. The representation is thus a category of identification, that is, of classification and distinction . . . (Lipiansky 1998: 145, translated from French by the author).

Collective identity emerges in differentiation to other identities; social identification is the other side of social demarcation. Therefore, every construction of collective identity has two dimensions—it points both internally and externally. The internal dimension is made up of those elements members of a particular community regard as being common to them all and which manifest the unity (the sameness) of its members; for their part, external elements are those with which the group establishes differences (and borders) toward neighbors—with their frequently negative mirroring—and confirms its own originality and specificity in relation to them.

Emphasizing the identity of the group and/or the internal sameness of its members is less a manifestation of the cultural and social unity of a group, and more a means by which the group tries to construct its unity, and to demonstrate it to others (Cohen 1985; Lipiansky 1998: 146). By offering its members an image of uniform totality that transcends the actual differences between them, the myth of sameness reinforces the foundations of group cohesion while separating them at the same time from other groups that it shows to be different.

So, cultural differences between communities are not consequences of their spatial and social isolation, but just the opposite, of their inter-action (Barth 1969). When groups communicate within some broader social context, they develop the need to set the borders between them. They distance themselves from each other by stressing some cultural elements, which can be shared by both groups, as being characteristic to them only. In this way, they underscore the fact that they are different and reinforce their decision on self-assertion. Researchers have pointed out that even imperceptible differences between groups can serve for their social differentiation. Pierre Bourdieu writes: "Social identity lies in difference, and difference is asserted against what is closest, which represents the greatest threat" (according to Blok 2000: 34). Since "that which is closest" also represents "the greatest threat," minute differences between neighboring groups can also lead to conflicting, antagonistic relations, to the narcissism of minor differences (Freud, according to Blok 2000).

The opposition that is characteristic to constituting the identity of a group can also be expressed through attribution of negative identities to other groups (Lipiansky 1998: 146). This is, in fact, attribution of positive identity to one's own group.

Because collective and individual identities are dynamic social processes, the understanding of identity that prevailed in the early studies of these processes was replaced by the expression "construction of identity" or the concept of "identification." These terms emphasize the dynamic feature of identity, its constant reshaping in the light of new individual experiences and changing social circumstances. They emphasize change as a process that is inseparable from identity. The term identification "highlights the active and processual dimension of attributing meaning to experienced similarities and differences between 'us' and 'them'" (Otto and Driessen 2000: 16).

In research into the social construction of identity, attention is paid to analysis of cultural content, which is given the status of the differential markers of the group. Identity is the cultural difference constructed on the basis of the cultural capital of the group, from which the group, in a particular social configuration in interaction with other social groups, will select a particular part of its heritage and imbue it with differential characteristics. The criteria of differentiation, as well as categories accessible for denoting oneself from the Other—genres (McDonald 1993) or idioms (Phillips 1994) with the aid of which one speaks of difference—will be defined by the local and broader social and political image of the times. The markers of a group's identity are not therefore completely arbitrary, but are the consequences of the mutual agency of "objective" cultural heritage and its subjective perception in the dialectical relationship of identification and differentiation of groups in interaction on the one hand, and, on the other, of categories in which, at a particular time and in a particular place, they most tellingly express the differences and define the identities of the groups.

In the opinion of Helge Gerndt (1988), the dynamic relation between the objective and the subjective is one of the most interesting issues in cultural analysis. For that author, it is a matter of understanding the play between perceptional and representational cultural reality. Applied to research into identity as a special type of representation, the question would be to which extent the self-presentation of the group—its declared identity—coincides with "objectively" ascertainable characteristics, both of their own and of the opposition group against which it is defined. Since identity is a subjective statement of the group about itself or the individual about her/himself, it seems to me that research into the constitution of representations—studying how they are typically expressed, and why those subjective truths or constructions of reality arise—is analytically more appropriate than their deconstruction in order to determine their "correctness" or foundation in reality, which is, in any case, "a difficult empirical question" (van der Berghe 1996: 355). In approaching identity from that aspect, it is useful to observe representations about Others and about oneself as stereotypes.

The word "stereotype" is derived from the printers' term for a plate cast from a mould; originally from the Greek *stereos* meaning solid (Ibid., 354). In (psycho)sociological studies, it relates to the fixed mental impression;[5] in ethnic research it was often defined as an overgeneralization about the behavior or other characteristics of members of particular groups (Ibid.); and in cultural research the notion refers to the entrenched images and conceptions that groups harbor about each other. "Stereotypes are not only firm and unbending, but are also value-judgement concepts that spring from prejudices, which are, in all cases, in a relation of tension and difference toward experiential reality. They deform reality, but they also create new reality, admittedly, most frequently a very problematic reality, for those, burdened by problems, who cannot break free of it" (Gerndt 1988: 11, translated from German by the author).

As a separate order of reality, (stereotyped) representations and identities as well as ascribed images of oneself and the Other place a series of questions before the researcher. How are notions of oneself and of Others expressed in a particular social configuration? To what extent does the notion of the other group influence the behavior of the individual in interaction with a member of the other group? Do contradictions arise between the two orders of reality—the reality of representations and the reality of interaction?

I shall be dealing with these questions on the basis of a study of Croatian migrants from Srijem to Croatia. The book gives analyses of the discourses that the Srijem Croats presented to their new neighbors, the homeland Croats in the locality of settlement and in the Croatian society as a whole on their arrival in Croatia, and the strategies of identification they chose—individual and collective—in the process of adaptation and integration into the local and broader social community. This case exemplifies how, in the reflexive process of delineating themselves from the old-settler population they have encountered in the new environment, migrants reinterpret cultural meanings and create new ethnic boundaries and individual and group identities. The local old-settler population is not exempt from this process; in asserting their differences, both groups engage in mutual stereotyping, finding material for the creation of stereotyped images about the other group in culture, and expressing them with socially available categories of difference. Let us take a closer look at the elements of this case study.

Case Study: The Srijem Croats

According to some estimates, between thirty and forty-five thousand people from Vojvodina, the majority of whom were Croats, although the migrants included members of other ethnic groups (Serbs, Roma, Slovaks, Ruthenians), moved to Croatia between 1992 and 1994 (Bičanić 1994, 1999; Černelić 1994). The new settlers with whom I spoke believe that the largest group—around twenty-two thousand—arrived from Srijem, while the others were mainly from southern Bačka, with a smaller number from Banat, all three regions in Vojvodina (see map 1).

It is difficult to determine the reliability of this estimate, among others, because it is based on the size of the Croatian population in the Vojvodina part of Srijem, while various estimations often fail to mention the exact territory to which the figures refer. My analysis of the 1991 census shows that on the territory of eastern Srijem (or the part of Srijem today in Vojvodina), excluding Zemun but including the city of Novi Sad (see map 3), approximately thirty-two thousand people declared themselves to be Croats.[6] If we assume, on the basis of statements of newly settled Srijem migrants, that some forty percent of the Croatian population moved out of Srijem, that would mean that some thirteen thousand settled in Croatia, and that the total number of migrants from Vojvodina is considerably below the lowest estimated number of thirty thousand.[7] Even when reduced, these numbers speak of a relatively significant coethnic migration of the Croatian populace, which is linked to the disintegration of Yugoslavia and the war for Croatian independence in the early 1990s.

Most of the migrants from Vojvodina came from Srijem, the eastern part of this region which has been united or disunited at different historical periods. Let us take a brief look at its recent history. After Srijem was completely freed from Ottoman rule in 1716 its largest part, called Srijem County (with its center in the town of Vukovar) in the mid eighteenth century was placed under the authority of the Croatian Parliament (*Sabor*) and the Governor (*Ban*) within the Kingdom of Slavonia and Croatia (itself part of the Habsburg Monarchy). A part of Srijem territory (with Petrovaradin, Zemun, and Mitrovica) was then included in the Military Borderland, which was administered directly from Vienna, and was thus outside the jurisdiction of the Croatian Parliament. After the abolition of the Military Borderland, the civil and military parts of Srijem were unified with Srijem County, which, together with other regions of Croatia, was within the framework of the Austro-Hungarian Monarchy until 1918 (see map 4). During the period of the so-called first Yugoslavia, between the two world wars, Srijem County ceased to exist as an administrative unit. In 1939, only a part of Srijem (the Šid and Ilok districts) was included in the newly founded administrative province—the Croatian Banate (*Banovina Hrvatska*). Srijem was once more incorporated in its entirety into Croatia during the brief period of existence of the Fascist puppet state—the Independent State of Croatia (*Nezavisna država Hrvatska*) from 1941 until 1945. With the foundation of socialist Yugoslavia, Srijem was administratively divided into three parts: the largest, eastern part was incorporated into the province of Vojvodina, itself a part of Serbia in the broader sense; the smaller, western part into Croatia; and the most eastern part, with Zemun and Batajnica, into Serbia in the narrower sense.[8]

Despite such complex and frequent changes in its administrative borders throughout the twentieth century, the Croatian population of eastern Srijem—that is, the part of Srijem that found itself in Vojvodina in the former Yugoslavia and, after the abolition of its autonomy in 1988, in the Republic of Serbia—right up until the exodus to the Republic of Croatia, lived under the conviction that Srijem belonged to Croatia. The national Croatian awareness of these people was strongly pronounced, as is clearly testified to by the statement below of a respected new settler:

> Patriotism lives within us—while we lived there, and now [here]. It is not important that I am not in Slankamen [eastern Srijem, today part of Serbia], but am in Ilok and Šarengrad [western Srijem, today part of Croatia]. That patriotism is Croatian patriotism. Now is not so important how long the state borders are, because Croatia is not only a state within borders. Croatia is a state within us, too, in our souls, our brains, and in our consciousness.

The migrants are not a homogenous group of people, either in terms of the place (village) or region of origin (Srijem, Bačka, Banat), or in terms of culture or ethnicity. As mentioned, the majority are Croats, but there are also an as yet undetermined number of representatives of other ethnic groups. Another factor introducing heterogeneity into the group is the difference in the duration of settlement in Vojvodina: some people are old settlers whose forefathers had for generations lived on that territory, while others are actually newcomers (*došlje, dodoši*) there, arriving in the region at various times during the turbulent twentieth century. There was a considerable influx of new settlers into Srijem (in the sense of the entire region) in the period between 1918 and 1941, during the agricultural reform program and the so-called colonization. However, at that time, only a small number of immigrant families were Croatian (Kolar-Dimitrijević and Potrebica 1994: 245). Croats from Bosnia-Herzegovina came to Srijem as displaced persons in considerable numbers during World War II. Further, during the agricultural reforms in eastern Srijem between 1945 and 1948, around one thousand families were moved from underdeveloped regions of Croatia to the districts of Zemun, Stara Pazova, and Ruma (Maticka 1990: 82–83). However, they could have included only a minority of Croats, since, of the total number of colonists in Vojvodina, only

3.17 percent were of Croatian nationality (Gaćeša, according to Laušić 1993: 94). After that organized colonization, Croats from Herzegovina, Dalmatia, and Bosnia came to Srijem looking for seasonal work. Beška is the only place in Srijem in which such a higher number of seasonal workers became permanent settlers (Bičanić 1999: 251–252). After the immigration to Croatia during the 1990s, many of those Srijem Croats—united by Croatian ethnic identity and Roman Catholic faith, yet different in origins—became newcomers in relation to the homeland population in the places in which they settled.

Forced Displacement

Although they were not forced out directly by war and military might, since there were no hostilities in the territory of Vojvodina where they lived, the context within which the displacement of the Srijem Croats took place make it an instance of forced migration. There was no alternative for the people who made the decision to move out.

I shall briefly mention here the reasons for their migration (spoken about directly by the settlers in chapter 4), referring to the testimony of the expelled Srijem Croats, which was collected and published by Milan Bičanić (1994, 1999), himself a settler. Regardless of whether they were living within Croatia or outside—in the other republics of the former Yugoslavia—Croats were delighted with the country's democratization set in motion in 1990 by the first free elections after World War II, and then by the proclamation of Croatia's independence on 25 June 1991. The war that followed in Croatia strengthened even more the affinity and support for Croatia on the part of Croats living in other parts of the former Yugoslavia (as well as of Croats throughout the world), but it also brought them a host of problems.

Reservists and young men of draft age were under the direct threat of mobilization in the Yugoslav Army, and as early as the second half of 1991, many of them fled or hid.[9] Srijem Croats were exposed to verbal threats, usually in anonymous telephone calls and threatening letters, slander, being brought in for questioning at police stations (which was often accompanied by physical violence and injuries), armed (grenade) attacks on their houses and properties, their property being stolen and being forced out of their houses, and there were also several reported murders and disappearances of persons (Bičanić 1994, 1999; Ritig-Beljak 1996). Fear was also instigated by the public statements and activities of members of the Serbian Radical Party and its leader, Vojislav Šešelj, calling for the deportation of Croats to Croatia.[10] The Serbian radicals harnessed the desire for revenge of the ethnic Serbs from Croatia, who had fled to Serbia during 1991 and 1992, and joined forces with them in attacking Croatian homes and forcing some farmers to exchange their holdings with Serbs who had left Croatia (Bičanić 1994, 1999; Duijzings 1995, 2000). The verbal threats and physical attacks that accompanied such extortion resulted in migrations of numerous Croatian inhabitants from eastern Srijem.

Since the majority of Srijem Croats had exchanged their real estate with Serbs, who were leaving Croatia and settling in eastern Srijem, they differed from all other types of migrants—refugees and internally displaced persons—in Croatia at the beginning of the 1990s.[11] In other words, unlike other migrants, they secured a roof over their heads and, since the majority were farmers who had also exchanged assets, they had an ensured existence. Only a small minority of Srijem Croats were forced to resettle without having contracted a property exchange. The Croatian Government offered them temporary accommodation in displaced persons' settlements, and after 1995, with the military reintegration of territory previously occupied by Serbs, also in the Knin area (see map 2).

Ger Duijzings (1995, 2000) established that the Church organized the resettlement of Croats from Kosovo in the 1990s. The same author claims that the exchange of populations between Serbia and Croatia was agreed upon between the Croatian and the Serbian presidents in the first half of 1992 (Hedl, according to Duijzings 1995). However, my research did not find reliable proof of the participation of the Church or the state in the resettlement of the Croats from Vojvodina, or more precisely, from Srijem. All of the former and current leaders of the Community of Croatian Refugees and Internally Displaced Persons from Srijem, Bačka, and Banat, an association of migrants from Vojvodina, claim that the state did not directly promote resettlement in Croatia. However, they do not claim that anything was done to halt the migration, although conflicting opinions about the migration were expressed at the first meetings between the migrants and the representatives of the Croatian authorities. This is how one of the founders of the Community described the first meeting between his delegation and the Croatian president, Franjo Tuđman, in the spring of 1992:

> The president put it like this: "We are not calling on you to come here, but if you do come, welcome! The doors are open to you! We have the room! You are our people!" Later I understood that, as president, he did not have the moral or political right to invite us, but we know that he could hardly wait for us to come.

It is not possible to precisely reconstruct Tudman's attitude several years after the event, particularly not on the basis of the statements of the leaders of the Community. For example, another man who was also present at the first meeting with the president, gives a different account of the president's words:

> The president put it this way, but let it stay only between us: "Tell the people to come! We cannot protect people, not as the Republic of Croatia or through the international community, so that they don't die down there [in Serbia]."

The migrant leaders claim the decision to migrate was left to individuals and the agreements reached within families. Indeed, the political party of the Vojvodina Croats—The Democratic League of the Croats from Vojvodina (*Demokratski savez Hrvata Vojvodine*), and particularly its president, Bela Tonković—were reportedly against the exodus and called on the Croats to stay in Vojvodina. Not even the Community of Croatian Refugees and Internally Displaced Persons from Srijem, Bačka, and Banat, founded in Croatia at the end of 1991, initially issued any guidelines that would have promoted migration, although some of its leaders openly supported the idea, convinced that the Croats in Vojvodina would be completely assimilated, living as they did in a majority Serbian environment.

According to one Srijem Croat, who moved to Croatia during the 1970s, resettlement in Croatia was linked with the fact of the creation of the independent Croatian state:

> You could say that I was a person who encouraged migration. . . . I felt that one could not survive there [in Serbia], so I encouraged people in that sense of the impossibility of surviving there. . . . You see, when we realized that a state for us was being created [Croatia] and that we would not be part of that state, we, who had suffered so much for the Croatian state. . . . Now that state will come about, and we will not be part of it. I knew how much every person there wanted to be in that state and, in that sense, that was the way in which I spoke. Look here, that was what [we] all wanted so much.

The Croatian state could have recognized that the manner in which the migration unfolded—the exchange of houses and property between the Croatian and the Serbian populations—was an acceptable way of reducing the share of the ethnic Serbian population in Croatia. In the words of one leading Srijem Croat, no matter how much his estimates are exaggerated, it was probably realized that the exodus would not only change the demographic picture, but also have considerable influence on the "voting machine" in Croatia:

Interlocutor: "What we-Vojvodina Croats-have done for Croatia is better than wars, because about fifty thousand of us have moved here, and we have sent at least seventy thousand of them [Serbs] there [to Serbia] without a grain of gunpowder—we exchanged our properties."

JČŽ: "How was it that many more Serbs left?"

Interlocutor: "Because we were aborigines down there who had large estates, while those here were clerks and workers, so that one of our families moved two to three of their families down there, when we exchanged estates. So that our people have exchanged five to six, two to three houses, two to three households around Virovitica. . . . That is our voting machine for Croatia . . . when you think that 50 thousand of us Croats have come, and if around 100 thousand Serbs have left, that is a difference of 150 thousand in the voting machine. That is a very strange picture, [but] a very positive one for Croatia."

One can assume that the Croatian authorities did not (publicly) either support or halt the exodus. Neither the state nor the Church organized resettlement in the sense that either of these institutions provided accommodation (except for a minority who arrived destitute) or employment for the migrating Srijem population. The resettlement from Vojvodina was entirely the result of informal exchanges between two ethnic groups at an individual level. Nonetheless, after the migration had taken place, the state played an important role in solving the numerous administrative problems of the migrant population, granting, for example, Croatian citizenship or legalizing the exchange of property (discussed further in chapter 6). However, there are dissenting views on this point. According to one leading migrant, the state's drawn-out solutions of such basic problems initially disheartened the migrants and caused them to doubt the correctness of their decision to move out of Srijem.

Resettlement in Croatia: Gradina Near Virovitica

Since the Srijem Croats largely exchanged their estates and houses with the Croatian ethnic Serbs who emigrated to Serbia at the same time, the majority of them settled in regions in which there had been a concentration of Serbian inhabitants until the outbreak of war—in northern Croatia in and around the towns of Virovitica, Slatina, and Osijek, Zagreb, and southern Croatia (Ravni Kotari in Dalmatia, Knin and the surrounding area, see map 2). Because of the chain-like effect of the two way migrations, the new settlers make up a considerable part of the entire population in the many places to which they moved. For example, the former inhabitants of Hrtkovci moved in large numbers into two villages, Kula (Galenić 1997) and Zvonimirevo, those from Golubinci into Slatina and its surroundings, and those from Slankamen to Virovitica and the surrounding area (all of these places being in Slavonia).

After a review of the available statistical data about the newly settled groups, and preliminary field insights in 1996, I selected as my case study group the Srijem Croats who were compactly settled in the village of Gradina, near Virovitica (see map 2). In subsequent research, I also included several families living in Virovitica, some of whom functioned as a unified economic unit with the part of the family living in Gradina, and leaders of the Community of Croatian Refugees and Internally Displaced Persons from Srijem, Bačka, and Banat living in Zagreb, Virovitica, and Zadar.

My interlocutors estimate that between 5,000 and 6,000 Srijem Croats have settled in Virovitica-Podravina County, information that was confirmed in a television interview in 1994 with Stjepan Mikolčić, who was then County Prefect.[12] The some forty families that settled in Gradina number around 150 members, who live in nuclear-family or stem-family households.

According to the census of 1991, Gradina had 1,058 inhabitants, of whom 778, or 73 percent, declared themselves as Croats; 235, or 22.2 percent, as Serbs; and 12, or 1.1 percent, as Yugoslavs. There were also two Montenegrins, seven Muslims, one Macedonian and two Hungarians living in the locality, as well as 18 people who did not declare themselves nationally, or their nationality was unknown.[13] After the departure of almost all of the Serbs in 1991 and 1992, Gradina is today inhabited by Croats in a larger percentage than before 1991, among whom the newly settled Srijem Croats are a large group.

Research into the mortality rate of the inhabitants of Gradina, carried out in the late 1960s and the early 1970s, encompassed interviews with the inhabitants about certain general features of the village and its inhabitants and established that there had been major migratory movements in that area in the past. In the late 1960s, 35.3 percent of the inhabitants had not been born in Gradina but had settled there (Sivački et al. 1986: 256). Half of that number was made up of settlers from Croatia, about 10 percent had moved there from Bosnia-Herzegovina, while 30 percent were originally from the nearby town of Virovitica. The survey did not establish the ethnic structure of the immigrants, nor was the region of their origin stipulated precisely. Judging from what the inhabitants of Gradina have told me, the settlers from Croatian regions were either from Croatian Zagorje or Dalmatia. The most intensive arrival of new settlers, according to the abovementioned research, took place in the 1920s and in the 1960s. The survey showed that two thirds of the migrations to Gradina were motivated by economic reasons, while the remainder were for marital reasons. When asked if they thought of themselves as Slavonians or had retained a feeling of belonging to the area in which they had lived previously, some 60 percent of the new settlers responded that they felt they were Slavonians, while 40 percent felt affiliated with the area of their origin (Ibid.).

The first wave of immigration has remained alive in the collective memory of the people, when the number of inhabitants rose by 27 percent (from 960 to 1,223 inhabitants) between 1921 and 1931, which was the highest growth in a ten year period since 1857 (Crkvenčić and Feletar 1986: 634). According to the statements of the locals, during those years, Serbs from Herzegovina and Dalmatia—the so-called *solunaši* or in the Gradina idiom, the *solunci*—colonized land somewhat distant from the old center of Gradina. These were veterans from the World War I Thessalonikki front who, because of their meritorious service during the war,[14] were settled on agricultural land as part of the Yugoslav agricultural reform program implemented between the two world wars. As a result, a rather large Serbian Orthodox community appeared in Gradina, which up to then was mostly settled by the Roman Catholic Croatian population. Religious differences were soon to be accompanied by the socioeconomic differentiation between the old and new settlers. The older people of Gradina tell vivid stories of that colonization and the privileges of the *solunci:*

> They were given estates of the landed gentry, they were given land fit for an earl. That's what they got! Each one was given nine large acres (*jutro*), that was ten acres, which is almost seven hectares of land, six to seven hectares of land they were given and they paid no taxes on it. During the time of the new Yugoslavia [after World War II] they also avoided it [paying taxes]. After land consolidation was carried out and various transformations of ownership [took place] they reduced the class [of the land] and what else do I know. So it was that we [Croats] came off second-best.

The newly settled *solunci* practically lived separately from the remainder of the village in Zmaj Jovina Street (today, Ban Jelačić Street), except for a few later settlers of the same or some other nationality. Territorial separation and ethnic specificity encouraged the aspirations of the Serbian inhabitants to also separate administratively from the old village, so that the new part of the village was given a new unofficial name—New Gradina.

According to what I was told by an elderly villager, up until twenty years ago, the two parts of the village were separated by boards which were later taken down, "but they [the Serbs] would never admit it [that Gradina was one and the same settlement]. They wanted to have their own."

After World War II, an agricultural combine[15] was established on the land between the two parts of the village, a new primary school was built, and a health station and a post office were opened. The old and the new settlements were spatially separated by the Roman Catholic church and the graveyard. Today, there are several shops in the village, along with a bakery and two agricultural chemical stores. There is a firehouse, a hunting association, a soccer club, an equine society, and a folklore group.

The most important activity of the inhabitants of Gradina is crop farming. Orchards and vineyards are generally not so important in the Virovitica region, while stock raising increased during the 1970s (Malić 1986).

When describing living with the Serbs, the statements of the people of Gradina diverge: some claim there was "normal coexistence" and cooperation, while others insist that the Serbs were in a privileged position, and that relations between them had never been good (see chapter 7). However, they all agree in their descriptions of the last few years of life with the Serbs, that the latter "turned the tables." The situation reportedly changed after the first democratic elections in Croatia in 1990, when the Croatian Democratic Union (*Hrvatska demokratska zajednica*), came to power. The Serbs allegedly started to leave their jobs, refused to play soccer in the local club,[16] planned their own elections in secret, organized village guard groups, and bullied Serbian families who recognized the new Croatian authorities and were engaged in the defence of Croatia. The result of all this was that only a few Serbian families stayed in Gradina, while Srijem Croats moved into the estates of the Serbs who emigrated to Serbia.

The new settlers share the Roman Catholic faith with the locals, but speak a different organic idiom—the Croats from eastern Srijem speak a Stokavian Ekavian idiom, which is not spoken in the region of settlement. Since the official standard language in the Republic of Serbia is Stokavian Ekavian, and the official standard language in the Republic of Croatia is based on Stokavian Ijekavian, the idiom of the Croatian settlers from eastern Srijem is perceived as a kind of Serbian dialect by the local population in Gradina (see chapters 5 and 7). Such a perception is the result of the nondistinction of two autonomous linguistic levels—that of the standard language (Croatian and Serbian) and that of organic idioms spoken by both the Croats and the Serbs.[17]

The Srijem settlers in Gradina came from several settlements: Slankamen, Golubinci, Kukujevci, Vajska, and Inđija (see map 3). According to the list prepared by the parish priest, Stjepan Biber, the largest group was from Slankamen. Of some forty houses with migrants from Srijem living in them, thirty-two of the families are from Slankamen, two of the migrant families have come from Kukujevci and Vajska, one from Golubinci and one from Inđija.[18]

Since the largest number of Srijem Croats have come from Slankamen, the old settlers in Gradina usually refer to them by the name of their original village—*Slankamenci*. This denotes all the newly settled Srijem Croats with the name of the place from which most of them have come. The locals are aware that this is a case of simplified identification; they know that the newcomers originate from various places in Srijem and that to designate them by a broader regional term—derived from Srijem—would be more appropriate than using a narrow, localized name. However, the name *Slankamenci* as applied to the entire resettled population, was being retained in Gradina, even some years after their arrival.

The resettlement of a large number of Srijem Croats in Gradina was confined to an area with sharp borders. They moved into the former New Gradina, more precisely into Ban Jelačić Street and the nearby Croatian Parliament Street. Prior to their arrival, this area of Gradina, by its position at the edge of the village and by the ethnic composition of the former inhabitants (largely Serbs colonized there after World War I), had been isolated from the rest of the village. This ghettoization was quite welcome to the new settlers, the Srijem Croats, but it did have certain shortcomings. It made it possible for them to be among "their own" in the early days, so they did not feel (or felt less) like foreigners. Although the setup of the place imposed segregation (unintentionally in this case), the ghetto is also an expression of the aspiration that being among one's own reduces the experience of radical otherness that is felt by a foreigner or by an immigrant (Raphaël and Herberich-Marx 1999); i.e., the isolation of the newcomers in the new part of the village contributed to the fact that they felt less like foreigners. However, as was noted by the Srijem Croats, the separate lodgings had a negative affect on the integration of some of the members of the group, and this is spoken of in more detail in chapter 3.

Polyphony, Hybridity, and Levels of Reading: Methodological-Epistemological Remarks

Having the objective of understanding the social situation that occurs in the encounter between the homeland inhabitants and the settlers, I applied qualitative research methods, primarily ethnographic field research.

My conversations with people were of the open type—they were not conducted according to a firmly set, previously defined questionnaire worked out in detail, but rather on the basis of several guidelines which, in keeping with the initial research idea, were connected with the organized activity of the settlers in Croatian society, and with their life in the Virovitica area. I allowed my interlocutors to speak about whatever they considered important, trying to develop an understanding for the meanings that they themselves gave to their lives prior to and after the resettlement. In fact, it could be said that the people with whom I spoke gave direction to the research and led me into the basic themes with which I deal in this book. They also influenced the fact that, during the research, I refocused my initial interest in integration into the recipient society to research into the processes of identification of the individual migrant and the group in interaction with the local homeland population. Since my interlocutors participated in the construction of the research topic, their statements given in the book are not mere illustrations of abstract anthropological theories, but rather the material upon which the interpretations are based, in a dialectical relationship between theory and (field) practice (cf. Supek-Zupan 1976). Their local knowledge and view of the situation is the source of the theoretical elaboration in confrontation, as Clifford Geertz would say (1983), with global, abstract knowledge. As participants on an equal footing in the interviews and research, they are not mere "informants" but "interlocutors," while for the same reason, the interviews could better be denoted as conversations or dialogues.

The book is the result of collaborative constituting of the research topic between the researcher and the subjects of the research. The interpretations and the research hypotheses derived from the field research were incorporated into the building of an ethnographically grounded theory (Strauss, according to Kaufmann 1996). The status of the subjects' statements, as the basic building blocks, is made evident by their ample use: whether long or short, they are presented in some parts of the book without interpretation. Readers are invited to interpret the statements themselves and, in a certain way, in completing the text, to produce their own understanding of the social configuration that comes about in the coethnic encounter between the new and old settlers. By presenting the juxtaposed voices and views of diverse collocutors—both the local homeland and the settlers' population—in a word-for-word form, the reader is offered various perspectives and active involvement in evaluating the author's interpretation and the perspectives of the diverse subjects, the co-creators of the interpretations.[19]

The narrative polyphony (Clifford 1983; Tyler 1986) presented in the book complies with the demand for cooperative production of ethnography (Marcus and Fisher 1986: 71) and with the comprehension of the interlocutor as a subject with a voice, views, and dilemmas, and her/his own specific attitude and interpretation of the situation and its cultural meaning. That demand has been broadened here inasmuch as I have given the reader an active role in (co)creation of the interpretation. Further, the polyphony is in keeping with the heterogenous and incoherent nature of culture within which no uniform viewpoint of all the participants exists—the native's point of view in the singular—but instead, a host of points of view (cf. Narayan 1993), which come about in the active relationship of the individual with culture and her/his own position in society. The book shows that the migrants' experiences are not identical, that their own interpretation of the situation and their position is not uniform, and/or that the experience of the settler in the singular does not exist; rather, there exists a host of diverse experiences. The settlers, too, claim that each individual destiny is unique. "We are a special story!" one woman said, while research showed that the "stories" also differed within the same extended family.

The method applied in this book approaches the ethnography of the particular: evaluating the particular experience—personal or familial—the interpretation is sometimes built upon the individual case, with sensitivity toward diversities in the opinions and attitudes of people. By paying attention to intragroup disagreements and differences, the ethnography of the particular avoids generalization and homogenization in anthropological writing, which then essentialize and freeze the experience of Others in an authoritative manner (Abu-Lughod 1991).

The narrative presentation of the statements of my interlocutors is not exclusively the consequence of a particular epistemology, but also of my wish to give the text a form that would be accessible both to the academic and the "ordinary" public, particularly the general public from Srijem and in the place in which the research was conducted. The result is a hybrid anthropological text (cf. Narayan 1993: 681) in which I have linked the ethnographic narration with theory. I tried to replace the scholarly discourse—set by a formula that introduces the thesis at the beginning and summarizes it at the end, highlighting the theoretical frameworks, and generalizing the statements—with a series of narratives that should give the reader a more lively presentation of my interlocutors and their viewpoints. The reactions to such hybrid texts were twofold, confirming Kaufmann's (1996: 116ff.) presumption about two levels of reading. The public informed about theory has read the text at the level of ideas and theoretical statements; the "ordinary" reader has read mostly the narrations and descriptions, without showing competence to assess the theoretical statements. I discuss this latter aspect in the epilogue.

My complex identity as researcher-scholar, professional,[20] and someone closely related to one of the new settlers, came to the fore in this research. I was a person who, knowing Srijem and having a familial bond, guaranteed a certain empathy and sympathy for the destiny of the migrants. The research was conducted in the midst of tensions between a certain insider position I held on the one hand, and, on the other, my wish to analyze the given situation from the position of an outsider. My hybridity sometimes confused my Srijem collocutors, in some cases perhaps making them more restrained in their statements, while in others they became very interested in me, particularly when they knew my kin and ancestors, and tried to place me in their Srijem village circle of acquaintances. In two cases, I was treated as a kinswoman: one woman constantly returned to the theme of her childhood and friendship with my mother, her distant relative; in another case I was "discovered" as a relative, even though a distant one, and became a frequent and welcome visitor whom they addressed with the familiar *ti* form.[21] On another occasion, the interest of one woman was prompted by the fact that she indirectly knew my relatives. However, that insider position also had its drawbacks: some of my collocutors expected me to become involved in the presentation and "defense of their case" in public. After I opted in my texts for the role of analyst of the social configuration and not that of advocate of the displaced group (cf. Ginsburg 1992: 137), their interest in my research somewhat waned.

The research was preceded by my personal interest in the destiny and experiences of my relatives on my mother's side, Srijem Croats who moved from the village of Golubinci in 1992, some of them settling in Virovitica and others in Zagreb. It was only in 1995 that this interest developed into a scholarly grounded project, on whose realization I embarked in 1996. Along with "objective" factors linked with my interest in interaction and integration, which required that both the locals and the settlers lived in the place of research, my choice of the location of the research was also influenced by subjective factors—the circumstance that my male relative had moved to Virovitica and that he had sound and ramified contacts in Virovitica and Gradina, both with Srijem Croats and with the local population. It seemed to me to be useful to choose the place in which he had settled. He introduced me to the field, to his friends and acquaintances, showed me hospitality during my stay there, and was himself part of the research and analytical process. After the first encounters he arranged for me, the network of my collocutors in both groups was easily extended.

It happened fairly frequently that the conversations were conducted with several people present: they were often married couples, either of the younger or older generation. I rarely had conversations alone with individuals. Sometimes the conversations were conducted in the presence of several generations of the same family, sometimes of several different families, and sometimes with Srijem Croats and the locals together. I went to Gradina and Virovitica over a period of three years (1996 to 1998), where I spoke several times under different circumstances with the same interlocutors from some ten Srijem and five local families, with around forty people who differed in age, gender, education, economic status, and occupation (the migrants are largely farmers, some have completed high school, others two year colleges, while some hold degrees). In 1998 and 1999, I spoke in Zagreb and Virovitica with ten or so eminent migrants, former and current leaders of the core migrant association, the Community of Croatian Refugees and Internally Displaced Persons from Srijem, Bačka, and Banat and its branches. The major part of my interlocutors are descendants of old-settler Srijem families from Slankamen and Golubinci, but others are members of first or second generation Bosnian-Herzegovinian settler families in Srijem, as well as people who moved to Srijem from Croatia after World War II. Both the Srijem and local interlocutors were largely open, articulate in their statements and attitudes, and very interested in recounting their "stories" and explaining their views on, and understanding of, the situation.

Since I stayed in Gradina and Virovitica on a number of occasions, along with conversations as the basic source of the material, I was able to practice other ethnographic methods to a certain extent: observation and participation in the interaction between the migrants and the old local inhabitants. My partially insider position, together with frequent stays in the field, made it possible for me to meet the inhabitants in informal, everyday situations, in which people, at least for a moment, forgot the reason for my presence. These proved to be key situations in particular parts of interpretation since they showed the one-sidedness of narrative sources in studying the process of identification. Research based on interviews and that in which the researcher observes and participates in interaction enable analysis of two levels of reality—the reality of the discourse and the reality of interaction (see chapter 7).

The Srijem Case as an Instance of Coethnic Migrations

My interest is in the treatment, acceptance, and incorporation of migrants in their "ethnic homeland" (Heleniak 1997) and in their efforts to reidentify in the new environment. An insight into several other cases of coethnic migration points out many similar problems and experiences of coethnic migrant populations.[22] The point of citing them is not to relativize the experience of the displaced Srijem Croats, but to incorporate them into a phenomenon of global proportions in the recent history of European and Middle Eastern countries.

The context of migration to the national state, which is also the migrants' "ethnic homeland" and the nation state in which they become a part of the national majority, is usually connected with the disintegration of multinational states. Several attempts at comparison of various population displacements engendered by transitions from multinational empire to incipient nation states have been made in the past decade (Brubaker 1995, 1998; Loizos 1999). A common denominator of those population displacements has been a process that Rogers Brubaker called by a term borrowed from Lord Curzon—"ethnic unmixing of peoples" (Brubaker 1995, 1998). The unmixing of peoples is a process by which formerly heterogenous populations in the incipient nation states—successors of a former multinational empire—are "sifted, sorted, and recomposed" into homogenous ethnic groups corresponding to new state frontiers (Brubaker 1995: 192). The reconfiguration of political space along national lines and the concomitant ethnic homogenization entail the migration of ethnic/national groups who have become national minorities in new nation states. The consequence of such migrations is the ethnic homogenization in both the emitting state and the state to which the groups migrate, hence the ethnic unmixing of hitherto mixed, multiethnic societies (Brubaker 1995, 1998).

The disappearance of the Ottoman Empire and the Habsburg Monarchy after World War I and, in our time, the disintegration of the USSR and Yugoslavia during the 1990s, prompted significant movements of coethnic populations to the nation states that are their ethnic homelands. After the disintegration of the USSR, forty-three million people were left living outside the ethnic borders of fifteen successor states to the Soviet Union. Nine million people, largely not of their own volition, migrated over the borders into the successor states, while some two million emigrated outside their borders. Three states—Germany, Israel, and the United States of America—accepted the largest number of immigrants, the former two by implementation of special programs for immigration of coethnic populations (Heleniak 1997: 15). Ethnic German populations experienced a similar fate in Central and Eastern Europe after World War II.[23] Let us take a closer look at several ethnological and anthropological studies of those cases.

Among the numerous population exchanges that came about toward the end and after the fall of the Ottoman Empire—between Bulgaria and Turkey, Bulgaria and Greece, Greece and Turkey—the latter and its consequences for the displaced populations were studied in detail. It involved the unprecedented compulsory exchange of 1.2 million Anatolian Greeks and around 400,000 Roumelian Muslims, which was agreed upon in a treaty between Greece and Turkey signed in Lausanne in 1923. One contemporary researcher has called that population exchange the first diplomatically agreed ethnic cleansing in the modern era (Aktar 1998). On that occasion, the population of Greece was increased by about one quarter. In order to consolidate its authority over the newly acquired regions, the state largely settled the coethnic migrants in northern Greece on estates that had been abandoned by the Muslims (Loizos 1999: 240–241).

In her study of a place with an immigrant coethnic population, Renée Hirschon established, almost a half a century after the migration, that the settlers used their Asia Minor origins as a differentiating marker, convinced in the superiority of their former way of life in comparison with what they encountered in Greece. The author claimed that in the new environment, the newcomers emphasized the minutiae of detail and differences that were of degree rather than of kind. The Asia Minor Greeks worked continuously and consciously at constructing a boundary and a sense of separate identity even in the face of minute cultural and social differences. Because of the conscious retention of a separate identity, they can be considered to be a minority group within the Greek society (Hirschon 1989).

For their part, the Muslims who went to Turkey with the assistance of the state were settled on abandoned Greek estates. However, taking possession of the estates did not progress without problems since the allocated houses and land had already been misappropriated by government employees or members of the local population, whose homes had been destroyed in the foregoing wars (Aktar 1998; Loizos 1999:

245). Researchers claim that the Turkish government did not have a systematic plan for the resettlement and for the refugees' transformation into a developmental force. After allocation of the property and minor initial assistance to the farmers, the migrants were left more or less to their own devices. Research has shown that the migrants had difficulties in finding their feet in the new environment, particularly because of a lack of social capital. Seventy years after their resettlement, Muslims from Crete living in the Smyrna region still retain their Cretan identity and regard themselves as "progressive" and "European" in comparison with their fellow citizens. They refuse to be called "refugees" because refugees, by definition, arrive without any property, while most of the resettled Cretans moved together with their movables and chattels (Loizos 1999: 246–247).

Throughout the twentieth century, Germany had an intermittent influx of ethnic Germans. For example, after World War I, some 600,000 to 800,000 ethnic Germans came to Germany from the territories ceded to Poland by Germany (Brubaker 1995: 200). The biggest exodus of ethnic Germans occurred after World War II from former German territories, which were incorporated into Poland and the Soviet Union. The massive flight started in the face of the Red Army advance and continued with forced expulsions between 1945 and 1949. By agreeing to the expulsion of the German population from Poland, the Allies aimed at avoiding future conflicts between the Germans and the Poles. This was considered a radical but necessary solution to the German-Polish problem (Benz 1992: 379ff.). In parallel, the Allied forces of Poland, Czechoslovakia, and Hungary were given the right to deport all persons of German origin, the so-called *Volksdeutsche*, or people of German descent living outside the borders of the Old Reich. Tito's regime also expelled all the ethnic Germans from Yugoslavia. Altogether, from 1945 and 1949, between eleven and twelve million Germans had to leave their homes and go to Germany, two thirds of them to what was to become West Germany, where they were designated as *Vertriebene* and *Flüchtlinge* (Münz and Ohliger 1997: 4–5). Yet, still about three million ethnic Germans remained in Poland, Romania, Hungary, and Czechoslovakia, or as internally displaced persons in the Soviet Union. They were the source of later migrations: during the West-East division of Europe, about 1.4 million of those so-called *Aussiedler* went to West Germany up until 1987. Their influx was intensified after the fall of the Berlin Wall, when about 2.3 million persons arrived in Germany (Münz and Ohliger 1997: 6ff.).

Studying this latter group, Regina Römhild claims that the ethnic Germans' move to Germany has been a disappointment to them. They explain their arrival in the country by the fact that "they wanted to live like Germans among Germans," but their expectations have been betrayed in the multi-ethnic German society—they have come to a multi-cultural society in which being German does not serve as an exclusive or unquestionable marker of identity. Expecting to find a culturally homogenous German nation state in which they would be welcomed does not correspond with the reality of Germany in which, as in the former USSR, they have found themselves in the position of a minority, admittedly not ethnically defined, but nonetheless a minority made up of immigrants (Römhild 1994: 120; 1999: 114ff.). Despite this group's official recognition as German citizens with the full rights that they have enjoyed since the day of their arrival in Germany, the homeland population of Germany—both the ethnic Germans and the other ethnic groups which live in Germany—perceive them primarily as "Russians" in daily interaction. Responding to this challenge, in their struggle to be accepted, many coethnic migrants start to defend their German-ness more forcefully than they did as a German minority in the former USSR (Römhild 1999: 114–115).

A politological analysis of the migrants' political activity has shown a rift in their identity: some coethnic migrants want to build up a separate Russian-German identity, while, for their part, others insist on the fact that they are Germans, without emphasizing their Russian origins. A survey conducted in 1994 showed that almost 50 percent of them had experienced antagonism from the homeland population, either at work or in their neighborhoods, while a third experienced it in contact with government services. Thirty-six percent feel they are not welcome in Germany, while another 55 percent tell they are only partly welcome (Klekowski 1999).

The case of Israel is specific because that state, since its foundation, has been constituted on the basis of the immigration of Jews from various countries throughout the world. Since 1968, the Ministry for Absorption has been active in Israel in easing the transition for the immigrants and facilitating their speedy integration into Israeli society. Despite that state institution and the absorption policy, recently immigrated Russian Jews—the largest immigrant group in the history of Israel, reaching 20 percent of the Jewish population—have not been successfully absorbed in practice. The resettlement of Russian Jews happened in two major waves. The smaller wave of about 160,000 arrived during the 1970s, while a much bigger wave of about one million persons occurred in the 1990s, in the post-Soviet period (Remennick 2003). The ethnic community of Russian Jews has become one of the strongest categories of group identity—they are called "Russians" in public—and conflicts have arisen among them between their ethnic Russian-Jewish identity and their more inclusive and general Jewish identity (Siegel 1995), and because of internal differentiation into earlier and more recent immigrants (Markowitz 1994). Larissa Remennick (2003) states that since the early 1990s, the dilemma of assimilation versus separatism faced by the Israeli-Russian community has largely revolved around the issue of Hebrew acquisition and usage, and that cherishing their cultural (believed to be superior to that of the Levantine and provincial Israel) and linguistic heritage, Russian-speakers resisted the attempts at their rapid "Israelization" from the outset. This highly visible Israeli-Russian community has given rise to abundant anthropological studies (among others see Remennick 2002, 2003; Yelenevskaya and Fialkova 2002, 2003, 2004).

Czech coethnic migrants have had somewhat similar experiences since, in migrations organized by the state, they resettled in Czechoslovakia from their Ukrainian and Belarus birthplaces at the beginning of the 1990s. Some 1,800 Czechs emigrated of their own free will, spurred on by the accident at the Chernobyl nuclear plant. The migration took place under the strict supervision of both the sending state and the state to which they were emigrating and, after months of preparation, during which the potential migrants were given information about Czechoslovakia and offered the choice of place of settlement. Once they arrived, they felt cheated: both with the compensation from the former USSR for the property they left behind, and with the locality in which they settled and the jobs they were given there. According to a team of Czech anthropologists (Valášková, Uherek, and Brouček 1997) who studied that immigration, the potential advantages of ethnic affinity between the settlers and the local homeland population were eliminated by two factors. On the one hand, the local population perceived the immigrants as "a foreign element," as foreigners born on the territory of the former USSR, with which the Czechs have negative associations because of the Soviet occupation of 1968. "Anyone who came from this territory was consequently not to be trusted, could be called a 'Russian' and could therefore be associated with the occupation forces," state the authors (Valášková, Uherek, and Brouček 1997: 101). The following comment of the homeland Czech population was also noted: "One group of Russkies has gone but now we've been landed with another lot" (Ibid., 61). On the other hand, the settlers regarded themselves as being different from the local population and "in many ways better Czechs than the Czechs among the autochthonous population" (Ibid., 93).

I shall mention just one other case of coethnic migration in Western Europe, in the colonial context and under the civic (and not ethnic) definition of nation, differing somewhat from the abovementioned situations, but similar in many respects with regard to the experiences of other coethnic migrants on arrival in their ethnic homeland. After Algeria gained independence from French colonial authorities at the beginning of the 1960s, over a short period some one million people from Algeria arrived in France. They differed in faith (Christian, Jewish, and Muslim) and were of diverse origins (Spanish, Italian, French, German, Maltese, Algerian, etc.), but were linked by French citizenship and their experience of life in Algeria, as well as by the abandonment of their homes and other property. Having settled in mainland France, whose citizens they were but with which they were not familiar, they found out their French compatriots did not welcome them, but, to the contrary, tried to limit their arrival and later on, passed over in silence their resettlement (Baussant 1998, 1999, 2002; Jordi 1995). For their part, the settlers claim that it is "completely impossible" to recount any of their stories to people outside, people who had never experienced exile (Baussant 2000). Feeling rejected as "second-rate Frenchmen/women" (Baussant 1998: 610), feeling as if they were in exile and not in their "rediscovered homeland" (Jordi 1995: 8), the Algerian French uncovered the cultural Otherness of France and found that they were separated from the homeland French by way of life and the world of tradition, which "shocked" them and often "caused them pain." In an environment that was hostile to them, the idealized picture of France, which had been created in Algeria through school textbooks, was demystified, and the picture of their lost birthplace in which everything had been better ("everything was lovelier: the Sun shone more brightly, the fruit and vegetables were larger, everything was better," Baussant 1999: 158, translated from French by the author) was made mythical. These images participate in the constitution of the collective memory that bonds all migrants and redefines their identity.

Notwithstanding the differences in the timing and the particular broader context of each of the coethnic migrations referred to, they show amazing similarities with regard to the events following settlement in the ethnic homeland. Despite the promises given by some of the host states, coethnic migrants have often been left to find their way alone in the new environments. The perception of differences—their own and among the homeland populations—leads toward emphasis on their diversity and a reshaping of their identity and, in some cases, also to the nurture of a feeling of superiority toward the homeland coethnic population. Despite their common ethnic affiliation (or, as in the French case, their common national denomination) with the majority population, they are perceived as foreigners, usually identified with the territory and the state from which they come, or are rejected as "refugees," a denomination they do not accept. If their numbers are high, they try to organize themselves politically and, in so doing, are haunted by a dilemma as to whether to do so on ethnic foundations, constituting a separate ethnic identity within the nation, or based on the acceptance of the more comprehensive national identity.

The extent to which the circumstances of the treatment, acceptance, and incorporation of coethnic migrants from Srijem in their ethnic homeland coincide with the abovedescribed situations of other coethnic migrant populations is quite astounding. I propose to subsume the encounter of those coethnic populations under a paradigmatic social situation of a type that was masterfully analyzed in an English industrial town by Norbert Elias and his associate John Scotson (1965). According to the authors, the particular configuration in which the local, long-settled population is obliged to live next to an immigrant population produces conflict and antagonism between them. The antagonism is, argue Elias and Scotson (1965: 156), inherent in the pattern which they form with each other and is beyond their control. I shall return to this analysis in chapter 7, while the next chapter serves as an insider introduction to the study that follows.

Notes

1. Under the influence of social-historical researchers into structures of *longue durée,* French ethnology gave early attention to mentalities, that is, the internal cultural world; consequently, Gerndt's claim cannot be applied generally to individual national European ethnologies.
2. In the old ethnological/anthropological conception, this corresponds with the understanding that culture is a given system, the backdrop into which the individual is thrown by birth, from which there can be no liberation and which is more or less the same for all members of that particular group.

3. The term "culture-builders" was made particularly popular in European ethnology by the authors of the book of the same name about building Swedish national culture (Frykman and Löfgren 1987). Also see Frykman (1999).

4. The question remains whether this was really so or if the individual in premodern society had a more active role in creating her/his identity.

5. The social psychologist, Gordon Allport (1954, according to van den Berghe 1996: 354) defines it as "an exaggerated belief associated with a category. Its function is to justify (rationalize) our conduct in relation to that category."

6. Calculations according to *Popis stanovništva, domaćinstava, stanova i poljoprivrednih gazdinstava 31. mart. 1991. Prvi rezultati* [Census of the population, households, and agricultural estates, 31 March 1991. Preliminary results], *Statistički bilten* 206, 1991, Novi Sad: Pokrajinski zavod za statistiku.

7. In an interview, the president of the Zajednica prognanih i izbjeglih Hrvata iz Srijema, Bačke i Banata [Community of Croatian Refugees and Internally Displaced Persons from Srijem, Bačka, and Banat] stated that thirty-seven thousand Croats had lived in Srijem in 1991, and that twenty-two thousand remained after the exodus (interview in *Slobodna Dalmacija,* 23 October 1995).

8. *Enciklopedija Leksikografskog zavoda,* vol. 7, Zagreb: Leksikografski zavod, 1964, headword "Srem"; *Enciklopedija hrvatske povijesti i kulture* [Encyclopaedia of Croatian history and culture], Zagreb: Školska knjiga, 1980, headwords "Banovina," "Slavonija," "Vojna krajina," "Okupatorska podjela Jugoslavije."

9. It has been estimated that, regardless of national affiliation, some 150,000 men avoided mobilization into the Yugoslav National Army (Morokvašić 1993).

10. In a documentary program shown by an independent TV station in Novi Sad about the migration of the Srijem Croats (broadcast on 23 May 2001), the remaining Croats mentioned Šešelj exclusively as the strategist of the spread of ethnic hatred and the exodus of the Croatian population from Srijem. As a guest on the show, Šešelj "admitted that he had entered the intensive care unit in the Novi Sad hospital in 1991, and demanded that all the Croatian nursing sisters who worked there should immediately leave the hospital. He also admitted that, by using propaganda methods, he had accelerated the displacement of the population." (From an interview with the author of the program, Marina Fratucan, given to the *National* news weekly. In Nina Ožegović, "Vojvođanska medijska heroina" [A Media Hero from Vojvodina], *Nacional* 291, 12 June 2001).

11. From the summer of 1991 until January 1992, the number of internally displaced persons in Croatia rose from 30,000 to 555,000 people. In other words, around 12 percent of the Croatian population had been driven from their homes. They were joined by refugees from Bosnia-Herzegovina, whose numbers rose sharply at the beginning of 1992: in April they stood at 200,000 and had risen to 350,000 in July (Čapo Žmegač 1996).

12. "Novi dom" [New Home], a Croatian Television production, 1994, script and direction by Stjepan Kolak.

13. *Popis stanovništva 1991. Narodnosni sastav stanovništva Hrvatske po naseljima* [The population census 1991. Ethnic structure of the population of Croatia by localities] 1992. Zagreb: Republički zavod za statistiku, 196–197.

14. During the agricultural reform program of the 1920s, some "1.5 million hectares of land" was allocated to 18,759 volunteer families, 6,788 colonizers, and 186,000 local entities interested in agriculture (*Enciklopedija Leksikografskog zavoda,* vol.1, Zagreb: Leksikografski zavod, 1955. 42, headword "Agrarian reform").

15. The Gradina combine was originally part of the Virovitica agricultural combine. It became independent in the 1990s, but was later declared bankrupt. It became private property in 2000, under the name Poljoprivredno dobro Gradina [Gradina Agricultural Farm].

16. This refusal was said to be linked to the change in the club's badge, upon which the chessboard pattern, the Croatian national symbol, replaced the five-pointed star, the symbol of Communist Yugoslavia.

17. Three dialects or organic idioms—Kajkavian, Chakavian, and Stokavian (named after various forms of the pronoun "what"—*kaj, ča, što*)—exist on the territory inhabited by the modern Croatian and Serbian nations. The first two are exclusively Croatian idioms, while the latter is common to the Croats and the Serbs. It is further subdivided into Ekavian, Ijekavian, and Ikavian (as e.g., in *mleko, mlijeko, mliko* [milk]). Serbs speak either Stokavian Ekavian or Ijekavian, while all three Stokavian subdialects are organic idioms spoken by the Croats. Furthermore, since the 1830s, we can speak of two language standardization processes in the modern meaning of the term; their aim was to create a means of communication for two emerging nations—the Croatian and the Serbian. Although basically independent processes, they ended up with similar results. In short, the modern Croatian standard was developed using the Stokavian Ijekavian idiom as its dialectical basis, i. e., the variants spoken by Croats in central Slavonia, and western and central Bosnia, with a strong influence from the highly developed literary language of Dubrovnik Baroque poetry. The famous Serbian ethnographer Vuk Karadžić, who proposed a radical language reform for the Serbs, founded the Serbian standard on the Stokavian Ijekavian idiom of eastern Herzegovina, which is very similar to the aforementioned Stokavian variants spoken by the Croats. However, with time, the Stokavian Ekavian took over as the Serbian standard, because it was spoken in Belgrade, the capital of the Kingdom of Serbia, and in Novi Sad, the most important cultural center of the Serbs. Since the official (standardized) language of Serbia is Stokavian Ekavian, Ekavian is perceived not only by the Croats but increasingly also by the Serbs living outside Serbia proper as the "real," "authentic" Serbian language, the language of all the Serbs, although there are Stokavian Ekavian organic speakers among the Croats, too—the Croats from Srijem for that matter living on both sides of the border between Croatia and Serbia—and there are Ijekavian speakers among the Serbs as well (most of them living in Croatia, Bosnia-Herzegovina, and Montenegro). Similarly, because they are incorporated in the respective standard languages, certain words are being perceived as either Croatian or Serbian, although they might be present in several organic idioms, be they Croatian or Serbian (e.g., *kruh* vs. *hl(j)eb* [bread]). It is precisely because of the lack of distinction of the two autonomous linguistic levels or categories—that of the standard language and that of organic idioms—that the local Croats in Gradina perceive the idiom of the Croatian settlers from Srijem as Serbian rather than Croatian.

18. According to the parish priest's list, some fifteen families from Bosnia, one from Kosovo, and one from Vukovar also settled in the village in the 1990s.

19. Although my interlocutors did not request that their statements be treated as anonymous, their identities are not mentioned in order to prevent any possible misuse.

20. My interlocutors were not able to fully differentiate me as a scholar-researcher and not a journalist.

21. In address in the second person singular, the Croatian language differentiates the respectful plural form *Vi* (*Sie* in German) and the familiar form *Ti* (*du* in German).

22. For a systematic comparison of several cases of coethnic migration, see Čapo Žmegač (2005).

23. On the postwar expulsion and exodus of the German minority from the former Yugoslavia, see, among others: the collection of articles, *Nijemci u Hrvatskoj jučer i danas* [The Germans in Croatia yesterday and today], (1994), and Scherer and Straka (1998).

Chapter 2

Srijem Croats Talk About Themselves

Exchanges

Interlocutor: "I saw what was brewing and I went to Zagreb [in Autumn, 1991], saw the house and said it would suit me. But that Serb came immediately [to Srijem] the next week, the one from Brdovac [in Croatia], and one thing and another, and said, 'Let's do it.' R. [informant's wife] thought we should go. We did it all in a hurry. You had to run for it now, you had to go. I was the first [to go] of the more prominent people in the village, you know. We packed almost everything and we left. However, when we arrived, the first thing was that the Serb didn't want to sign the contract, he said he didn't have time. We unloaded all our things. He said, 'We'll do it' [sign the contract], and I had left six horses at home, a new tractor, and another that had been completely overhauled. Everything I had was left down there . . . the land. However, I didn't think so much about that. When we went into the house, then R. [informant's wife] started . . . , my daughters started crying. And then, when my heart opened up. You know what I'm like. Damn it, I wailed with grief! It was awful. I said: 'We're going home!' And then V. [informant's daughter who lives in Zagreb] arrived, and tried to convince us not to go. Out of the question, not a chance! We're off home! We just couldn't do it. Only then did you see what it is [what it means to resettle]. So we went back. . . . The Croats were happy that we had come back. Overjoyed! The Serbs said nothing. But one of them had tears in his eyes. . . . I got the sack, R. [the wife] gave notice herself. . . . Then [the idea] was not to go [for the family not to move out again]. Will I go, won't I go, will I, won't I, will I, won't I, but you see it, how things are. Eh, and then it came—Vukovar fell [a town in

north eastern Croatia, under Serbian siege for three months in 1991],
the peace treaty was signed, Croatia was recognized, miracles, a circus.
But I saw that it all amounted to nothing, it was no good, that everything was going the way it was and . . . They started, Slankamen [a village in Srijem] had already moved out. Everyone was losing his or her
bearings, and then I saw that simply . . . we had to go. But for a time,
that realization that you have to do it . . . And then I started looking
for a house and land to exchange with ours. And everyone knew I was
going, but nobody said 'Don't go!,' 'Where are you going?,' 'Hang
on, where are you off to!' . . . You think about it, you have to go. You
see you must. And then I had no luck. I just couldn't find a house.
Those villages that left—Slankamen, you know, they communicated
more [had more information about houses]. . . . I come to look over
a house, I look at four . . . five. And then, when I'm on my way back,
I'm all happy that I haven't found one! Going home happy! I tried,
but I couldn't [find anything]. You go, and pray to God you won't find
anything. I think, that was . . . that made you shudder. I remember
when I went out [in Srijem], it was springtime—that was the time
when I had to go to do the rounds of the fields. For God's sake, I go
over there—there, you know, we had land right by the village and I
went there. As far as the vineyard. I didn't believe that a man could cry
so much [laughter]. It's really strange! I'm there, walking, and the tears
coming down like strawberries. It's terrible. And that's it. I mean, you
know, they just pour out of you, it's all . . . and it's awful. So it goes,
you struggle, and struggle, and what now? But it all came to a head,
became clear, I simply won't, I couldn't, I didn't want to be with them
[to stay and cooperate with the Serbs]. . . . And then we did it: I came
upon this house by chance, quite by chance!"

[The owners had already moved to Serbia, a family whose house
had been damaged in the war had moved in temporarily. The people
with whom the exchange was agreed saw the interlocutor's house in
Srijem at almost the same time. The exchange was carried out in
April 1992.]

Interlocutor: "We did it in about ten to fifteen minutes [agreed on the
exchange] . . . I said, how are we going to do it, what will we do? He
said, 'mine is a better house.' I said, 'I'll give you two acres of land,'
here in the village. I said, 'Is that alright?' Then I gave him another
acre for the bedroom furniture because R. [the wife] exchanged the
furniture. I should never have allowed it but f—k it all. . . . So it was
all finished, completed, quite fairly, correctly. Everything. We did it.
And the contract on Monday morning. You couldn't get the semi-
trailer [for the removal] for another two or three days. There just
weren't any [available]."

[The man transported the horses in a hired lorry, while the family stayed in Srijem to await his return. The removals were done through Hungary, since the direct roads between Serbia and Croatia were closed. Although he did not have an official passport for transport of livestock, he managed to convince the customs officers to allow him to transport the horses across the Yugoslav-Hungarian border, and then across the Hungarian-Croatian border. He spent four hours on the latter since, despite the property exchange documents, the Croatian customs officers thought that it was a matter of livestock import. After a 24-hour journey, he had a brief rest and set off back to Srijem to organize the move of his family.]

Interlocutor: "I go to the border. The Customs officer tells me that there is a message that my family has crossed the border into Hungary. I start crying. [He cries.] I left them there, afraid that something could happen. I left on Tuesday morning, and would have been back on Wednesday evening. However, they already loaded up [the semi-trailer] on Tuesday, I had asked for a jumbo lorry to transport the trac-tor. I went back [from the border]. They [the family] arrived around eleven or twelve. Now I had to go back [to Srijem] to return the lorry [that he had hired for transport of the livestock] and go back by car [the interlocutor's automobile had been left behind in Srijem]. I, M. and R. [the persons who exchanged their house with the interlocu-tor] met up in Subotica [northern Vojvodina]: they returned the lorry and I drove the car [to Croatia]. The sixth day after I left, a group [of militant Serbs] came to Golubinci [interlocutor's village in Srijem] and shouted: 'Where are you, Ustascha?' A R. [the person with whom the interlocutor had exchanged the house] went outside and told them that I had left."

A man about 50 years old, originally
from Golubinci, holds a degree

Interlocutor A: "We exchanged around 28 to 30 acres in one lot, with two Serbs."

JČŽ: "Is it good land?"

Interlocutor A: "It's good land."

JČŽ: "How do you evaluate the exchange of the land?"

Interlocutor A: "It's not the same as our land for orchards. We gave four to five acres of orchard land for bare land, but still, it's alright."

JČŽ: "How did you negotiate it?"

Interlocutor A: "Acre for acre. An acre there, an acre here."

JČŽ: "Did you try to get something for the orchard?"

Interlocutor A: "No, nothing. We didn't know then. At that time, you ac-cepted what the Serbs offered, they were better prepared than we were.

They had thought about it. We had not thought about it at all that we
would have to exchange. We abandoned it all, just like that."

JČŽ: "Hadn't you ever thought about moving out?"

Interlocutor A: "No. I never thought that we would ever have to leave."

. . .

JČŽ: "And you weren't able to organize transport of your things because you
had already left Slankamen?"

Interlocutor A: "Well, no. At the time that we moved [the beginning of 1992]
they did not allow us to take our things."

JČŽ: "Who didn't let you?"

Interlocutor A: "Well, those at the border—the Serbs. So that we then exchanged everything for everything."

Interlocutor B: "But M. [their daughter-in-law], she wanted to [to move] earlier. She felt something. She heard something. He [interlocutor A] said,
'Are you mad?'"

JČŽ: "When was that?"

Interlocutor A: "Well, it was in '91. In Spring. She said, 'Let's get out of
here. We have our lorry so let's move our things.' So I said, 'What,
you would move just like that!' I said, 'What!' We didn't even think
in the seventh or eighth month [of 1991] that we would be moving."

. . .

JČŽ: "Did that everything-for-everything exchange function well?"

Interlocutor A: "They [the Serbs with whom the exchange was agreed] were here.
They were here [when the people from Srijem arrived]. But they took their
things. They took with them all the better things." . . .

JČŽ: "Did you check what they took with them?"

Interlocutor A: "Yes, we were [here] when they were taking things out. We
were here in this house, and they were in the one across the way. They
had two houses."

Interlocutor B: "But their son and daughter-in-law came to our place in
Slankamen so that we could not take anything. When I asked her about
the curtain, I said to M. [the woman from Gradina], 'I don't know if
the curtains and the carpets will be staying there?' She said, 'You know
what'—she was sincere, she wasn't a rude type of woman—'you know
what, I don't know what my family will take and what they will leave
behind, but you,' she said, 'you take any of your things you want.'
I immediately took down the drapes. I didn't buy carpets, we have
wall to wall carpeting, I didn't touch any of them. V. [interlocutor's
son] said 'Nothing Mama!' And that's how we agreed that he wouldn't
. . . [take things]. He says, 'That's what we agreed.' When I came [to
Gradina, in Croatia], there were four, six chairs, five actually, here, a
dining-room table, while our house had a complete dining-room as
full as, as full as . . . Look, just as far as the chairs are concerned, we

left 32 chairs, [we found] five chairs here and four shaky ones there. We had nine rooms!" ...

Interlocutor A: "We exchanged one of the tractors with one Serb, and then we found that other Serb and exchanged [a second] tractor with him, and the combine harvester, and other things, a corn picker and I don't know what else. We left ours there, and got his from the man here. That was alright."

JČŽ: "Do you think you lost out materially in the exchange?"

Interlocutor A: "I don't know, we say we did [lose]. Our people from Slankamen say we have had a loss of half. But we say, if it's 30 percent it's alright! What's important is that we all got out alive, and we will lack for nothing."

> A man and a woman about 30 and 60 years old
> respectively, originally from Slankamen, farmers

Interlocutor A: "He [the Serb with whom they exchanged property], when he came, when he saw our house, he said, 'I have to admit that your house is better' and he gave us two."

Interlocutor B: "God forbid, it's bigger—I mean our house, it has more rooms and is much better furbished, and it's newer and better preserved and maintained. But theirs [house] ... is eight years older. And those pipes had burst."

Interlocutor A: "But it's not really so bad, except for the facade."

Interlocutor B: "And what about the mud? Where it's cracked, that wall is all damp." ...

JČŽ: "Do you think that your house and property exchange has been a success?"

Interlocutor B: "Well, there, many say that we are among the most successful ones [regarding exchange]. K. [another family] are the very best. So, I think that this here, this house is small but there's room in the other one [the other house they received in the exchange] ... I think it's the same as what we had. Except for the *kotobanja* [farm building], it's not so close, but these buildings, it's about the same."

Interlocutor A: "We did well with the land, it's just that the land here is quite far away."

Interlocutor B: "We gave twenty two acres, he gave us thirty because of the orchards, because the orchard land is of better quality."

JČŽ: "So that's what you managed to agree?"

Interlocutor B: "It is, yes, we agreed, we agreed and went to conclude the contracts. We have ... we still haven't transferred those land deeds."

...

JČŽ: "Did you transport the furniture and other things, or did you exchange them with the former owner?"

Interlocutor B: "We brought the furniture for this room with us."

Interlocutor A: "We brought as much as could be loaded on one lorry. That's what we agreed, I mean that when he [the man with whom they agreed the exchange] transported his things there, he would return ours. If it was too much for one lorry then he would go once more and we would cover the cost of the fuel."

Interlocutor B: "We paid for the fuel and for the lorry-load he brought."

JČŽ: "Did you get all the things that you agreed you would take with you?"

Interlocutor A: "He said when we were talking here, he said, 'You will get your things if you come in one year or two, or five, or ten.' He said, 'Your things will be waiting for you there.' But there you are, that's what he said when he was here."

Interlocutor B: "Good, but we also agreed that they be left there [that some thing would stay in Srijem]. Because V. and Đ. [son and daughter-in-law] only brought the furniture for one room. But the rest, the kitchen furniture and the furniture in the other room, were left there, that's what they [the people they exchanged with] left behind. . . . We left the furniture for one room, we brought it for this room, the bedroom furniture was left, along with our dining-room furniture, and the newly fitted kitchen. . . . And then they say 'What can you do!' Ah, well. When I think of it!"

> A married couple about 70 years old,
> originally from Slankamen, farmers

JČŽ: "Did you exchange approximately the same things?"

Interlocutor A: "Listen, to be frank, I got the house in Virovitica for the house there [in Srijem], but I lost everything else. . . . So that we really lost out. We did not finish the harvest [the yield in the year that they moved], we didn't do the picking; we left the earthed up turnips and the corn and the watermelons, everything was left, and the vineyard and everything, we left the vineyard ripening."

Interlocutor B: "That year [the first after migration] just passed by us, we didn't have a harvest [they moved before picking time, in July 1992], and we had nothing."

JČŽ: "Did you exchange acre for acre?"

Interlocutor A: "Approximately. Here [in Gradina] I first exchanged with B. from here. It was all scorched land. I gave him an extra acre of land for this parcel of land and this barn that was here, and we exchanged everything else for land. We exchanged with some M. from Zvonimirovo [the neighboring village]. That other land [was exchanged], also for land. I received again good land. Fairly. We have more of the land together in one spot and better quality, and it's better quality than many others here have. Only M. got better land than I did. . . . But I said, children, you have to be careful—if you make a mistake you can't fix it later. So many of them would fix things now! But there's no way, no way. Now when they went back and exchanged things again, ha, how could they do it now! But you shouldn't leave [anything] behind! When we came here: our old dishes—peasant ones—we need them for the ducks, and the chickens, you need the old baskets. You can't put everything in the lorry. There was not enough room in the lorry. . . . We traveled by way of Hungary, and there's the customs, and the lorries. I also made a bit of a mistake: my nephew . . . he had a lorry, he would go cheaply, he would go for 500 German Marks. That's what a small lorry costs! But we should have taken a big one [a lorry] for 1,000 Marks. As much as that had to be left behind [chattels in the value of 500 Marks]—I had to leave more than if I had paid 500 Marks. What I left behind was worth perhaps 4,000 Marks!"

> A married couple about 60 years old,
> originally from Golubinci, farmers

JČŽ: "Did you see the house in Gradina before you agreed on the exchange?"
Interlocutor: "I did, and we easily agreed about everything [the interlocutor and the former owner]. He was so agreeable. I couldn't have even an inkling that things could turn out the way they did. House for house. He did not have any land but I would find land [to exchange], which I did. However, he would pay me if I let him have two acres. But he did not have the money here, nor his car, the money and the car were in Crvenka [in Serbia], his daughter and son were there. That's what he looked like [someone who would keep his word]. Eh! And I agreed. We agreed on the amount of Marks. Everything was alright. We came to Crvenka, . . . but he said nothing. . . . He never said he would not give anything [the money], but kept saying, I'll pay, but he never gave it to me [the money for the land]. But then, when we were leaving, he would not allow us to load up some of our things that it had been agreed would be left [to make up for the fact that he did not pay for the land]. . . . Two freight wagons of corn were left behind, I didn't shell it. And when I found my feet here and found a buyer [for the corn], he wanted to buy it but when he got there to see what it was like and to evaluate it, S. [the man the property had been exchanged with] took out a pistol and said 'I won't let you have it.' I phoned him, 'S., what's going on?' He said if I came he would let me take it. How would I dare to go there!"

> A man about 60 years old,
> originally from Slankamen, a farmer

JČŽ: "How does this house compare with your house in Srijem?"

Interlocutor A: "It's an older house, yes it is. There is cane in the ceiling, whereas we put up a [concrete] floor [laughter on the part of the Srijem Croats present], two actually, three—counting the one over the basement. When I walk here the stove shakes [striking the floor with her foot]."

JČŽ: "How large is this house compared with your house in Srijem? How many rooms are there?"

Interlocutor A: "There are fewer rooms [a sigh]. There are less because we had two in the loft there. We had two rooms and both had lovely large halls, and the upper and lower three by . . . My goodness, how large? Three by four, I guess, no, six, three by six in metres. And the upstairs and downstairs halls. Ceramic tiles everywhere, and I put up wallpaper. My daughters helped. . . ."

JČŽ: "Did you ask the house owner here for a supplementary payment for the value of your house? Was that done?"

Interlocutor A: "Yes, people did it. We were stupid, not to write it down. We extracted a bit, but we should have got more, that wasn't it . . . There [in Srijem] we had guttering and the house had a stucco facade, and . . . They gave us two cows and one calf and two sows, supposedly, because our house was a better one."

JČŽ: "You don't think that was enough?"

Interlocutor A: "No, it wasn't, how much does just a facade cost! And then there's the wainscoting we need here. We built everything new there. We built the house in 1981. And everything, as they say, built with concrete. We didn't need wainscoting. From the street here, you can see all the beams."

Interlocutor B: "Here, when it's raining, you sit here and it falls on you and that's it. What now? F—k . . . What can I do now? I'm not going to kill myself . . ."

Interlocutor A: "We have a roof over our heads."

A married couple about 70 years old,
originally from Slankamen, farmers

JČŽ: "To what extent do you think the Srijem Croats adequately exchanged their land and houses?"

Interlocutor: "Well, you see, it's like this, they were . . . it's hard to know how and in what sense to measure those values. Those people who came to a town from a village . . . just in that respect things are more valuable in towns. However, these people of ours who exchanged village for village—that can't be compared at all. For example, our villages, they had completely installed infrastructure, you don't know how to compare it. However, something happened that I foresaw, it happened that the economy of Yugoslavia fell apart, while Croatia more or less survived or was less affected. And today, when those people look [at the situation], in many cases if they were to sell what they have here they could buy there, because everything there has lost its value, there, for example, an acre of land was ten thousand Marks, now it's one thousand, not even a thousand. That's the way things have gone."

A man about 60 years old, originally from Hrtkovci,
has been living in Croatia for some twenty years

One's Own and Other People's

Interlocutor: "I said to my daughters: Are we going to exchange our things? I won't sleep on Serbian couches! I am taking my own! And even if it's not my room, when I put my things in it, it will be easier for me. That's what happened. We included it in the contract that we were exchanging our cabinet. But she [the Serbian woman with whom she exchanged her house] said, 'My shelves are bigger, my cabinet looks better,' said that former lady of the house. But it wasn't, I could see that her furniture was smaller. Our furniture—here where the cabinet stood was 4 by 4.60 metres, and there was this much room on both sides [she indicates the width]. And hers [cabinet] was combined with some color like this and brownish, and . . . But, they convinced me that it would be damaged in transport . . . so I agreed and we put it in the contract that we were exchanging the cabinets. I went home, but M. [a neighbor in Slankamen] used to drop in at my place, and I kept saying, I said, 'I don't like her cabinet. Even if it is more beautiful, I find *my* cabinet more beautiful. It is *mine!*' [the informant strongly emphasizes the word 'mine'] And she said, 'Grandmother M., just you take your shelving.' . . . I listened to her, even though she's younger [laughter], and I brought my cabinet and I'm happy! Oh, N. [the woman she was exchanging with] was so angry!"

Interlocutor B: "It meant a lot, when you saw something of your own here in everything that was new, something of your own. It meant a lot."

A peasant woman about 70 and a woman about 30 years old
with a high school education, both originally from Slankamen

Interlocutor: "Now, it's all like some sort of current, like a wave when I remember all that it was like [resettling]. We were not aware of everything that was going on and what it was like."

JČŽ: "How long did it take for you to become calm?"

Interlocutor: "I . . . I couldn't settle down. Every time I would take hold of the door handle, I would start to shudder and shake. I would think, my God, my own house, my own house! I would think, why [did we have to leave]?"

A woman about 60 years old,
originally from Slankamen, a farmer

JČŽ: "What do you like in Gradina?"

Interlocutor: "I couldn't say that I like anything. But then, I like it, just that the children, that the children . . . that all our kin are here! There, that's what is dearest to me. But otherwise, what can we do! I tell you, our fruit, our peaches, our vineyards, our apples, everything we had, was all left there! Everything was left behind!"

A woman about 80 years old,
originally from Slankamen, a farmer

Interlocutor: "It's not like Srijem soil [in Gradina]. I was saying to K. [a neighbor, a local woman] when we plough in the autumn, in the vegetable garden . . . and when it freezes, I never let anyone in with a harrow or a horse, and certainly not with a tractor! I have never let a tractor with a harrow into my vegetable garden. In spring, I take a rake and as I plant so I rake: it was never lumpy, the soil was like ash. She [the neighbor in Gradina] perhaps does not believe me, eh? But here [in Gradina] we have really hit the jackpot with the vegetable garden—this was once the land of some earl or something—and something made of brick stood here, so we keep on ploughing up bricks. I have already picked out a pile of bricks from the vegetable garden! You can't strike once with the hoe without hitting a brick, every time, and pieces of brick, and when my husband was ploughing there one day he ploughed up a huge, entire brick. If he goes a bit deeper and . . . Well, I told you, there's nothing like my vegetable garden! Nowhere! And not so much grass grew in it. Here, here's grass and grass . . ."

A woman about 70 years old,
originally from Slankamen, a farmer

Interlocutor: "They [grandmother and great-grandmother] crossed the bridge on foot. And grandmother took across a shoot of rubber-plant. That rubber-plant arrived in a very ordinary bag, like that, with a little bit of water on the roots. I told her on the phone, I said, 'Mother, at least bring me a shoot.' The rubber-plant was huge, at least just one shoot. And she brought it in her bag and how fine it is now. And that big philodendron arrived in a pot. Grandfather brought it somehow on the lorry when he came. D. [her husband] teases me now, that I have to change the soil—it's already huge, up to the ceiling—I have to change the soil. 'Don't change it,' he says, 'that is Slankamen [soil] in the pot.'" [laughter]

A woman about 30 years old, originally
from Slankamen, high school education

Interlocutor A: "Listen to what I am going to tell you now . . . at one time, my father . . . my father, when things were disappointing here, in the first year of our stay, came to us and said, if only there could be some possibility for him to go back to Slankamen, and so on. A. [the interlocutor's wife] said to him, 'Well, alright, I know, but how could you go back to Slankamen when your children are here? We have no intention of going back to Serbia.' He said [the father], 'Yes, but *my* house is there!' [with strong emphasis on the word 'my']!"

Interlocutor B: "And it was like that for two years. We had it for two years . . . whenever—you just saw them crying [grandfather and grandmother], it was always 'my house, my house.' I was already . . . Alright then, how long are we going to have this house business?"

A married couple about 50 years old,
originally from Slankamen, both hold degrees

Nostalgia

Interlocutor: "Dreams are stronger than reality, you can't suggest to a man what he should dream. Never in my life, in these ten years, I have never dreamt about Slankamen, but I often dream about the Danube, I almost always dream about the Danube! A little time passes, and then once a week or once a month I dream about the Danube. To me, the Danube is nostalgia, and when I first went to Vukovar, after they [the Serbs] left, when it was liberated, I immediately ran down to the Danube. It was winter, and I immediately ran down to the Danube to wash my hands. And to me, when I saw the Danube, to me it was as if I was back in Slankamen! And Šarengrad [a town in eastern Croatia] was the only place that reminded me not of Slankamen, but it was perhaps closest to the Danube, and it lies on the water itself [and that is why he bought a small house there]."

A man about 50 years old, originally
from Slankamen, high school education

Interlocutor: "When I go down to it [the Danube]—that air . . . The water feels as if it were the sea. But on the Drava River [now in his vicinity]—it's nothing."

A man about 50 years old, originally
from Golubinci, holds a degree

Interlocutor: "Look, nostalgia for your birthplace. That's normal. . . . Sometimes I ask myself, Lord, what would it be like if we were perhaps [laughter] to go back? You know, it's a different feeling: they [the internally displaced persons in Croatia] have been displaced for those six years and suffered and now—now they are going home! But we are staying behind! There are no houses for us there!" [the woman speaks in a low and sweet voice]

JČŽ: "Hasn't the house in Gradina become your home?"

Interlocutor: "Yes, it has, but you know there's always something, there's
something there in a person's subconscious mind . . . And, you know
what, it's very strange to me—I always say that what we left in Slankamen is our house, and this one in Gradina belongs to Š. [the name of
the former owner] [laughter] . . . But you know what surprises me:
simply when I am at the seaside during the summer and now when I
want to say something quickly—'Now I have to go . . . ' I never say
'to Gradina!' I have never said to Gradina! I'm always going to Slankamen. It's . . . I'm telling you, I find myself saying so many times that
I'm going to Slankamen. I find it so hard to say 'I'm going to Gradina.'
. . . I have caught myself so many times saying to my mother-in-law:
'Now when I go to Slankamen' . . . and then she starts laughing. Then
I see that I have made a mistake. Ohh, to Gradina!"

> A woman about 30 years old, originally
> from Slankamen, high school education

Interlocutor: "Something interesting now. I spent [some time] there in Buda-
kovac [a village near Gradina]—I was there from March right up until
All Hallows in 1993 when I came here [to Croatia], I slept there non-
stop. Now I look at it like this, you're here every day and working. But,
I am not interested in that path beside the field. I don't find it beautiful.
It's not the same grass to me! F—k it all, it's not the same and that's it!
While there [in Srijem]—it's stupid to say it—but I must have, must
have known every blade of grass on the way to the vineyard and to the
field [in Srijem]. I mean, it's . . . I can't make myself . . . [love it?], no way.
I don't know what I would, what I would do if they gave me an English
park, I just don't know. It's strange! . . . Let's say, I have now come somehow to like the house [that he exchanged]. I feel good in the house. But
now I'm looking for something else—you know I have lived in Zagreb,
Vukovar, Belgrade, down on the coast. Where to live is no problem to
me. But that house of mine and the yard, and the garden, that's . . . , you
can't exchange that with anything. There's nothing . . . I'm telling you!
I know exactly . . . And now I'm going backwards and that's so great to
me: I am going back to when I was small, and that huge vineyard, an
acre and a half, with my uncle, my father, my grandfather, and I see the
cows there, and the little road, and a fruit tree or so . . . That is, that is it
. . . and I mourn deeply for those times. And they were good times and
people loved each other, they did not hate each other, there was not this
race for money."

> A man about 50 years old, originally
> from Golubinci, holds a degree

Chapter 3

Identity Building in
the Local Environment

It depends a little bit on each individual—what position he takes in his environment, and, you know, these antagonisms are then overcome, people accept it and so.

> A man about 30 years old, originally from
> Slankamen, with high school education

In this chapter I will analyze individual identity-building strategies with the help of which the newcomers to Gradina attempt to bridge the chasm between their earlier and current life, with each having its own value code (cf. Camilleri 1998: 253–254). The chasm has emerged as a result of the drastic change in their life and in their social circumstances which they experienced because of the forced migration. Striving to make sense of their earlier and new experiences, the settlers find ways to relate their experiences to each other so as to redefine their understanding of themselves both as persons and as members of the local community. In the context of migration, identity-building strategies serve the purpose of reevaluating and redefining personal identity in a new social and cultural setting, and thus establishing social identity in the new environment. They are not the same for all the settlers from Srijem—the strategies they adopt are different, even within a single family. Settlers may reject the host society, and may demonstrate the capability to participate in it in different ways; both of these are two specific and individual ways of dealing with the new setting.

I shall present three identity-building strategies used by the Srijem settlers in their new setting. Elderly people treat the migration with resignation; they view the new environment with a critical eye and judge it ethnocentrically, leaving the role of initiators of social incorporation in Gradina to their offspring. They see their own role in the new environment only through their offspring, explaining that their decision to move was clearly determined by their care for their offspring. The second type of settlers' reactions is similar in some of its attitudes. It shares the ethnocentric evaluation of the host culture and the host society with the first type, but differs from it in the verbal rejection of any possibility of settling in the new environment. Looking back, such a person lives in her/his idealized world of the past, physically in Gradina, but isolated from it, her/his mind and spirit somewhere else; her/his emotional state may be described as sorrow, and the strategy s/he employs is based on ontological identity, on irreplaceable values that the person had integrated before the migration (cf. Camilleri 1998). In contrast, some people are very active in their attempts to integrate into the host society. Their identity-building strategy emphasizes the personal as opposed to the collective identity of an individual as the basis of integration into the new environment. Using a "civic" strategy of inclusion, they define their experience outside the experience of the group with which they moved, building their identification and integration strategies on a pragmatic acceptance of the new environment.

Most of the settlers I talked to employ the first strategy, which may vary depending on the age of their offspring, their own age, whether they live with their children or not, whether they still work, etc. The remaining two types are not as common—their representativeness does not lie in the number of cases they cover, but in the personal experiences they represent, which can, in turn, be interpreted as an example of possible immigrant reactions. Hence, the ethnography of the particular (Abu-Lughod 1991) emerges as the most appropriate exposition method in this chapter, because we find members of a single family who interpret their migration experience, the possibilities of adapting to the new environment, and their role in it in completely opposite ways.

"If they are doing well, we are doing well too": Resignation

I can't tell you and remember full of sorrow what and how we left. Yes, all this beauty, all this beauty; that soil of ours, I tell you, it is as loose as soot when we work it. And here, the climate is different, everything is different, the air, and everything. Our Slankamen! Oh, God! Fruška gora! What beauty! The Danube, you know, nearby, three kilometers away.

There's not a thing, not a single thing we can do. I can only say: "Thank you, my Lord." Again, I can only say, I'm grateful that there's children, grateful that the children are alive.

A woman about 70 years old, originally from Slankamen, a farmer

Resignation is the basic attitude of older settlers from Srijem, both men and women, toward the new environment. They are strongly attached to the village they were forced to leave at an old age, the village where they left "all that was best and most beautiful," and where, they are quick to point out, they left all the possessions that their ancestors and they themselves had acquired over the years ("*our* inheritance," "*our* house"). For them, this migration has signified a caesura in their life, after which, because of their age and their unfamiliarity with the new environment, they believe they can hardly go on living their life where it had been broken off before they left Srijem. Therefore, in redefining their own identity in the new setting, the elderly rely on their children. Let us examine the elements of their identity-building strategy.

The Srijem farmers and fruit producers managed to take advantage of the agricultural market boom of the 1980s and became successful crop producers or fruit and vegetable retailers. Fruit retailers from Slankamen, for instance, would go to large nearby and distant cities, such as Zemun, Belgrade, Novi Sad, etc. Hard work in the summer months, practically with no rest, ensured a relatively high living standard, and they primarily invested their earnings into newly built houses and yards.

Their estimates of the financial losses they suffered in the exchange vary; sometimes they estimate to have lost as much as 30 to 50 percent. There is no way for the researcher to check the accuracy of their statements and the situation seems to vary considerably from family to family. What may be more important than their financial loss is their loss of ownership, the loss of the feeling that the house where they live and the land they farm were earned by them (see narrations in chapter 2). Although they have become legal owners, they do not experience the "new" property as their own but as "somebody else's." An elderly man talked about going back to Slankamen for two years, explaining curtly: "But *my* house is there, *my* house is there," while a woman said that she could not stop thinking for a whole year about the house she left in Slankamen: "Every time I would take hold of the door handle, I would start to shudder and shake. I would think, my God, my own house, my own house! I would think, why [did we have to leave]?" (see chapter 2). Another elderly woman, when I asked her whether the house she moved into in Gradina would ever become hers, answered "not really, not really."

For an elderly person from Srijem, his or her house represents tangible assets, and it may be the result of their life's work and investment; it is in every way owned by the family that built it, as prescribed by the old as well as the more recent tradition of the region, and by the family members' participation in decisions about its appearance and furnishings. It is also much more than that: it is a method of achieving and maintaining the status of the family in the village community; in a rural setting, the status of the family would be mirrored and displayed to others by their house (Bourdieu et al. 2002; Schnapper 1976: 489). In this sense "my" or "our" house is irreplaceable for the elderly settlers from Srijem; its value is material, social, emotional. In short, incalculable, therefore it may take a long while before the elderly accept the houses they moved into in Gradina as their own, or, indeed, it may never happen. Let us consider a short statement about the house which was left behind, although its written form can never reflect all of the pain and sorrow with which the old women uttered her words:

> Oh, the house we had in Slankamen! With two businesses, two shops! Oh what a house that was! And where we are now! You have seen it. What can we do! Thank God that the children are alive. That's all.

The category of beautiful is subjective par excellence. What a person has earned, built, bought by himself is beautiful; what is your own is beautiful: "I don't like her cabinet. Even if it is more beautiful, I find *my* cabinet more beautiful. It is *mine!*" said an elderly Srijem woman (see chapter 2). Since nothing they have come across in Gradina has been made by them or is the result of their choice, every cabinet, every flower brought from Srijem (still planted in the Srijem soil), every detail brought from their own house is a small but very important pleasure in the life of elderly Srijem women.[1]

For the elderly, nothing can replace the cultural or natural setting of Srijem. One woman compared her old garden in Slankamen and her new garden in Gradina, and concluded, full of longing and sorrow: "There is nothing like my garden there [in Srijem]!" Another one compared landscapes with almost poetic rapture:

> When I left, when we passed Subotica [a town in Vojvodina], lo and behold! . . . all was white with snow, and so beautiful. You can't see the end of it. You can't see a single tree. You can't see . . . And I think, oh how beautiful this Srijem and this Bačka [are], and what a wonderful life!

And, you see, [these people] here like nothing but greenery and trees, and they say they are better for you.

Stressing the pronoun "ours," one of my male narrators said excitedly: "When they show those fine horses, those customs over there and when I see those beautiful front gates—and when I see all of that—*ours*—I still care! I could wail with grief! I still care!" The pronoun "ours" is crucial in the relationship of the elderly people from Srijem toward their new and old environment. There is nothing in Gradina that could make up for the fact that they were not born there, that Gradina is not their "mother country," and that they are foreigners there. Let us consider a conversation between two elderly women:

Woman A: "We have everything here, doctors and everything. Our doctor's office [in Gradina] is more beautiful than the one in Slankamen. Like a small hospital. They can take your blood there and everything. We did not have that [in Slankamen]. We did not have any of that . . . We also have a church and a school."

Woman B: "It's not bad, everything is nice and neat, but that's of no use, it's not *ours!* You know, we were not born here, no no, we were not born here, oh, oh, oh."

The people from Srijem have experienced a drastic break in the space and time of their life, they lost their familiarity with the world, and their memories are filled with intense feelings which exaggerate the characteristics of their home region (Raphaël and Herberich-Marx 1999). They suffer for what they have lost, for familiar things that seem "more beautiful" in comparison, because of the very fact that they are theirs. This is why a comparison of the appearance of the village, the church, the layout of the garden and the house, the location, quality, and size of the fields and of livestock in Srijem and in their new setting will necessarily be unfavorable for the latter. Let us consider the following narration:

JČŽ: "You do not like this yard?"

Interlocutor: "I don't like that it is so wide and that there is so much in this yard; grass in the summer and he [the husband] cuts it down for the pigs, and nettles on that side under the cherry tree. When I was sick, I could not take care of all of that. Last year I weeded several times, and then once again, I do not like that there are nettles. Where we lived there was our house, a small planting area, and there was Brompton stock, and those nice tulips, everything was so nice . . ."

If they mention any good points concerning their migration, a part of the older generation will say that they are pleased to have moved to Croatia. Given that the eastern part of Srijem was an integral part of Croatia in the more recent past, i.e., from the eighteenth century to 1918, and in the Independent State of Croatia, and given that by its Croatian inhabitants it was not considered part of Vojvodina or Serbia in the former Yugoslavia (for more details see chapter 1), the people from Srijem (not only the elderly) have learned from an early age from their parents that Srijem is part of Croatia and that they are Croats. Therefore, they are at least satisfied with the fact that they have moved to Croatia, where they claim to belong:

Interlocutor A: "We like it that we have come to Croatia."
Interlocutor B: "Yes, we like to have come here. We [are] real Croats! That's that! I don't like to go . . . I wouldn't like to have gone God knows where. Because we are Croats! We love our own!"

They talk about their own Croatian nationality and the Croatian nationality of all people from Srijem with pride: "When I would go to Osijek [a town in Croatia], when I would see the Croatian flag—yes there was a five-pointed star on it, but it was Croatian flag nonetheless[2]—I was so happy my heart leaped like this [he shows how]!" [laughter]

This elderly man believes that his love for Croatia and the creation of the independent Croatian state would have been reason enough for a decision to move, even if there had not been any coercion.

The feelings of my interlocutors are ambivalent: on the one hand, they claim that, being members of the Croatian nation, they are happy to live in the newly created Croatian state; on the other hand, they have not come to terms with the fact that they have left their material possessions and their social capital in Srijem. The satisfaction of living in their "mother country" seems to provide the elderly with nothing more than a verbal consolation for the arising circumstances, a means to persuade themselves that the migration has its positive aspects. If there had been an alternative to the migration, everyone would have gladly chosen it. According to my interlocutors, a possible alternative would have been for the eastern part of Srijem to become part of the Croatian state once again. In that case, they would not have been forced to move, which is what the following 80-year-old woman believes:

I wish that this difficult time had never come. I like it, you know, I like it that we can call this our Croatia and that we are Croats and that Croatia

is ours. But I keep thinking, if only there had been no such great migration, you know, if only we had been left alone. If only, like a long time
ago, Croatia had stretched to Zemun, it would have been different. But
instead, this migration and this torture, oh, oh, oh. When I look at where
we are now, oh my; and you must have seen the water leaking over there,
and oh, what a house we had left. [sigh]

Today (1996–1998) most would decide to go back, on the condition
that their fellow villagers would also go back, and that the Serbs living
in their houses would return to Croatia. Let us consider a few opinions
of elderly people from Srijem:

Interlocutor A: "I would prefer if I could go back there, not alone, though, but
if all of these people who were there would go back. Who would want
to live with them [Serbs from Croatia] over there? I mean we could live,
with those Serbs—our Serbs, but with these Serbs we couldn't!"[3]

Interlocutor B: "You know what, let me tell you something from the heart, like
a woman! If they were to say 'Everybody go back to their house!' I would
go too, even if I had to walk all the way!"

Sometimes these conversations are accompanied by jokes at their own
expense, which reflect the moral strength of these people. Slight mock-
ery at their own expense on different occasions, as will become evident
later, is one of the ways in which the people from Srijem cope with their
difficult situation. Three older women talking:

Woman A: "I would go back! Not that I wouldn't! I certainly would! To my
home village, to my fatherland, as they say. But only if my people would
return too!"

Woman B: "But you have just managed to learn a bit of Croatian."

Woman A: "Only if my people would return! I have learned a lot of Croatian."
[laughter]

Woman C: "You would be in trouble! They would not understand you!"

Woman B: "And then you'd want to come back here."[4]

There are two aspects that are characteristic of the life of elderly people
in Gradina. The first is the compact migration of a considerable number of people from Srijem in the so-called new, peripheral part of the
village, which used to be populated by Serbs before their arrival. The
isolation enables the elderly, less mobile, and less active settlers, to feel
that they are among "their own people," even though they are no longer
in Srijem. They welcome homogenous settling in a separate part of the
village and they do not often have to be in the other part of the village to

come into contact with the local inhabitants. Every time they go out to the street, every afternoon they sit on a bench (that some have brought with them from Srijem!) on the sidewalk in front of their house or yard, they have the opportunity to feel as if they were "at home." Apart from "grumbling" they also "amuse themselves":

> Thank Lord, that's what I say. When I go out to the street here, there are plenty of us, us people from Slankamen, a street full of us. We all have great . . . so to say amusement when we go out to the street. The whole neighborhood gathers round, we are all together. We have to forget all that was, that's how it has to be. Hard, hard times and a hard life. And I say thank Lord that it isn't any worse than this.

In a strange landscape, in what seems to them a street of unusual yards and unusual organization of agricultural areas, their segregation has a salutary effect in so far as it reduces the experience of radical otherness which they feel as immigrants (cf. Raphaël and Herberich-Marx 1999). Living in a kind of ghetto gives these older settlers an opportunity to strengthen networks established in their home village and to create new connections with immigrants from villages other than their own. Even here, on the periphery of the village, the settlers from Srijem experience otherness with respect to their co-settlers,[5] but to a lesser extent than in encounters with the local population. It can, therefore, be expected that the marginal position of the resettled part of the village will favor homogenization of immigrants from various villages in Srijem, and that it will perpetuate the perception of immigrants as newcomers with respect to the local population.

The second favorable circumstance in the life of older migrants is their decision to migrate with their offspring. Being used to living with their offspring in stem-family households (and living for them), the older generations cannot conceive of the possibility of living alone and they connect their future with the future of their children and grandchildren. The adaptation of their offspring to the new environment provides them with confidence that their decision to move was not a mistake, although their sorrow for their home region remains:

JČŽ: "Do you feel better when you see that your children are coping well?"
Interlocutor: "Certainly. My heart fills up with joy when I see my children. What can I do? Life has to go on for the children. What would we do without the children; that's what we are used to. . . . What would we do? That's how it has to be! We are with our children, and thank God for that, but the sorrow still remains."

Older people accept life in their new environment indirectly, through their children, without taking part in the integrative social processes that will affect or that have affected younger people. Believing that it is too late for them and that their time has passed, they reject the possibility of their own adaptation, but do not doubt that their children, and especially their grandchildren, will assimilate into the new community.

Although they are still able to work, these people allow their adult offspring to take over most economic activities and social action in their resettlement community, which is discussed in detail in the following chapter. The elderly possess wisdom that some younger settlers might lack. Although they believe they can teach the locals various new things, they are not aggressive and they adapt when they consider it to be better than standing out, because one should not be the odd man out, "a white crow among black," they would say. They believe that, being newcomers, they should repress their discontent, keep it to themselves, and join the majority: "The village is always stronger than the wedding procession [laughter]. . . . A man is by nature such that he has to communicate. If you want to do that, you must adapt. If you won't budge, then it's all over."

One of the first things they accepted from the locals is the village patron saint, St. Elias. They celebrated the patron saint of their native village only the first year after they arrived, when they asked the priest to celebrate mass.[6] They unanimously agree they could not demand that Gradina change its patron saint, because the local population "would really take offense." Besides, they all come from different villages, which had different patron saints. And as their religion is common to all of them, they say it is all the same whether they celebrate St. Michael (as in Slankamen), St. George (as in Golubinci), or St. Elias (as in Gradina):

> What now? You can't! You can't drive a nail through a brick wall. You can't, no you can't. You have to accept. A bride who comes into her husband's family house has to change her life immediately. After a while everything is as the bride says, but today [at the beginning] it can't be. It can't! It is still clear that there is someone older in the house. These people are older here, and we must respect them. And it's all the same—St. Elias or St. Michael.

Although the community's acceptance of religious customs and behaviors is easier because both the local population and the settlers are Roman Catholics, the elderly settlers believe that it is too late for their social integration. They have left their friends, acquaintances, relatives, and neighbors in Srijem, and they can only engage in short impersonal

conversations with the locals. Some of the newcomers have not even con-
sulted the local population about cultivating soil, but have learned on
their own, some by trial and error, what the quality of the soil was and
what changes they needed to make in their way of cultivating it.

The elderly people from Srijem cannot converse with the natives because they lack the social competence created while living in a particular
environment; they do not know the village or its inhabitants, or their
relationships, they do not know which of them are friends and which of
them are on bad terms with one another, in short they to not know "the
old stories." Here is what an elderly couple says:

Husband: "This can't be done overnight or in a short time. A man must grow
up somewhere to create all that. When I came here . . . I mean, I do have
friends here. People have accepted us. But I grew up over there and I
know that place, and I do not know this place. So what can I talk about
with them [the local population]? I can talk about that it rained, about
the crop, if it will be good, I mean I can talk about all that, but I can't talk
much longer than that . . ."
Wife: "The old stories—that's what we don't know, and the people, anybody. And
they [the local population] when they meet they know their own. And we,
people from Slankamen, when we meet here, oh, we mostly grumble."

The older immigrants' comparison between the natural and cultural setting of their home region and their resettlement community clearly il-
lustrates their sense of a rupture in space, a destroyed intimacy with the
world that they previously left only in exceptional cases and temporarily, a loss of the psychological and emotional safety provided by material goods, and above all their attachment to their home region, their
soil, and the possessions that they themselves acquired. Now they are
forced to live in an unfamiliar environment, both immediate and not-
so-immediate, in a house whose dimensions and layout they still have
to get used to, surrounded by unfamiliar things. Despite the fact that
they have become legal owners of the houses, they do not consider them
their own. One woman says she feels as if she were among stolen things.
I speak of the resigned identity of older settlers because for the older
people from Srijem, their children and grandchildren are the source of
their current identity and self-evaluation, and it is through them that
they have accepted their life in Gradina.

The impossibility of getting over everything that was left behind cor-
relates with a negative attitude toward the new environment and closed
attitude to the local population. However, older people from Srijem share
the attitude that as a minority they should adapt to the native majority;

that is, they should not stand out. Generally speaking, they believe they have been accepted, and that there have been no serious problems in their relationships with the local population. Several older people stand out because of their especially tolerant attitude toward ethnic and cultural differences, which emphasizes the common humanity of all people.

"We will never get over It": The Srijem Sorrow

There is still a small part of us who have stayed home on their land. These people still speak the Ekavian dialect, like they did in Slankamen. They have not yet changed anything in their old way of life and work. They still do everything as if they were still there. They are only physically here. Is this the reason that they do not work anywhere? I don't know.

A man about 30 years old, originally
from Slankamen, with high school

This is how a man from Srijem, himself well incorporated into Gradina, described some of his fellow villagers. His characterization goes to the heart of how some of the settlers live in the new environment: looking back on Srijem and the villages they left behind, they are turned toward the past, which they idealize, and freeze images created before the political turmoil that brought about the abandonment of their home region, and they are convinced they "will never get over it" and that "they will die with this burden." These people from Srijem are extremely critical toward their new environment and they depict it almost exclusively negatively; they overlook even the most evident positive characteristics that their family members draw their attention to, and they claim that they will never be able to "get accustomed to it." A young farmer from Srijem is the main representative of this attitude:

Interlocutor: "The younger people will adapt, but we won't. I am thirty years of age, but I can't adapt, no way. These youngsters who go to school here, they will learn. They will associate with the old locals, they will mix with them, get married with them, and we can't do that."

JČŽ: "Why can't you do that?"

Interlocutor: "Because I have spent the best years of my life there, and I can't forget that! . . ."

JČŽ: "Such a young man, and he can't change?"

Interlocutor: "No he can't, he can't. Maybe if there were one—two—three houses here, and if there were a few of us, maybe it would be different. But like this, no way."

This man has identified one of the important factors that make it difficult for him to adapt and accept life in the new environment. The people
from Srijem settled in the new part of Gradina as a larger group, entirely occupying a street that had been on the periphery of the village,
isolated from the rest of the village even before their arrival, and have
therefore been exposed to intensive contacts among themselves and have
been marginalized in relation to the center of the village. The agricultural
orientation of most of the people from Srijem[7] and the advanced age of
a considerable number of them additionally minimizes contacts with the
local population; this leads them to maintaining regular contacts with
other people from Srijem, speaking their organic idiom in which they
were enculturated, and most often discussing the past, their forced migration, the life in Srijem in comparison to their life in Gradina, etc.

Looking back on her home village where she occupied a certain social
position in the local relations, an elderly woman remains uninterested
in the new environment where she has not managed (nor has she tried)
to gain a similar position. Moreover, she considers it more important to
assess her current social position in relation to the position she used to oc-
cupy in her home village than in relation to the present social setting. Although she has lived in Gradina for several years, this woman is still in the
liminal position, that is, in between the two places of settlement: she has
been removed from the place where she spent her entire life and settled
in an unfamiliar one, where her status remains to be achieved. She de-
termines her position using the standards of her home village and suffers
because of a feeling of loss of social position as a result of being settled in
the peripheral part of Gradina. According to her opinion, the fact that her
house in Gradina is next to an (unfinished) Serbian Orthodox church and
a graveyard lowers her status in her home village of Slankamen. A positive
evaluation of this location within Gradina is of little comfort to her, and
her husband keeps apologizing for not having noticed when choosing the
house that it was next to a graveyard.[8] The rather sad narration of this
women is interrupted by the laughter and irony of those present, and by
her and her husband's attempt to laugh at everything themselves. Self-
irony is a means to overcome their torment and sorrow, a way to relax and
accept their situation. For instance, one of the participants in the conversation suggests what the woman should do if she does not like the view of
the Serbian Orthodox church: "You should put a curtain there, and you
shouldn't look. When the plums bloom, you won't see it!"

Contacts with "one of us," which is what people from Srijem call one
another, sometimes go beyond the boundaries of the resettlement community. Every opportunity is used: a funeral of a friend or a relative as

far as two hundred kilometers away, even of a person one has only heard of, is an opportunity to meet people from Srijem and obtain information about events in all of Srijem and in their home village. My young interlocutor who refuses the possibility of adapting to the new setting says:

JČŽ: "These meetings with other people from Srijem connect you?"
Interlocutor: "Yes, we see each other, and we talk about this and that in Srijem. You always hear new things and so."
JČŽ: "Are you interested in this information?"
Interlocutor: "Very much so."
JČŽ: "Are you interested in what is going on in Slankamen?"
Interlocutor: "Of course. We can hardly wait for someone to arrive to hear whether there is something new in Slankamen: who died, what happened at Christmas, what happened at Whit Sunday, what is new with this person and that, how they spent St. Michael's. . . ."
JČŽ: "It seems to me like you've never left Slankamen?"
Interlocutor: "Well, yes."

This young man lives only physically in Gradina, but his heart is somewhere else, in the community that he was forced to abandon. He is still more interested in news from his home village—various village events, who died, celebrations of important village holidays, etc.—than in the possibility of inclusion into social networks in the resettlement community and of eventually developing the competence to take part in local conversations and events with the native population. Information from Srijem transmitted orally or by video images gives this man an illusion that he still has not lost contact with his home region. At the same time, it takes up so much of his free time and emotional engagement that there is no need for him to seek those items in the new environment.

Attending funerals of deceased people from Srijem confirms the traditional importance of the funeral as a local social event. The difference lies in the fact that in this case, it is not just a gathering of former fellow villagers and relatives who are now scattered through various parts of Croatia, but also of people from neighboring villages who may never have been in contact with the deceased or with his family. Attending a funeral of an unfamiliar person brings together a community wider than the village community, and results in connecting people from different parts of Srijem. It is not important whether someone is from the village of Kukujevci, Slankamen, or Nikinci: "No, not at all, as long as he is from Srijem, it does not matter from which village, he is one of us!" said my young interlocutor. In the immigration situation, village affiliation, which used to be the identification reference point, has been combined with the wider regional affiliation.

Because of intensive contacts among people from Srijem, these settlers have more difficulty in changing their native Srijem dialect. While this is understandable for the elderly, and hardly anyone will hold it against them, younger persons who resist changing their idiom attract attention, both of their peers from Srijem and of the locals. My interlocutor, who rejects the idea that he could accept life in Gradina, admits to not even trying, as opposed to his wife who attempts to use the local dialect for the sake of her children.

In addition to claiming that he is unable to adjust as well as to socializing mainly with people from Srijem and refusing to change his idiom, my young interlocutor is very critical when comparing the lifestyle in Gradina to his home village. He considers the difference between these two settings to be "big, big"; so big, in fact, that the very possibility of comparison is questionable ("It can't be compared"):

JČŽ: "Which differences come to mind first?"
Interlocutor: "First of all we had concrete yards there. Everyone did, even the poorest people, if they could not have concrete in their yard, they at least used bricks to lay it with, and here there is nothing like that, nothing. Also, in Gradina we have a town water supply, . . . while the villages all around here do not have a water supply at all; they still have electric pumps and wells. To us that's unthinkable, we can't imagine things being like that. For example, take Dijelka and Ada,[9] where our people from Slankamen live, they have to go to the third or fourth house—if they have a good well—to fetch drinking water. One of our people says 'I am cleaner getting into the bath than when I get out of it,' the water is of such bad quality. No sign of a town water supply! There [in Srijem] we had a church, a post office, a doctor's office. We have them here in Gradina, but the nearby villages don't. . . ."
JČŽ: "The differences are big?"
Interlocutor: "Yes, they are. We are not used to this type of life. We in Gradina, we are still okay, but the villages around here where our people from Srijem moved, that is very bad, very bad."

There are also differences in certain customs:

Interlocutor: "Well, for instance, funerals are different where we come from. We do it differently than they do. In Srijem, women sing when the deceased is taken out, and things like that. We do it differently than they do."
JČŽ: "Do you think that these differences are important?"

Interlocutor: "No, they are not that important. But we stick to ours; we have not accepted theirs from them."

When asked whether they would accept some customs from the local population, my interlocutor and his grandmother answer:

Grandson: "There's nothing to say, our customs are better than theirs."
JČŽ: "Not all customs are the same?"
Grandson: "Oh, no, not at all. We keep our customs, they keep theirs."
JČŽ: "Do you think that can be done, two customs alongside each other?"
Grandson: "Sure it can be; everyone observes their own."
JČŽ: "But other people's customs should be respected!"
Grandson: "Oh, we respect them. We sure do. We just observe our customs. . . ."
JČŽ: "Since it is you who came here, shouldn't you accept the local customs?"
Grandson: "Perhaps."
Grandmother: "We do accept them, what can we do."
Grandson: "We do accept them, but not so much. We accept theirs and they accept ours."
Grandmother: "We like it that something is the way we do it, but only that which is better."
JČŽ: "How can you say which is better?"
Grandmother: "Oh, no, I am not referring to religion and that, that is common, that's all there is to it. But customs like things we eat and things we do. For example, we always make an aspic dish for Christmas and for Candlemas, and they don't."

On another occasion, I asked again whether they would accept any of the customs from the local population, and I got the answer that there was nothing to accept from them. As a matter of fact, said my interlocutor, a person does not change; once he has learned the way to do things, he does them in this way, and that cannot be changed.

Observing the differences between farming, customs, foods, etc., has the purpose of separating Srijem Croats and the local population (see chapter 5) and defining the personal identity by relying on an imagined Srijem identity. Perceived differences are a starting point that allows a negative evaluation of the local population and emphasizes the progressiveness of the Srijem Croats, not only in their customs but in other domains of life as well. Ascribing a negative identity to the local population only strengthens this man's belief that he himself cannot adapt. After all, why would he change when "they are worse than us!" Looking back at his abandoned home, drowning his individual identity in the collective Srijem identity built on the differences from the local population, he points out the irreplaceable values and habits incorporated before the migration, and the impossibility of a person changing. In this way, he gives coherence to his experience and his life: keeping the self-definition that he had until then, he refuses reidentification in the new setting, emphasizing his ontological rather than his pragmatic identity (cf. Camilleri 1998).

A narrative about the Other is in fact a narrative about oneself— how the man sees the world and his place in it; it is a narrative of self-identification based on ethnocentric judgments of culture in the resettlement community. I consider his ethnocentricity, although it is still unremitting six years after moving, a transient and transitory phenomenon caused by the sorrow for his home region, his familiar and idealized lifestyle of a rich villager from Srijem, and his sorrow for a mythic, exaggerated image of the old life, which he "cannot forget as long as he's alive." It is a rationalization for his inability to adapt to the new setting and his lack of acceptance of the forced migration. Unlike the older group of Srijem Croats, parents and grandparents, this man is not old enough to accept the new life with resignation, lean on his children and grandchildren, and integrate into the new environment. Considering his age, his rejection of the new environment and his claim that he is too old to be resocialized are unusual. His sorrow is so strong that it is not penetrated by the detachment present in the humorous remarks of the resigned elderly at their own expense and at the expense of other people from Srijem.

His wife, who thinks differently than he does, has commented on his attitude on an occasion when her husband was physically there, but, considering his words, absent in spirit:

Wife: "There, you see, we manage to get by somehow, we have gotten used to it, but, you know, there are some of these people from Slankamen who keep feeling sorrow." [looking at her husband and laughing]

Husband: "We will never get over it. . . . We will die filled with this torment. . . ."

Wife: "He feels so old, he feels old and all of that bothers him so much, I don't know why. You can't look on it like that. You must watch your children grow, you must watch them accept it, how they are accepted, and things move on. And the fact that we feel sorrow for some things, well, you know, maybe our folk used to feel sorrow for some other things that couldn't be."

"There's no going back, you have to go forward": Integration

You don't go to complain to anybody. I did not complain to anybody, that's personal. People from Gradina need not know. When they ask me how I did, I say I did fine. Whether this is so or not, that's none of their business. We have not burdened anyone with such matters.

A man about 30 years old, originally
from Slankamen, with high school

Some other young people take an attitude that is completely opposite to the attitude of the young man who feels sorrow for his home region and rejects integration. Agriculture is not their primary occupation; they have completed secondary education, two year post-secondary education, or vocational education. In a stem-family household, these people are the middle generation, they actively work and they take over the leading role from the older generation in earning a living. I will describe this integration strategy on the example of a younger married couple. Their strategy relies on the settlers' activism, on the individualization of both the settlers and the local population, and on a complete inclusion of the settlers into the new environment.

The couple builds their integration, which they consider successful, on a positive relationship toward their new setting and on conscious efforts to be accepted in it. They take advantage of different institutions and seize any opportunity to meet with the local population and to establish contact with them: the church and religious rituals, their work and social activities, friendships that their children make, etc. They mention the church as the first institution where the local population and the settlers came into contact. This was the place where contacts with the local population were made, and it was here that the settlers were first invited to visit the locals at home, which they consider an important step in their relations with the native population. The integrative influence of religion was increased after the Virgin Mary appeared in Gradina on 13 June 1997 to children of the local population and the settlers, including this couple's son. Common prayers were organized in the village for a period of several months after the apparition, at first in the houses of those who witnessed it, and later in the houses of other villagers, at their own request. Prayer groups in which both the local population and the settlers took part were very well attended.

The couple's jobs, which are not connected exclusively to their house and to working the land, allow them to communicate with the local population to a larger extent than the farmers can, both in the village where they settled and outside it. Their frequent contacts with the native population, both direct and through their children, enabled them to increase the number of their acquaintances and to possibly make friends. As they got to know the local dialect, they changed their own speech, and they noticed the differences between their ways and the way in which the local population works, their local traditions, mentality, and expectations.

Although the native population and the settlers can understand each other without difficulty, the main obstacle to establishing closer contacts with the locals for this group of settlers was their idiom. It was their idiom that immediately gave them away as settlers. Because of the effect of their work environment and because of their efforts to make their children's linguistic transition easier, the settlers who maintained a positive and activist relationship to the new environment accepted the change in their speech. In my conversations with them in the summer of 1997 and in the winter of 1998, it was evident that the process of acquiring standard Croatian had begun. Sometimes, they still use their native dialect or an expression typical of it, and in situations when they communicate with people from their home region, they often go back to it. There are cases where the new dialect has prevailed over the old: for example, a young woman is persistent in using the new dialect, regardless of the communication situation she is in: whether she is talking to the researcher, her family members or to the locals.

The settlers who have spent time away from their native region and who speak other languages find it easier to accept changes and the need to adapt. Here is what a man oriented toward integration in the host society says: "And then I realized when I came here. Just like I had to speak Swiss German[10] there, I knew when I came here that I would have to change my speech. I must behave the way they behave here."

This man's son quickly learned the local idiom and introduced it into his home. Sometimes children correct their parents and the parents, in order to avoid ridicule, try to exercise care in their speech. According to the belief of both parties—the settlers and a local teacher—there have been no problems in accepting the immigrants' children in school, nor have they been in any way isolated from the other children. There are also other ways in which children act as a powerful integrative factor for their parents. Children associate outside school, which gives their parents an opportunity to meet, and some children encourage their parents to meet and pay each other visits.

Gradina also offers other possibilities for the settlers and the local population to meet and communicate: in the local firehouse, the hunting club, the soccer club, the village administrative institutions, political party organizations, the folklore group, etc. The locals rate the settlers' participation in the local events and institutions unfavorably, because they do not believe that the settlers accept their invitations as often as they should. However, integration oriented settlers with an active attitude have assumed a leading role in some local associations. For instance, because of the husband's training in folklore, which made him the leader of the restored local folklore group, this young family from Slankamen got the opportunity to get to know almost the entire village: children active in the folklore group and their parents as well as the older generation of the local population, whom the new leader of the folklore group visited in order to restore an old local dance. Both the husband and the wife bear witness to a very good beginning of their social integration in Gradina thanks to their work in the folklore group:

> Thanks to the children I met all Gradina, and I am on great terms with everyone. Many people from Virovitica also know me. A great way for people to meet me, and for me to meet them. My wife and I are accepted here. . . . I know that if I want to visit anyone in Gradina, I know that every door is open to me and that they will accept me, and I am on good terms with everybody. . . . I have made many friends here and we have fitted in really well.

Not only is this couple aware of the role that the activity in the folklore group played in their inclusion in the social networks in the village, they are also aware of the general integrative potential that the presentation of different folk customs may have. This man from Srijem does not only practice local dances with the folklore group, but also dances from the larger region, including Dalmatian dances (there are people of Dalmatian origin in the area). For their performance at a folklore festival in the region of Slavonia, he prepared dances typical of other parts of Slavonia as well as Vojvodina. His effort to present the folklore of the region inhabited by a population of heterogenous origin, dialects, and traditions seems to be a strategic move designed to not only help in the incorporation of the Srijem population into the host society, but also in fostering the multicultural environment in which they live.

These immigrants have accepted the fact of their migration: "There's no going back, you have to go forward," they say. Turning toward the future is not devoid of memories, because the past cannot be forgotten. However, their integration in the host society by taking part in social networks evoked less painful memories of their home region; and their wish to return or even visit Srijem disappears. The husband and the wife say:

Husband: "I do not complain; I like it a lot here."

Wife: "We can't complain to have come [here]. Nostalgia for our home region will always remain."

Husband: "Nostalgia, yes, but I am not drawn to go back. In the beginning I was really drawn to see what it all looks like, because I went away in time [before the changes that the immigrant Serbs have brought to the village]. But with time, as I fit in here, I do not think of it any more, nor do I want to think of it, nor is it of any interest to me any more. All of that has passed."

Wife: "We talk about it more when we meet with people from Slankamen. As far as some kind of sorrow is concerned—it's not like we feel terrible in this environment and like we want to [go back]—we don't feel like that at all. It's more of a normal nostalgia for your home region. We will suffer as long as we live, but there is no disappointment or bitterness. I hear some people who are bitter. I don't know why, they must have some personal problems."

For this couple, accepting the host society and culture is not incompatible with preserving one's own culture. It will not lead to neglecting their Srijem traditions, but will move these traditions from the public to the private sphere, the sphere of family life; while in the public sphere, they will adapt to the community in which they live. These settlers choose an identification strategy that is typical of a national integration of civic society, with the only difference that it functions as local integration. French society is a specific example of this model. Until the 1980s, French society was based on a strict separation and distinction between the public and the private domain. All manifestations of ethnocultural differences among French citizens, including those of religion, were kept in the private sphere. In the public sphere of the centralized state all citizens formally had equal political and social rights. According to Gérard Althabe, this is "a powerful assimilatory model in which each person living in France participates, thus reproducing the distinction between one's own private life, in which expressions of one's ethnocultural specificities are set apart, and public life, in which the individual participates based on formal identity only." (Althabe 1996: 223, translated from French by the author)

Some of the Srijem settlers choose the assimilation model of integration. They do not want to remain visible as settlers in the host society, and they do not want to be integrated based on their specific cultural characteristics and their collective identity. Such inclusion would imply preserving their old identity and the presentation of the individual as the bearer and representative of the Srijem identity, i.e., the identity of the group of Srijem settlers who moved to Croatia in the 1990s.

These people do not want to act as the representatives of the resettled group in the host society nor do they want to present themselves in this way. Their strategy is individual; they want to be included in the host society as individuals formally equal with all other villagers, regardless of whether they are locals or newcomers. Repressing their own cultural characteristics in the public sphere, settlers show their acceptance of the rules and norms of the new environment. Accepting the norms of the resettlement community entitles them to use the institutions that the new community offers; it entitles them to "civil rights" in that community, specifically the right to participate in the local community on an equal footing with the local population. The end result of this strategy is the impossibility to distinguish the settlers from the local population in the public sphere. The culture of origin is repressed into the private sphere, and the immigrant accepts the culture of the host society in the public sphere.

In accordance with the strategy of individual integration, these Srijem Croats do not accept generalizations about themselves or others, being aware that the identity of a person is not just a result of her/his membership in a particular group. They do not want to be seen by the local population primarily as the members (representatives) of the Srijem settlers, and, as a result, they view the locals as individuals and not as a nondifferentiated, alien group of people. Therefore, when asked whether he could remember a conflict with the local population, my integration oriented interlocutor replied by individualizing the native community: "Individually looking, I did come across some minor things several times. But I can't say . . . if I see a drunken person I can't say that everybody is drunk."

For this couple, their individual integration strategy prevails over the usual mechanism of mutual perception of settlers and locals as foreigners, as described by Simmel (1984: 59). They treat their migration and all the difficulties that arose from it in the same individualized way, as their personal problem and not a social one. They believe the responsibility for its solution is a personal and not social (institutional) matter: "Nobody can help us; we have to do it on our own."

As a logical consequence of this attitude, their migration cannot be viewed as the cause of demanding special rights in the wider society, such as organized social aid or economic support of local, regional or state authorities to the immigrants, etc. This attitude is shared by a portion of the Srijem settlers' leaders, which will be discussed in chapter 6.

In a small environment, an individual's social involvement as a citizen, without emphasizing her/his ethnocultural characteristics, is an integration strategy acceptable to the local population, because it does not divide the village and the community into "the native population" and the "newcomers," into "us" and "them." Using this strategy, a newcomer shows that s/he wants to become part of the local community; and it makes the host society accept her/him more easily.

Attempting to be included in the new environment, these younger settlers with secondary education or associate degrees are on the road to social integration in their resettlement community. They make a deliberate decision to be active and change their "give-away" speech. The ghettoization of the Srijem Croats in the separate part of the village does not pose an obstacle for them. The opportunities for interaction with the locals are not geographically limited like in the farmers' case, and arise in their work, in various interest groups in the village, and through their children. Cultural integration is preceded by inclusion in the local social networks. It is safe to assume that the choice of a strategy which emphasizes individual inclusion in the new environment and encloses one's own specific cultural characteristics into the private sphere will result in a cultural division into the public and the private sphere of life, i.e., in the assimilation in the public sphere and the maintenance of ethnocultural characteristics in the family domain. Alternating cultural codes is a strategic component of their identity redefinition in the new environment: the pragmatism of the strategy they selected opens the door to integration and enables them to reevaluate their own experience.

Ethnocentrism of the Newcomers

These three identity-building strategies of the settlers from Srijem who live in Gradina can be viewed as paradigmatic of the relationship of newcomers toward their new environment.

Shutting out the new environment and using their age to justify their inability to accept its norms and achieve social integration, the elderly live in isolation in their part of the village. Their resignation finds refuge primarily in the identification with their offspring, whose successful integration they believe to occur, beyond a doubt. In accordance with the expectation to spend the rest of their life in their children's shadow and passive in relation to contemporary events, the elderly take over the identity of their children, which will be discussed in detail in the following chapter.

Some people consider their Srijem identity inadaptable to the new environment, and reject any possibility of its redefinition so as to integrate in the host culture and the host society. This is the way in which a person from Srijem protects the coherence of his own identity: by refusing to redefine himself, he highlights his specific and unchangeable identity. In other words, he emphasizes his ontological identity (which is based on an imagined collective identity) in relation to his pragmatic identity.

Finally, the third case of identification is completely opposite to the previous one: considering collective identity secondary to individual identity, considering collective values and identities pragmatic rather than transcendental, and believing they should not be emphasized in the new environment, some Srijem Croats are open to the new environment and are involved in individual integration. They are represented by younger migrants who are not farmers. Their strategies bear witness to the dynamism and flexibility of identity in everyday situations.

Depending on the identification strategy they adopt, the newcomers' opinion about the new environment and its population changes, along with perceived difficulties, integration prospects, and the perception of the host population. Immigrants with an active attitude to integration claim they have made good friends with the local population; those with a negative attitude claim that the locals are difficult to make friends with; and those who are resigned say that they have nothing to talk about with the local population. Depending on their identification strategy, the role of ethnocentrism in self-identification of the Srijem Croats also changes: some reject ethnocentric judgments, others express them, but they do not determine their identity-building strategy, and for others still, ethnocentric judgment represents an excuse to reject integration.

According to the Italian ethnologist Bernardo Bernardi (1994), ethnocentrism is a necessary part of identity construction in individuals and groups, because each of these constructions includes a positive relationship toward one's own heritage and a pride of one's own heritage. However, when one's own culture starts to be evaluated higher than other cultures, when it becomes an absolute criterion of value and progress, when the pride of belonging to an ethnic group/nation turns into an exaltation of one's own group and a lack of respect toward other ethnic groups/nations, it becomes "a social disease which can lead to violence," that Bernardi terms pathological ethnocentrism. The boundary between the two types of ethnocentrisms is difficult to draw. The ethnocentrism of some Srijem settlers is not pathological because it does not turn into a lack of respect ("We respect them," they say) or into violence toward the local population.[11] Their ethnocentrism is not aggressive toward the other but tends to be self-destructive: their insistence on the supremacy of the Srijem identity prevents the restructuring of personal identity and integration into the host culture and the host society.

The success or its lack thereof in the exchange of estates is not a very important factor in ethnocentric judgment: the ethnocentric attitude has been expressed both by those who believe to have made a relatively good exchange of their house and their estate and who did well economically immediately after the migration as well as by those who were dissatisfied with the exchange. However, as a result of the economic situation in the country and especially as a result of problems in agriculture, the overall standard in the second half of the twentieth century was on the decrease. In these circumstances, a comparison of the wealth in Srijem with the current worsening situation was necessarily to the detriment of the latter. If we were to seek social explanations, the inexistence of migratory opportunism in some of the newcomers should be understood in this light (Brewer and Campbell, according to Bernardi 1994), i.e., the reason why they refuse to adapt to the new environment and its ways of behavior and why they stress the superiority of their culture and the place of origin. A superior opinion about their culture is a usual reaction of (forced) migrants; it includes idealizing their home region, their abandoned houses, and the life in their place of origin (for other cases of coethnic migrations, see chapter 1). These explanations of the lack of migratory opportunism in some of the newcomers should be combined with individual differences among people; according to one of my interlocutors: "It is personal, it depends on the person itself, and whether the person is introverted or communicative."

These people find the apparent motive for their refusal to adapt in the alleged inferiority of the local culture. Their ethnocentrism includes reasoning which should explain their refusal to change their speech, accept local customs, and take part in the wider local social networks. The alleged superiority of their own culture serves as a justification for the lack of acceptance of the local culture and society. Since it is an interpretation of their own position, ethnocentrism, even in its strongest form, which is evident in the young man from Slankamen who refuses any possibility of adaptation, remains on the verbal level and is dissolved on the interaction level, where the man maintains close neighborly relations with the local population. It has been observed that despite the ethnocentric rhetoric of some of the Srijem Croats, they do participate in the local social networks and have close relationships with the locals, which includes having work colleagues, friends, and even godparents among them. This will be discussed in chapter 7.

Notes

1. This applies to life of women in general, which points to a gender difference in the degree of connectedness to one's home and one's house.
2. The Croatian flag had a communist symbol—a five-pointed star—until the democratic elections in 1990. This is when it was replaced by the Croatian coat of arms consisting of alternated red and white squares, popularly called *šahovnica* (chessboard).
3. Srijem Croats are unanimous in distinguishing between "our" and "these" Serbs, see chapter 4.
4. Narrators here refer to the fact that their organic idiom is Stokavian Ekavian, and that they had to learn the Croatian standard language when they moved to Croatia and acquire a somewhat different vocabulary of Croatian (see chapter 1, footnote 17).
5. See chapter 7 for narratives about the mutual unfamiliarity and differences of settlers from different villages in Srijem.
6. Each village had a particular patron saint. On this day, special mass was usually celebrated and there were celebrations at home, with many guests. See Čapo Žmegač (2000a: 530).
7. In the case of this young Srijem Croat, his farming activities could have played an important integrative role because, as he had the machinery, immediately after being settled in Gradina, the local population called him to work their land. Several locals that I talked to pointed out that he was professional and good at doing his job. But, according to his own opinion, he did not integrate into the Gradina community.
8. In villages in Srijem, graveyards were located at the periphery of the village and people who lived near graveyards were the lowest in the social hierarchy. In Gradina, the narrators' house, although close to the graveyard, is also very close to the administrative center of the new part of the settlement.
9. Villages of resettlement close to the town of Virovitica.
10. This man spent some time working in Switzerland.
11. There were several physical conflicts between the local population and the newcomers, but all of my interlocutors claim that they were individual and caused primarily by the individual traits of those involved.

Chapter 4

The Older Generation
and the Migration

The Serbs made us do this [migrate], this is their idea. They came; they raided our houses and drove people away. I tell you, when I came here I was the first one, and I never even thought about exchange, that I would exchange my house. Only after I came, my people came, a year after I came, they came and exchanged their houses. . . . But, when . . . people started, those farmers that are deeply rooted in their land, I am not saying they look at things narrowly, I am just saying that they are deeply rooted, well, when they had to leave their houses and their estates, I saw that there was no going back and that something terrible would come.

A man about 45 years old, from Beška, a driver

In this chapter, I will examine in detail the situation of the older generation before and after their migration. Firstly, I will discuss the reasons for the migration as well the role and the responsibility of the older generation of Srijem Croats in making the decision to resettle and in choosing the resettlement site in Croatia; secondly, I will consider the changes that occur in their lives and the lives of their children and grandchildren in the new environment. This chapter is based on conversations with the elderly population, 65 years of age or older, and encompasses the population of Gradina and Virovitica, because their good financial status allowed many families to exchange or buy houses in both locations. Similar to other texts in the book, no attempt is made to generalize the situation of the older generation, but rather to describe particular experiences of migration and life in the new environment of ten or so older farmers from Srijem.

Before the Migration:
"There was money! What a life! Real life!"

At the end of the 1980s, Croatian peasant families in Srijem were extended and three-generational: they consisted of two nuclear, vertically connected families living in the same dwelling. Patrilineal inheritance was the rule, just like in other peasant communities where Croats lived: the family surname and its real estate property were passed on through the male line, and the newlywed couples resided patrilocally. When daughters got married, they would leave their home with a dowry of clothing, footwear, bed linen, tablecloths, furniture, etc., and sometimes livestock. In addition to the customary textiles, some were also given a piece of land or money. Money was favored, because it meant that the land would continue to remain in the hands of the sons of the family (Čapo Žmegač 2000b: 498). The system of a "single child"—the preference whereby families only have one child—was famous for its deliberate limitation of the number of births from as early as the nineteenth century, and it has remained characteristic of the region until today. Here is a self-critical and regretful statement of an older Srijem woman on this subject:

Woman: "If I only had more children. [I had] only one son, that F., only him. Silly are the women who have a single child. That isn't good, it sure isn't. . . . And there, I was foolish and I only had him."
JČŽ: "Is that what you wanted?"
Woman: "Well, that's what I wanted. Oh, oh, not good. Lucky is the mother who has more children!"
JČŽ: "Why have you made this decision?"
Woman: "I don't know; I don't know myself why it is like that. Perhaps for him to be the owner and inheritor—a single child."

If there was more than one male child, there were no norms whether the oldest (the primogeniture principle) or the youngest (the ultimogeniture principle) son would inherit the estate. The son with whom the parents had a better relationship or who showed interest in agriculture stayed to live in the house with his father. During the 1970s and the 1980s, he, and his brother if he had one, would get an education, so that frequently the son who was to inherit his father's estate learned a craft or trained for some other non-farming job. Here is what a married couple says about this:

JČŽ: "Which child stays with the parents at home?"
Wife: "The one who inherits stays. That's mostly how it used to be. There were those who didn't want to be with their parents. Well, we bought our older

son a house—he would go to school. . . . We would educate him, so that B. [the younger son] could stay on the land. Later it happened that he went to school too."

Husband: "She only wanted for her children to go to school."

Wife: "So that they become . . . That they are not ignorant like me. That was my wish. I see that the gentlemen live well, and the peasant's bread is hard to earn."

The members of the extended family would farm together on the land that belonged to the father who, if he was still able-bodied, was in charge of making economic decisions in the family farming business. And the business, according to the narrations of the Srijem Croats, flourished at the end of the 1970s: "There was money! What a life! Real life!"

Working and living in a family collective is connected with the common cooking and dining of all family members, which took place under supervision of the mother(-in-law). The younger generation could gain some autonomy from the earnings of the husband or the wife outside the family estate, and from having their own bedroom in the roomy houses where they lived.

The second type of household before the resettlement were households which consisted of aged parents whose grown up children had left their family home. A research conducted in Vojvodina in the 1970s showed that as many as 38 percent of farming households were run by the elderly, i.e., by people over 65 years of age.[1] After schooling, the children would leave their parent's home, having decided to live from non-agrarian work, and the parents would be left to run the estate by themselves. They helped their offspring economically, supplying them with farming products, often commuting between the village and the city, and sometimes staying with their children for shorter or longer periods of time.

The events of 1991 and the later resettlement to Croatia struck at the very roots of this well established life punctuated by the concern about the crop and by family events; a life in which the older generation was still holding the economic reins.

Reasons for Leaving Srijem and Making the Decision to Move

The first chapter discussed some general reasons for emigrating; I will discuss them in more detail here according to the narrations of the Srijem Croats in Gradina and Virovitica.

In the fall of 1991, Yugoslav military airplanes with the mission to attack Croatia flew literally over the heads of the people living in Srijem, especially in the villages next to the Croatian border—in Kukujevci, Šid, and Morović (Bičanić 1994,1999). Arms and tanks were amassed which would later be used in the attack on the town of Vukovar,[2] on Eastern Slavonia, and on the entire Western Srijem. Let us consider the testimony of a man concerning the period when he still lived in eastern Srijem:

> It was 15 or 16 August of '91. Me, your aunt and uncle were pruning grapes in our vineyard. . . . The planes were flying all the time. It was a corridor. It was very interesting. Where the vineyard was, it was beautiful, beautiful! It is interesting when it happens. Every plane that takes off from Batajnica [a military airport close to Belgrade] flies directly over my vineyard. Every plane! It's a corridor. And when it lands, it goes to the left, towards Indija. That was their landing corridor. And then the evacuation [of the army and the army forces] from Croatia and Slovenia began, and there were three or four transport planes, big ones, that circled, because the airport simply couldn't take [them]. And they were flying, and you watch it all. . . . You see, I was pruning my grapes. It was around ten minutes before six or thereabouts. As I look up, and it is flying, and I say to your aunt, "F—k it, these are going to Vukovar." Later on I found out—that was the first plane that attacked Vukovar!

The Srijem Croats living in Vojvodina were not merely passive observers of the Serbian aggression on Croatia. They were in danger of becoming active participants in the attack. Male family members were getting draft notices for the Yugoslav National Army:

> I couldn't allow my son to be drafted into the Serbian army. It was really the Serbian army; it was only called JNA [Yugoslav National Army]. Everybody knows what happened. There's no need to repeat that now. . . . And that [was] for sure one of the real reasons for which you had to [move].

After an initial disorientation, and even after short periods of time spent in the army ("Up to, oh, say the end of '91, there were our people who were in that army"), younger men started running away in order to avoid being drafted. Typical places for younger men to run, which they thought to be a temporary escape at first, were Croatia, Hungary, and Bosnia-Herzegovina. They were joined by somewhat older men who were politically active and who gave their clear support to the political changes in Croatia.

The narratives of the Srijem Croats primarily bear witness to the fear that had taken over the civilian population, both men and women, of all ages. Fear, one of the basic emotions and a very intense one, was what accompanied the actual and the anticipated appearance of danger (Povrzanović 1992: 74).

Based on the testimonies of the Srijem Croats, I continue by enumerating the elements of the social production of fear[3] in Vojvodina in the early 1990s, which resulted in the decision to move away. At first, fear spread because of phone calls in which people were threatened and called *hadezeovci*[4] ("Phone calls: the phone rings once. A question: 'Hey, what's up hadezeovac?'") and *Ustasha*.[5] Later, assaults on property and people were becoming more frequent: explosive devices and bombs were planted into people's yards and people were physically assaulted or called for police "interviews." Rumors about events in the neighboring villages, transmitted orally or through the media, and memories of World War II of the older population were two factors that additionally caused fear in people and they started to "run away." Srijem Croats themselves testify to this best:

Interlocutor A: "Slankamen somehow remained without incidents, so to say. We ran away."

Interlocutor B: "We left immediately . . . as soon as they started bombing. . . ."

Interlocutor A: "That's because that . . . bastard . . . from Pazova, that guy Ulemek kept coming to Slankamen."

Interlocutor C: "One extremist Serb, he really was. He somehow had it in for Slankamen. Why, what bothered him, I have no idea. Anyway, that was his game. . . . Nova Pazova,[6] you know, is not that far, and then they were supposedly always getting ready to attack Slankamen, and so all of us were just leaving. Look, it was more psychological than anything else. It was, like, you know, you get scared away, you get phone threats, and you simply leave."

Interlocutor B: "You get scared away . . . You don't want to get hurt."

Interlocutor D: "Where we lived [in Slankamen] no one was killed, no one was beaten, but you know what they say, when they said boo, we ran away. That's what it looked like. But the people from Kukujevci, they are a bit tougher, they didn't want to. They [had] victims. That would have happened to us too, if we hadn't accepted what we had [to do]. Us, if we had not accepted that, it wouldn't have gone [like this for us] . . . You know, we had no casualties. They planted a bomb in the house of the guy who was the president of the association of Croats from Vojvodina. Luckily, he was not home. . . . No one was hurt. That was the beginning; that was the winter of '91."

Children were also confronted with problems: in class they were subject to Serbian propaganda, and Croatian and Serbian children would make the same accusations against each other like the adults:

The eldest [grandson] was in the first grade. As we are sitting at the table having lunch he says . . . This guy from Zagreb came, a refugee, already, it was the fall of '91, a Serb. He moved from Zagreb, sold the house in Zagreb and bought one from Serbs over there [in the village of Golubinci]. Bought it. There was no exchange yet. He says [the grandson], "You know what the Serb said . . . What's up *mupovac!*"[7]—"So what did you tell him?"—"What's up Chetnik!"[8] What can you expect? He said to him, "What's up Chetnik!" straight away. We did talk about those Chetniks at home and that, trouble was already brewing. But he was so young, and immediately accepted it, and said it just like that. And that's why I, as they say here, decided to go with the flow: let's go. I am a sick man; I couldn't stay alone without my children. They want to go. So let's go!

In some villages it was a particular event that led to interrogations and persecutions of Croats, which later intensified because of the beginning of the war in Croatia and the actions of the Serbian Radical Party. For instance, during the 1991 First of May celebration in Slankamen, the Croatian flag with the Croatian symbol of the chessboard was flown on the building of the Croatian Peasant Home.[9] Here is a narration of a young woman:

Our village in Srijem was a very strong Croatian base. In '91 on 1 May we started hoisting the flag. We had it in our Croatian Peasant Home— there was a committee that voted for the proposal and supported it that our Croatian flag with the chessboard[10] was to be simply flown together with the Yugoslav flag. So that there is, so to say, their [Yugoslav] flag, but our chessboard too. So here comes 1 May, early morning, I believe, and the chessboard is flying smack in the middle of Slankamen. You can't imagine how touching it was! Everybody came outside! All of us enjoyed it, but we were also scared because we had to take this side. And it was flying like that the whole day. But then, somewhere in the afternoon the police came, a police patrol . . . and they cut down the flag by force. But that's when the revolt started: people simply started to come out of their houses; started going to the Croatian Home, "Why are they doing this? [taking down the flag], that's not nice, we're entitled to that."

The foundation and the activity of Croats in the Democratic League of the Croats from Vojvodina[11] in Beška, Slankamen, Kukujevci, and other villages posed a threat to their peaceful life. In 1992, Serbs from Croatia came, and, together with the Serbian radicals under the leadership of Vojislav Šešelj, a Chetnik "duke," openly threatened the Croats, forcing them to the exchange. Here is a testimony of a woman:

It was easy to get by [in Virovitica], because we used to be harassed over there. And Serbs from here [from Croatia] would come and they would say: "Do you want to exchange? You have to! You'll leave carrying bags, plastic bags."[12] And they would threaten us, it was horrible. From the time they sawed down our flag until . . . we came in '92. It was—on the 14th [of February]—it was four years ago. Until we came we used to sleep in different places. . . . We would hide in rooms, and we went through all sorts of things, and they would threaten us, especially my husband, because he would spend a lot of his time . . . in the Croatian Home.

The Srijem Croats are unanimous in distinguishing "our" from "the other" Serbs;[13] with the former, their long-standing neighbors, they allegedly had no problems until the end of the 1980s and the beginning of the 1990s. They hold it against "their" Serbs that they did not protect them from "the other" Serbs, i.e., from Serbs who came from Croatia, whom they consider the main culprit for their forced migration. An elderly couple from Slankamen, answering the question whether they had good relations with the Serbs before the war started in 1991, states:

Wife: "Well, one had to."
Husband: "There weren't any Serbs there, and then when you go to the market . . . And those people, they [Serbs] were not very nasty to us like those that came from here [Croatia]. It was different then, those that came. Over there in Slankamen there were not many Serbs,[14] so that we did not come into contact with them."

Distinguishing "good" and "bad," "ours," and "the other" Serbs is the result of the fact that the Srijem Croats exchanged their estates and houses with Serbs from Croatia, usually with difficult and often unsuccessful negotiations after which the people from Srijem felt cheated. Moreover, it should be kept in mind that the Croatian Serbs, who did not accept the new democratically elected Croatian government and who were exploited by the radical Serbian politicians in Serbia, in fact started the Serbian rebellion in Croatia.

Some of my interlocutors suggested that their removal from Srijem had been planned. Allegedly, Serbs from Croatia several years before the actual events photographed and made video recordings of Srijem villages in order to "divide up" Croatian houses and estates more easily:

It turned out at the end that students some five or six years before [roughly in 1986 to 1987][15] simply walked through Slankamen and simply took pictures of people's houses. I don't know if you were aware of that. For instance, a student would come to your house and say, "We are students, we are trying to make some money to go to school, and we would like to take a picture of your house. Would you be willing to buy [the photo]?" "Yes," people say, "of course! Our own house!" It's a great keepsake. But then later they would have albums full of our photos!

Despite the atmosphere of fear and pressure, and the war in Croatia, the decision to resettle was not an easy one to make, especially for the elderly. It meant more than leaving material goods—newly built houses and land that had been in the family for generations; rather, it meant leaving spiritual values, their roots, and the pride connected with their "centuries-old home." To many elderly women, mothers, and grand-mothers, the decision to move was incomprehensible.[16] A 65-year-old woman with only five grades of primary school described her resistance to moving in the following way:

> Me personally, I could not accept that. I mean, how can we leave our fa-therland, and the war, and . . . And then Grandpa [the husband] decided that we should move, and I said no, no. He was angry. I kept stalling, don't go, things will settle down. And the war, why would we go, I mean, how can you move where there's war! You would be going to war.[17] You know, that was somehow very unacceptable to me. . . . I didn't want to. I keep shouting, "Calm down children." I didn't want to. "Calm down!" I thought it would pass. Why would we move! . . . I didn't . . . It was all completely unclear to me, how come? Why? Why are they killing people here [in Croatia]? And why would we go where they are killing people? [I am] a peasant woman with five grades of primary school. Do you see? I couldn't accept that. I mean, why? It will settle down, and, my son, you can move, but as for us—whatever God's will, whatever God's will.

When the decision about resettlement was being made, men mostly talked about leaving: "It was a nightmare: To go? Not to go? And there's no way you could sleep soundly. Today you're going, tomorrow you aren't. Where are you to go? What are you to do? Should you do this or that; should you go here or there?" Photos of numerous refugees leaving their homes in haste with their essential things in plastic bags, which started appearing on Croatian television screens in the fall of 1991, frightened these well-off Srijem Croats that the same fate would befall them if they did not make a decision and prevent it. There were other factors too: old age, illness, and concern for the future of their children. Here is a narration of an elderly man from Srijem:

> I came mostly for my children's sake. But I came for my sake, too. I was sick. So why would I have someone slaughter me, someone murder me?

If I have to die—then that's that, everybody has to die. Whoever's alive has to die, there's nothing more to it. But still it was terrible when I saw those people on the TV, those people with plastic bags, when they put them onto a truck somewhere there, in Baranja, and they took them off, and searched them, and took their gold and everything. And then I realized: it's over. When I saw that truck later, people from Slankamen moving, this person and that person left. But when I saw those people being taken off the truck and all their gold and money and everything taken, then we started immediately, immediately [to move].

One of the motives to move, mentioned by all the members of the older generation, is their concern for their "children." They use this noun generically, as a term covering all of their descendants, encompassing children and grandchildren. On the one hand, their decision to move is motivated by their responsibility for their descendants and their wish to ensure a better future for them, and on the other hand, for their own life in old age.

Since the grandfathers were the owners of the house (or houses) and estates where they earned their living together with their son's family, their rejection to resettle would have made it impossible for younger generations to resettle or would significantly decrease the younger generation's standard in Croatia. Although there are cases when, not being able to decide to leave their rich estate and their house, parents and grandparents did not follow their children (who were, consequently, forced to stay in Croatia with their relatives or get by in other ways), these cases are rare, and some of my interlocutors condemned them.

The parents mostly made the decision about collective resettlement after the middle generation declared they wanted to move away. The abovementioned woman who resisted resettlement finally accepted it, with the explanation that they should go because of their children. The following quotation, just like the previous one, clearly shows that moving away for the sake of the children is inseparable from their concern over who would take care of them in their old age:

You have to go with your children. What can I do, when B. [the son] goes—I have to go, too. . . . You know, you have to go with your children! What will we do when we get old, who will nurse us? The children have to go, you should accept that!

And while grandparents follow their children and grandchildren, those whose children left their homes and their native region earlier decide to go after them. Many had children who lived in Croatia or abroad, where they moved because of schooling, marriage or work. The new political situation at the beginning of the 1990s, and especially the war in Croatia, made contacts with them more difficult—telephone lines were dead, direct passage from Serbia into Croatia was temporarily impossible because of the war, etc. Many had already considered moving to be closer to their children, and the war only sped up that decision; others had only just started to think about moving at the insistence of their children, if not near them, then at least somewhere in Croatia where mutual visits would be possible. An elderly couple does not believe they would have moved had there not been for persuasion from their daughters who live abroad:

Woman: "We should have moved to the seaside. It would have been better! For us. Well, you see, we only have two daughters. And they are not here. They would [come to visit] more there [at the seaside]. Now they tell me 'To hell with your Gradina! You want us to come?! To hell with your Gradina!' [laughter] Why then have you made me go and exchange the house!?"
JČŽ: "So they wanted you to do the exchange?"
Woman: "Yes, it was them."

The Resettlement: The Grandfathers Deciding

Once the decision about the resettlement was made, it had to be implemented, and a place of settlement had to be chosen. Relying on the economic power stemming from their ownership of the house and land, still in full productive force, fathers and grandfathers played a key role in this phase as well. If there was time, the decision concerning the choice of the resettlement site was not made hurriedly, because "once you make a mistake, you can't put it right." One of my elderly interlocutors claims that "whenever it was the youth [middle generation] who decided on the exchange, it was bad." That is why he assumed control in this matter. However, exchanging a house was not the kind of business in which a person of Srijem would do well; on the contrary, buying a house was a completely unknown type of trade for the Srijem Croat:

Cause look, a peasant could buy a cow, he could buy a horse; he knew what acre of land was good and all that. But who, who . . . When was there trade [house-trade] from the beginning of time? My God, exchanging a house?! There's no such thing! You have to be careful about the door frames, and see what is where, what type of wooden floor, what type of water installations. When you come you must see a lot of that, see everything quickly, and make your decision.

Male members of the family traveled to Croatia looking for suitable property. They went to regions where Serbs lived, taking many well-trodden paths and connections of the first resettled Srijem Croats ("Whoever came first, we followed them like sheep"), looking at what was being offered, making and sometimes canceling contracts with the Serbs. For the Srijem farmers who settled in Gradina and Virovitica, the basic precondition for the exchange was that the region where they were going to move was agrarian, that it had farmland ("We can't do anything else, the two of us, but work the soil"), preferably fertile and divided into larger parcels. Farmers by vocation, they hoped that the farmland, just like in Srijem, would enable them to earn their living in the new region:

Interlocutor A: "A few of our people exchanged for the seaside; there was a lot on offer to us, Zadar, and whatever, on the coast. But we largely came here, most of us came right here because the Srijem people are farmers, and there's land here . . . What would we live off of?"

Interlocutor B: "You believed that this land would somehow ensure your living, your existence, at least your survival. And then when things settled down a bit we would see what we would do and how."

The Srijem Croat, who has an "agrarian soul," remains attached to the land even when s/he obtains a college education:

I am some sort of an engineer. But the agrarian, the peasant aspect, I guess, still remains in me. When I came here [to Croatia] I didn't try to go to the center—to Zagreb. I lived in some type of a large center there [in Belgrade], but you are always attached to the land which seems to mean something in your subconscious, some type of security.

For a person from Srijem, the land is more than a source of earning a living and a feeling of security. It is a pleasure, and makes a person proud because of the effort he devotes to its cultivation. A veterinarian explains:

You see, when I set the plow, for instance, or the break when I go to work. When I set all of that and when I start plowing or when I do that, and then I turn around—having worked like a horse, I mean it's hard work driving a tractor all day long—and then I turn around and I see that everything is so nice, I think to myself what else do you need [in life], you

fool. And then I look again, and then . . . It's so beautiful! It's so beautiful that it's plain wrong! [laughter] And that's it. Your heart fills up. It's
wonderful, really wonderful! . . . People can't understand that! They can't
understand that! And I talk to myself. . . . Your [my] heart fills up! When
you get really tired, in the evening, when you see what you have done and
how much you've worked . . . You sleep like someone [has] given you a
thousand German Marks today.

The assessment that the Gradina region had good farmland was an important reason why the Srijem peasant decided to settle near the town
of Virovitica. There were other factors that influenced the choice of the
settlement site: a lowland landscape similar to the one that they had left
("I am not used to mountains, you know. Srijem is flat."); the presence
of other people from their village ("My husband came here. There were
many people from Slankamen here. And nowhere else [did he want to
settle]! And there will never be anywhere else."); and developed communal services in the village ("First I went to see if there was a church,
if there was a doctor's office, and if there was a school. What does it
matter when the children come, what do I do [if there is no school]? I
mean, that was the most important thing, the main thing that there was
everything here in the village.").
     This last thing was especially important; it defines the "civilized na-
ture" of the resettlement site that is of special concern to the grandfathers because of their grandchildren who will live there:

> This place, Gradina for me—as well as Suhopolje [town nearby]—they
> are civilized . . . Because I was always afraid that my grandson would say,
> excuse my language, to hell with my grandfather who brought me here.
> That's what people used to say—the grandfather took them wherever! So
> that my grandchildren would not say, "See what my grandfather did."
> There are some here, some grandchildren who will curse for years to
> come that they went to some godforsaken place.

For this man, the fear of making a mistake is primarily the fear for the
future of his descendants. In any case, "they are the ones who'll stay, and
us, we have lived our life," said an elderly woman.
     However, not all elderly Srijem Croats are satisfied. A feeling of dis-
satisfaction is present among those people who live without their descendants and have no opportunity of comforting themselves that their
decision to move was the right one for their children. For instance, the
abovementioned elderly couple, who moved away at the urging of their
daughters who live abroad, complains that their grandchildren find it

uninteresting to visit their grandparents who moved to a small, completely unattractive border village in the north of Croatia. This is the reason why the grandmother keeps thinking about the fact that it might have been better had they moved somewhere to the seaside where the grandchildren would have wanted to come more often, and the grandfather dismisses it with a wave, unconvinced that it would have been any different. The situation in which the daughters or the grandchildren show no interest to visit them causes family disputes and mutual grumbling: the elderly complain because the children persuaded them to move, the children and the grandchildren complain because of the choice of the resettlement site.

In the New Surroundings

Resettlement causes significant changes in family life. For some extended families it meant the end of cohabitation of the middle generation with their parents and the youngest generation with their grandparents. Namely, some of the Srijem Croats exchanged their house for two houses, while others exchanged their house in the town and were trying to get another one in the country, closer to the farmland which remained their main source of income. Others still already owned a house in Croatia: they acquired another one in the exchange, so that part of the extended family separated.

The primary significance of separate dwelling resides in the fact that it enables the middle generation to run their household independently. Autonomy from their parents and parents-in-law is psychologically important both for the son and the daughter-in-law. Separating from the mother-in-law has multiple meanings for the Srijem daughters-in-law: for the first time, although possibly in middle age, they have the opportunity to own their household and to run and organize it by themselves, and take care of their children alone with their husbands. For the first time, they are no longer under control of their mother-in-law, away from the not-always-harmonious cohabitation circumstances, never as harmonious as the older ethnographic literature and romantically inspired defenders of extended families would have us believe (cf. Rihtman-Auguštin 1984), just like, for that matter, some of my interlocutors. This narration of an elderly woman bears witness to the fact that residential separation from the parents and the parents-in-law could be important for the daughter-in-law:

> We were all together in one house there [in Srijem], and here we mostly got [houses] both in Virovitica and in the country. And now, our youth must be

in Virovitica because of the children and the school, and the in-laws—they are in the country working the land. And then, D. [a Srijem woman] talks about that, . . . and says, "We should love Tuđman . . . because he separated us from the father-in-law and the mother-in-law!" [laughter]

Residential independence is the first step for the separation of parents and their adult children, but it does not mean complete independence for the middle generation if it still lives from farming. The middle and the older generation still work together in running their farm located in the countryside where the parents live. There seem to be no rules as to the division of economic roles in the common household: in one family, the ownership of the land by the old father-grandfather is the basis for his participation and his dominant role in the economic decisions, although the son's role is growing more important. In another household, the son has taken over the decision making. The division of labor and the roles in production depend on the type of activity: depending on the type and the manner of distribution of their products, part of the trade is taken over by the eldest generation and part by the middle generation. For instance, an older woman sold her own products retail in front of her house and on the market in Virovitica, while wholesale and supplying the local town markets and stores was taken over by her son.

If the middle generation tried to find their way out of the insecure farming business in taking up employment outside farming and if they neglected their contribution to the family farming business, some elderly people tried to continue the agrarian production in a narrower scope, counting on only sporadic help from the younger generation; others completely withdrew from economic activities. The main cause of this is not their physical incapacity due to old age but the unfamiliarity with their new surroundings, including conducting business and the local population, and their perception that their time has passed. "We are getting along, because of our children. They are the ones who work, and we work with them. Otherwise the two of us—me and my wife—we would have had a difficult time getting along."

In an unfamiliar situation which they cannot control, the elderly find it easier to leave part (or all) of the economic and social activities to the middle generation, especially the part connected with contacts with the local population. Older people from Srijem, as I have shown in the previous chapter, show reserve in their social activity in Gradina and have little contact with the locals. This does not mean that they do not have their own opinion about the new environment and its way of life. They keep it to themselves, suppressing the wish to influence the new environment by discussing some of its characteristics. The reason for this is their offspring whom they could harm in this way; the elderly believe that the young should be in control: "I did not allow him to [the husband to criticize the priest]. . . . I mean, who is calling the shots here—the younger do. . . . I did not allow him to say anything," said an elderly woman.

Decisions are left to the children in other areas of family life, too. For instance, if everybody still lives together in one house, the older generation does not interfere in its refurbishment.

Just as they connected their decision about resettlement with the concern for the future of their offspring, they now view their own life in the new surroundings through the prism of how well their children manage: "If they are doing well, we are doing well too." Sorrow and difficulties connected with the resettlement are gradually replaced by their resignation connected with how well their children are coping: "Of course that all of this was difficult! But what can we do now!? I was crying my eyes out for a year here, I couldn't stop crying. Now I can see that my children are settled, they are working, so why would I . . . ," explained an elderly woman.

The older people are passive observers rather than active participants in the new life; they find their pleasure and peace with their children and grandchildren, they are observers of integration processes taking over the middle and the youngest generation. In their parents' and grandparents' view, the children and the grandchildren are those who should be active, living, and creating in the new surroundings; for the elderly, the life of their children and grandchildren is a way to extend their own life, which they consider to be over or somewhere else, in the region from which they emigrated. Therefore, they come to terms with their destiny, even claiming that they like living in Gradina.

For the older people, their descendants are the source of their current identity and self-evaluation. Identifying with their offspring and establishing a (social) identity through them is their strategy of living in the new environment; it gives meaning to the other part of their life, the part in which the frailty brought about by old age has been supplemented by the unwanted resettlement, with consequences such as the change of their familiar setting and habits, people and customs, a new social order, etc. Their attitude toward their current life is not active anymore because they believe that it is too late for them—it "may take a generation for a man to stabilize, to get somewhere," said an elderly Srijem Croat. Therefore, their life has meaning inasmuch as it is directed at helping their offspring; it is often subordinated to them. This may also explain the dissatisfaction of the abovementioned elderly couple who moved at the urging of their children, and now their children do not visit them: these (grand)parents can do very little for their offspring, because they do not live with them. Not having them in their view all all times, they cannot witness their (well-)being, and the children, in turn, have not kept their promise to visit them once they have moved. Feeling lost, these aged peasants do not accept the new environment and they wonder about the sense of their resettlement.

From Domination to Dependence

The elderly made their decision to move away with more or less resistance and have given it more or less thought. This decision, made in an atmosphere of fear and threats, was meant as support to their offspring with whom they generally lived in common, extended, multiple-generation households. The decision to move away made by the elderly was connected with a responsibility to the son, inheritor of the estate, and his family who remained to live with them. Parents have no such responsibility or commitment to the children who had left their parents' house earlier, regardless of their gender; they settle in Croatia independently of their parents, alone, or, in the case of women, within other families extended on the husband's side. The resettlement of the elderly, then, is closely connected with patrilineal descent and the distribution of assets. The second characteristic case of the resettlement of the older generation is motivated by the fear that the political situation will make it impossible for them to see their offspring who had already left the parents' home. The elderly Srijem Croats, therefore, try to move closer to their children, regardless of their gender, and their families.

In both situations, in a general atmosphere of uncertainty and persecution at the beginning of the 1990s, the elderly were also prompted to move by the fear of illness and old age. The fear of illness on the one hand, and the concern for their children on the other, are elements of a silent intergenerational contract and its expectations. The parents and grandparents are expected to support their [male] descendants; that is to say, they have the responsibility to provide for them. The descendants have not been exempt from their traditional role of caring for their parents in old age and in illness. Research of the older farming population in Vojvodina conducted in the 1970s showed that around two thirds of the older subjects believed they should be taken care of by their children, while one third of them believed this should be done by society (Dimković 1977: 64). Some twenty years later the former expectation still holds true among my interlocutors.

Caring for their parents is a type of intergenerational exchange with a delay: the younger generation expects their parents' help when they have not yet become independent and/or established; the parents, in turn, expect the young to reciprocate in their old age. Giving and reciprocating are part of an unwritten intergenerational contract, which practically made it impossible for the parents/grandparents to decide to stay in Srijem. This is the reason why few elderly have decided to stay in Srijem despite their children's migration. Perhaps their decision was influenced by the assessment that the son cannot carry out his part of the intergenerational contract.

At the moment of making the decision to move, the grandparents, because of their economic power, are not just the guarantors of family ties (cf. Attias-Donfut and Segalen 1998: 12), but also the guarantors of material survival of the family: the middle generation has no goods to exchange with the Serbs from Croatia. If the older generation had not given their consent to emigrate, the younger would have had a hard time getting by, and would have suffered a significant fall in their standard of living in Croatia.

At the time of the resettlement, the older males were still at full economic and physical strength, and therefore played an active role in making the decision to resettle and in choosing the resettlement site. However, after resettlement the situation has changed considerably for the older generation: they are no longer dominant in economic or in other family issues. The middle generation tends to start living independently, which is the first step to complete independence. The (grand)parents, on the other hand, age, and it is increasingly difficult for them to cope in the new surroundings, and they entrust their children with the economic and social activity in the new surroundings. Economic activity is organized in various ways, but they all share a limited role of the older generation.

It is difficult to separate the effect of aging from the effect of the emigration on the older generation; they both work in synergy, contributing to the withdrawal of the older generation from activity and dominance in economic and other aspects of family and social life. It is safe to assume that the resettlement simply sped up the biological basis of the process of the exchange of generation roles, in which the earlier givers increasingly become receivers. Both the social fact (resettlement) and the biological fact (aging) contribute to a resigned, passive relationship to life in the new surroundings, which was discussed in the previous chapter.

Being aware of the process of generation change, the elderly describe their current role in the family as passive, transferring the meaning of life to their offspring. They express the opinion that it is "the children" who give meaning to their current life; it is the children that make it rich. Their life philosophy in the new environment has been summarized in the statement of a grandfather who said "[I] moved and [I am] suffering for my children," and in the question of a grandmother: "What are we to do without the children?" Here we are in a world of aged landowners who have experienced a radical change in their life, which sped up their withdrawal from economic and social activities.

Notes

1. In the 1970s, the social position of old peasant households was an important social and political issue and it was therefore the subject of public debate. Research showed about 80 percent of old Srijem peasants believed that they had been left to themselves, which brought the researchers to the conclusion that little has been done in the region concerning organizing the improvement of the social and economic position of old peasants (Dimković 1977: 63).
2. A town in the north eastern part of Croatia, which lived under siege and constant attacks of the Serbian and Yugoslav army in the fall of 1991 for three months, and in which, after its fall on 18 November 1991, mass murders of wounded civilians in the hospitals were committed, and the whole Croatian population was driven out. In the memory of the Croatian people, this town became the symbol of the 1991 to 1992 war suffering.
3. Maja Povrzanović (1992) wrote about social production, the roles, and the consequences of fear during the spring of 1991 in former Yugoslavia.
4. The name was coined from HDZ [ha-de-ze], the acronym of the Croatian Democratic Union, a political party formed at the end of the 1980s, which, under the leadership of Franjo Tuđman, won the largest number of votes in the first democratic election in Croatia in the 1990 and enjoyed great support of the Croatian population outside of Croatia.
5. Ustasha movement, a pro-fascist movement, whose leader Ante Pavelić came to power in the Independent State of Croatia with the support of Italy and Germany in 1941. In the war of 1991 to 1992, the Serbs used this name for Croatian soldiers and all Croats in general.
6. A little town in Vojvodina, the center of Serbian nationalists.
7. The name used for a member of the Ministry of Internal Affairs, derived from the Croatian acronym of the Ministry (MUP). Since Croatia did not have an organized army in the early days of its independence, members of the police, called *mupovci,* participated in the defense of The Republic of Croatia.
8. Chetnik, Chetniks (pl.) are military formations and groups organized in various periods when the Serbian regime wanted to realize Serbian territorial interests over the territories populated by the non-Serbian population. During the Serbian aggression on Croatia in 1991 and Bosnia-Herzegovina in 1992, various Chetnik and similar paramilitary groups were formed; they worked together with the Yugoslav National

Army—which became predominantly Serbian—and they attacked and slaughtered civilians (*Hrvatski leksikon* [The Croatian Lexicon], Vol 1, 1996: 213, Zagreb: Naklada Leksikon d.o.o.).

9. The Croatian Peasant Home in Slankamen was founded under the name of "Croatian Library" in 1902. In 1938, the Croats bought a house where they located the library and they put a sign that read "Croatian Peasant Home" on the front. Later this institution was registered as the Culture and Art Association "Stjepan Radić." The sign on the front of the building was taken down by Serbian extremists in 1992.

10. See chapter 3, footnote 2. When the decision was being made about flying the new Croatian flag with the Croatian coat of arms instead of the five-pointed star, there was a discussion among the members of the Croatian Home board: "People were in two minds whether to put it up or not. They were aware of the consequences, and finally that flag was hoisted after all."

11. A political organization founded in 1990, which represents the interests of Croats in Vojvodina.

12. In the early days of the war in Croatia, the plastic bag was a powerful metaphor evoking images of people forcefully driven out of their homes, people who managed to take with them only a handful of things contained in a plastic bag. For ethnographic analyses of everyday life during the war, see Čale Feldman et al. (1993).

13. However, because of all they went through, some of them today speak with considerable bitterness, making generalizations about all Serbs:

"I didn't even know to distinguish [between Croats and Serbs], but once we went through all that . . . Two Chetniks entered our house. . . . I never hated anyone. Okay, everyone loves their nation, of course! There is only one God, I never . . . And now I am so hateful of them that I can't even tell you, horrible, horrible. That they looted so much, that they are so arrogant and I can't stand them. My daughter, my child worked, she bought herself things, and the Chetniks came, and they took everything from our house, whatever was nice. And that's how we went through that. And then that . . . Chetnik who moved into our house, he said to my father 'Go while you are still alive, there is nothing for you here, no pruning your vineyard!' He didn't even make an exchange with us, and he took our tractor. And that, trust me, I say that I hate these Serbs so much. God forgive me, but when I am desperate . . . When they [came], [we had] a full freezer of food . . .—they ate all of that. They simply moved into our house to rob us, to take anything from us, and we didn't even make the exchange with them. . . . From that time, believe me, I can't stand them. I am really bitter. I am so bitter at them. I don't like to hear a Serbian name, I can't. God forgive me, but I can't. . . . There, I am bitter and that's that."

14. The 1991 census shows that there were a considerable number of Serbs in Slankamen. In New Slankamen, there were 23.4 percent (697) Serbs and 66.5 percent (1980) Croats; in Old Slankamen, 41.3 percent (238) Serbs and 39 percent (225) Croats. The rest of the population included Hungarians, Slovaks, Roman, others, and persons who did not declare their nationality. In both parts of the village combined, there were 26.3 percent Serbs and 62.1 percent Croats (*Popis stanovništva, domaćinstava, stanova i poljoprivrednih gazdinstava 31. mart. 1991. Prvi rezultati* [Census of the population, households and agricultural estates, 31 March 1991. Preliminary results], *Statistički bilten* 206, 1991, Novi Sad: Pokrajinski zavod za statistiku). My narrators' statements show that despite a relatively large number of Serbs, the Serbian minority was not socially noticeable; Croatian people in Slankamen experienced it as a Croatian village. Socially speaking, a considerably larger grouping

of Serbs in Golubinci was insignificant as well: allegedly in this village there was a rivalry between Croats of different origin who lived in two different streets, and not between the Serbian and the Croatian population.

15. Another interlocutor claimed that in May 1990 there was a photographer who went to Srijem villages and photographed houses, and that these photographs were later found in the exchanged houses by the Srijem Croats.

16. More difficult acceptance of the decision to resettle among older women was also noticed by other researchers of forced migrations (Duijzings 1995; Loizos 1981). Women with whom I talked during my research, especially the older ones, were not as active in the nationalist movement as their spouses. Some of them pointed out that in Srijem no differences were made between Croats and Serbs, but after the events in 1991 to 1992, they drastically changed their opinions (see the statement in note 13).

17. The war in 1991 to 1992 was fought only on the Croatian territory, and the Srijem Croats were moving there from Serbia, where there were no war operations.

Chapter 5

Constructing Difference, Identifying the Self

Croatian nation building lies within me, not in me but in, in . . . Because when we arrive [here] with that [awareness], we can invoke hatred and, around Virovitica, we already have. That antagonism. Just because of that, because we have brought a better way of working the land and a better Croatian-ness, a more vital Croatian-ness. I'm not saying better, but . . . perhaps a more intense Croatian-ness, more open, and more religious . . .

A man about 50 years old, from Slankamen, a farmer

Previous chapters have indicated that a smooth integration of the migrants into the local community is neither easy nor a foregone conclusion. Similar to other coethnic migrants—for example, Greek, German, Czech, and the like—the Srijem migrants, after settling in their "ethnic homeland," realize that life in a different sociocultural milieu has made them different from the local population, and, consequently, that shared ethnonational belonging does not guarantee their customs, worldviews, and mentalities will resemble those of their new co-citizens. Differences that they perceive between their mores and those of the people in the area of settlement serve as the basis for evaluating local culture and society. Six to seven years after settlement, a part of the newcomers evaluates local culture negatively. In chapter 3 I have interpreted their ethnocentric discourse as a rationalization for their impossibility to integrate into the host society, arguing the inferiority attributed to the local culture serves as a justification for the inability of coethnic migrants to adjust to the local community. The reason behind what might be termed unsuccessful accommodation on the part of some migrants lies in their refusal to come to terms with the circumstances of their forced migration and loss of status. In addition, their ethnocentric discourse is a consequence of the tendency to ideal-ize the homeland from which they were forcibly driven out. This is also exemplified by other coethnic migrant groups.

The ethnocentric discourse of the Srijem Croats is analyzed in this chapter as a function of the creation of the collective identity of the migrants. We encounter it in the poorly adapted Srijem Croat who longs for his previous life and birthplace, among the members of the older generation of farmers in Gradina, as well as among a dozen Sri-jem migrants, mostly with advanced or degree-level education, who live in Virovitica and do not make their living from the land, and among many of the people interviewed in the documentaries about Srijem mi-grants made by Croatian Television.[1] Whether they are young or old, farmers or intellectuals, rather well-off or of modest economic standing, whether settled in a smaller or larger locality, these people have a nega-tive perception of local culture and of the local inhabitants, and point out the incomparability of their previous way of life in Srijem and their present way of life in Croatia.

Their perceptions and points of view are elements of their collective self-identification, which grows out of the process of encounter and in-teraction with the local population. By differentiating themselves from their new neighbors, they transform the local population into some other people and set up barriers against them, while at the same time recon-structing their own identity and the image they hold of themselves. The ascription of identity to the Other relies on cultural logic—the logic in which culture is the basis for identifying the other group—whereby per-ceived cultural differences are given the status of a fundamentally dif-ferent characteristic, that is, of an unchangeable substance rooted in the other group. Enumerating what is, and what is not, the cultural difference or similarity between themselves and the local population, the migrants identify the latter as some "other Croats." The principle of distancing and differentiating the Other also functions in the opposite direction. State-ments by local inhabitants about themselves and their Other, the Srijem immigrants, are quoted at the end of this chapter to enable the reader to compare them with the statements by the migrants themselves (see also chapter 7). By quoting them without any commentary or interpretation, I want to offer readers an opportunity to form their own view with regard to both the statements of the locals and the migrants, and the interpreta-tion that I have suggested in this and other chapters.

While interpreting the migrants' perceptions of the locals, my interest does not lie in the discrepancy between an objectively ascertainable reality—economic, social, and cultural—and a subjective perception of that reality. Rather, my aim is to show how perceived differences between the locals and the migrants are typically expressed in the migrants' representations. I want to discover the symbolism in which belonging to one's own culture and the frontiers to the Other are expressed. Therefore, the subject matter of analysis is not the objective cultural, content but a certain genre (McDonald 1993) or idiom (Phillips 1994) in which immigrants express their identity by ascribing differential identity to the other group. The idiom in which a collective identity is being cast is made up of "popular models," a complex group of ideas that people hold about their social identities and relations (Phillips 1994).

Attribution of Difference and Symbolism of Collective Identity

The Croats from Srijem come up with quite a long—and for them obvious—list of differences between the area of settlement and the area of origin. Some are expressed with astonishment, some with sorrow; frequently they contain a value judgement, and are defined as crucial markers, as the distinctive traits of the local as opposed to the migrant population. Above all, differences appertain to the main areas of life—economic issues, the characteristics of villages, households, traditions, language, and mentality.

All of the migrants, from farmers to intellectuals, point to differences in agricultural practices, specifically in the types of soil, crops, and land cultivation techniques. The differences are conditioned by geographic and pedological factors and require accommodation. Sometimes it is a matter of very subtle, or as Blok (2000) would put it, "minor differences," which are, moreover, negatively evaluated:

Interlocutor A: "Their fields are full of weeds. . . . After they reaped the wheat, they weren't seen again in the fields until it was time for deep ploughing. But we were there [in Srijem] working, ploughing twice, ploughing deep, and our fields were exemplary."

Interlocutor B: "They simply sow, but never dig up around corn. Not so much as a blade of grass is allowed in our fields, especially in K.'s and Ž.'s fields. Real models of how it should be done. That's the way it is with most of us, but not with them. Now, they are starting to do it a little bit."

In an effort to explain economic differences, a man asked himself, hesitantly, about the feasibility of comparing two geographically distant areas—eastern Srijem and northwestern Croatia—and moreover, two politically and socially distinct systems—the former Yugoslavia in the 1980s and the Republic of Croatia in the 1990s. Namely, he was not sure whether the decisive impact on the economic situation in two regions should be ascribed to geographic and pedological or to sociopolitical factors:

> So, the properties range from ten to, what should I say, thirty or forty acres. But the fact is, how can I explain it to you—I see that they can hardly make ends meet here if they have ten acres. We, too, find it hard to make ends meet here with as much as twenty acres. But, it was different there [in Srijem]. No, there . . . Conditions were different in Juga [Yugoslavia] at that time. You see, I think that you can't compare it with now. And the soil was different, of a different quality, different yields per unit of land, and the market near at hand. . . . It can't be compared. We have come here to what is practically the poorest part of Croatia, but we didn't have much choice at the time that we had to go.

The newcomers have introduced the cultivation of watermelons, *bostan,* which traditionally has never been a crop found in northwestern Croatia, and have induced many native inhabitants to do the same. A farmer, not lacking in humor and distance from the situation, tells jokes about how the locals learned from the migrants how to plant watermelons: "They didn't plant watermelons, they simply didn't know how. My neighbor across the road—he is a Serb—asked 'How do you know when it's ripe, can I cut out a small wedge and put it back if the watermelon isn't ripe?'"[2] [laughter]

The newcomers believe that they also "bring" a new approach to labor, which is characterized above all by their hard work and resourcefulness. Those traits are said to be a heritage from the not so distant past in which they were, in their own words, treated as "*kulaks* and enemies of the state" by the Communist authorities. This forced them to become resourceful: "We have learnt to be like otters" (an expression in local parlance indicating the epitome of resourcefulness), said a man with a university degree, who, upon settlement, became a farmer. Mostly independent at the time of their life in Srijem, those farmers cultivated and sold their own produce, frequently on a large scale, not refraining from entrepreneurial risk practices. It is especially in these characteristics that they perceive a significant difference in relation to the local farmers in the area of settlement, who are said to work only to satisfy their own needs.

A couple from Srijem, both of whom hold university degrees, had this to say:

Husband: "The crucial thing is that we have a particular mentality, you know, and we came to a completely different environment. It took time for them [the locals] to get to know us. They us, and we them. We were appalled by their way of life—how they lived, how little they produced according to our standards. But they regarded us as megalomaniacs. As if we are now out to get everything, as if we think we will get rich overnight. There was also some malice, and they gloated when we did not succeed. Yes, on the whole, things didn't succeed [laughter] and so . . . OK, now they have got to know us and we them."

JČŽ: "What is the difference in mentality?"

Wife: "Well, it's hard to say. I think we are . . . In general, the people from Srijem are more agile, what can I say! They are ready to come to grips with problems. We think these people here are . . . What can I say . . ."

Husband: "In an economic sense we were more aggressive because we have been used to that, to all sorts of undertakings. When I started to plant those orchards, first of all I brought about a thousand seedlings. Let's try it, to see how it goes! [A local inhabitant] asks me: 'Are you going to eat all that?'—'I am not a cow to eat apples from a thousand trees!'—'To whom are you going to sell them?'—'I'll sell them to someone, presumably someone will buy them!' . . . Still, after the War [World War II], they treated us a bit like *kulaks* in the part of Srijem from which we came. We were a bit like enemies of the state then, and we have learnt to be like otters and to cope."

This couple is not alone in stating that the people from Srijem are accustomed to working on a broad scale. Compare the following statement by a Srijem immigrant in Gradina about Srijem Croats arriving with loads of goods that they transported in large trailer trucks, which testify to their previous and current affluence:

JČŽ: "How was it in the beginning? Did the locals visit you?"

Interlocutor: "Yes, they visited us in the beginning. They came to see if we needed any help, we made friends . . . They thought that we were [poor] . . . but when they saw how we worked and compared it to how they worked, when they saw that we were more advanced . . . They keep one cow, but when I came I bought eight cows, I delivered 100 liters of milk [daily delivery to the dairy buy-up station], while they had ten. They immediately said: 'Huh, how come he has 100 liters?' . . . They said we were like carpet-baggers. But we are not carpet-baggers, we are semi-trailer people [laughter], because we came with semi-trailers, not carpet-bags."

JČŽ: "Who said that?"

Interlocutor: "One of our Srijem people. He says, 'Don't you take us for carpet-baggers, we are lorry people. We came with lorries.'"

That man interpreted in developmental terms the perceived difference in
entrepreneurial spirit (" . . . when they saw that we were more advanced
. . ."), whereas an 80-year-old woman, albeit with some hesitation, interpreted it as a difference in the industriousness of the two groups:

Woman: "They [locals] say, those crazy people from Slankamen,[3] they work a
lot. Yes, they say, those industrious people from Slankamen, they really
work hard." . . .
JČŽ: "Isn't the local population hard working?"
Woman: "Yes, they are. But I don't know, somehow not the way we are. But
when they get used to it, they'll do things differently, too . . . when they
see how much corn our people harvest, how much wheat they thresh,
because everyone can see it."

Although the elderly woman hesitates, she gives a value judgement, in fact,
a stereotype that generalizes at the level of the groups, attributing extreme
assiduity to Srijem people, doubting if the local population has a similar
characteristic. I heard a host of similar value judgements about their own
and the other group regarding the settlements—in Srijem and in Croatia—particularly about the way the land was tilled, along with comparisons about household amenities and the way the yards were kept.

The villages in eastern Srijem from which the migrants came had
between 2,000 and 4,000 inhabitants, with some even larger than that.
In the Virovitica area in northern Croatia, they settled in smaller localities, with, on average, from 200 to 500 inhabitants. The exceptions
are Gradina (1,058 inhabitants) and Suhopolje (2,741 inhabitants).[4]
Village communal infrastructure is directly linked to size. According
to my interlocutors, each village in Srijem had a water supply system,
telephone lines, pavements, at least one shop, a public health and veterinary station, and a church, and was almost like an urban settlement
with respect to the available infrastructure. While speaking about this, a
50-year-old teacher is trying to explain the lack of urbanized settlements
in the Virovitica area:

When one of our 60-year-old farmers came here and saw a village with
thirty houses, he immediately realized that it is impossible to build pavements here and impossible to build the infrastructure a settlement needs.
Inevitably such a village does not have a public health or a veterinary
station, does not have village attributes, does not have a church, a shop,

does not have anything! Then comments were made: "Why are there such villages, why a village with twenty houses, why a village with fifty houses?" Time passed before I could explain to my father that this was because the Serbs took possession of the space here, that this is why they built so many villages. It's a part of Serbian policies, not part of Croatian policies. Those parts of Vojvodina that were under Hungary were obviously urbanized as far back as in the eighteenth century, while there is still no urbanism here even today. . . . One cannot establish infrastructure in these villages, it's impossible, impossible.[5]

A young settler in Gradina, quoted in chapter 3, emphasized that it was incomprehensible to the Croats from Srijem who had settled in smaller villages that their new settlements did not have a water supply and sewage system. Though he acknowledged the advantages Gradina offered in comparison with the smaller villages in which Srijem Croats were settling, his overall appraisal of life in Gradina was negative, as were the judgements of many other settlers. Their views were strongly influenced by the television documentaries that Croatian Television shot about the Srijem Croats, one in particular that dealt with the underdeveloped infrastructure in certain smaller villages in the Gradina district, which aired in 1994. The interviewed migrants who had settled in those villages stated that they had come from a "much richer and better environment to a more backward one." As we have seen in the previous chapter in statements by older settlers in Gradina, Gradina has all the amenities that are needed for a "civilized life": a water supply system, sewage, telephone lines, a post office, a public health station, shops, etc. These amenities were one of the reasons for settlement in Gradina. Nevertheless, there are settlers in Gradina (and also in the regional center of Virovitica) who seem to overgeneralize in their appraisals of the poor communal infrastructure in the area as a whole.

A further significant difference noticed by Srijem Croats relates to the organization of the villages. The assessment is frequently linked to the fact that the migrants have moved from a central location in the village of origin and had to settle on the outskirts of the village of Gradina, in the so-called New Gradina.

Along with statements about the differences in the way in which space and the location of outbuildings on the plots around the houses are organized, many people, in completely separate conversations, stressed what they regarded as one of the core differences—the appearance of the farmyards in the Virovitica area and in Srijem. Apparently, all the yards in Srijem were paved with brick and, more recently, with concrete: "Everyone, even the poorest man—if he could not afford to have concrete, at least paved the yard with bricks. But you never find that here, never," said a young man from Srijem. The paving made it possible for them to walk around their properties in (leather) slippers, a habit which they do not want to give up even after migration. An anecdote is told that a man from Srijem continues to walk in his slippers—taken as a marker of his identity—in his new surroundings. According to a primary school teacher: "The peasant there [in Srijem] walked around in slippers because his yard was nicely paved. Here he needs boots to go out. . . . He is used to wearing slippers there, so he wears them here, too." The paved yards are not only a matter of aesthetics and tidiness, but also a marker of development[6] because they ostensibly protect against infestation by rats.

The underdevelopment of the area of Virovitica in comparison to Srijem was evident to my interlocutors in still another characteristic: metal stoves that burn sawdust and are used for heating, which can apparently still be found in the villages around Virovitica. "Not everybody in Srijem had central heating. That's normal . . . but they used coal and there were tile stoves. I can remember that sawdust heaters were used in Srijem back in the 1960s."[7]

In any case, according to one man from Srijem, the Srijem Croats were more advanced in every regard: "in their farm mechanization and their labor, the way they tilled the land—in every respect." Another man, living in Zagreb today, offered an explanation:

Interlocutor: "In Srijem, culture was higher. I asked myself why this was. Then I realized what the answer was: Vienna and Budapest were centers of culture, for centuries, isn't that so? And the Danube was the main artery. White ships that came—transport, and civilization spread along the rivers, until the railway and highways came."

JČŽ: "What did your higher culture consist of?"

Interlocutor: "In general, in everything. Now I'd have to enumerate. Well, the culture of living, the culture of communicating with other people, the work culture. I was stupefied when I came here and saw that people here were still sowing wheat by hand—in 1991! I mean, I cannot explain this to you, for you are an intellectual [i.e., you will not understand]. Corn-sowing machines—in Vojvodina we have been using a pneumatic machine for twenty years, which takes grain by grain and tosses it. Here, they . . ."

JČŽ: "Srijem and Vojvodina, more generally, were the two most advanced regions in the former Yugoslavia."

Interlocutor: "Not only with regard to agriculture. There is also the way of thinking. . . . *Švabe*[8] were the first to bring threshing machines. Švabe were the first to bring bicycles, the first motor-bikes. That happened in Srijem, because all of Vojvodina was full of Švabe. Hungary was an advanced country, it is in our neighborhood, do you understand? That culture has left its traces. That is a matter of civilization, it's not only a matter of an ethnic group. But to consider it all here—it's embarrassing to even talk about it, because people will say: 'Why did you come to us in Zagreb to lecture us?' . . . It does not mean that we want to demean everything that we have found in Croatia. No, what I am talking about is the truth. . . . We compare, generally . . . how can I put it . . . the culture of living . . . Take orchards—we had plantations of orchards, in the 1980s we had 2,000 acres of plantation peaches in the Slankamen area alone. Do you know how much that is? That's a small California!"

Perceived differences in customs and mentality were expressed in statements ranging from those without value judgements to those with value judgements and generalizing stereotypes. Some differences were presented as a defining characteristic of ethnic identity of the self and the Other. For example, the population from Srijem practices a common greeting, which is of religious origin—"May the Lord (and the Virgin) be praised!," to which one expects a counter-greeting "May He be praised eternally!" It is not used by the local population, who, when addressed by it, respond with "May the Lord be praised!," which causes laughter and sneers among the newcomers. The migrants link this greeting with their ethnicity, claiming that it was their distinctive feature in the old country, setting them apart from the Serbian population.[9] With the change of social context, the previous ethnic marker has become a social one: whereas in Srijem it identified and separated Croats from the Serbs, in Gradina it is a symbol of the social division between the locals and the newcomers.

Even with regard to the common religious denomination linking the settlers with the natives—the majority of Croats are Roman Catholics—which might be expected to facilitate their integration,[10] the newcomers discover differences between themselves and the locals. The differences pertain to some details in greeting the priest when he goes on his household blessing rounds. A primary school teacher speaks: "Back home, when the priest comes to bless the household, all of us wait for him outside the house. Waiting for him is a sign of respect to the priest. But they [locals in the area of settlement] don't do that, he goes alone from house to house, and they don't wait for him."

The differences sometimes intrude upon the ritual itself. For example, an elderly farmer settled in Gradina informed the priest about the customs and expectations of the Croats from Srijem, criticizing him for the lack of ritual elements during household blessing visits. While recounting his criticism, the man was actually comparing contemporary ritual in Gradina with the former ritual practised in his village of origin in Srijem, which he remembers from the period between the two world wars:

> When another priest came and blessed the houses—two years ago—we all came inside, he did everything and when he was leaving the house, I said: "Sir, I could find fault with you, I could reproach you for something! When you step out into the street now, someone could ask me: 'Was that man begging?'" He didn't have anything! A parish priest! No altar boys, no robes, he didn't even have any holy water! One has to prepare everything for him, he only comes to take the money. . . . He did not carry anything, only the Book [the Bible], only the Book, and I made my objections [clear] to him . . . And, last year, last autumn, he brought four or five children with him. They don't ring any bells, they don't sing, they don't do anything! . . . I remember when in the old Yugoslavia—that rotten old Yugoslavia—when the priest, Pera Masnić, came. They were all dressed from head to toe, in that long cape, they had everything, there were four altar boys, bells, holy water, incense. You could smell it—the entire house smelled of incense. Here you have no idea about who was in the house! Just someone to collect the money, if you ask me.

Furthermore, the Croats from Srijem argue that they are "better believers" and that they have maintained the practice of their religion to a greater extent than the local population has done. However, they do understand that religious traditions were abandoned to a certain extent during the Communist period. Compare a statement by a middle-aged farmer and poet from Srijem:

> That was what the [Communist] policy was then, but we hung on, we went to church more, we did not cave in and we baptized our children. When we came here—to Croatia—people with beards and moustaches[11] were being baptized. Now you find children who have already finished school being baptized because it's free [to practice religion], it's Croatia now.

Differences appertain also to communication and people's habits, according to a man from Srijem:

> The way of behavior, communication, teasing, jokes—all of it is completely different. We noticed it immediately. In Tovarnik [a village in western Srijem]—people eat and drink more at the inns. Here everything is quite empty, except for a couple of drunkards who come to the inn. It is not the custom here [to go out to the inns]! People have different customs here.

Some claim that people in Virovitica visit each other less and communicate less:

> Nobody has contacts with anybody here. In the street, they just say "Hello," and that's the whole story. Here the yard gates are locked and unlocked—when you enter the house and when you leave it. There is not much contact. It's something we are not used to. I have never had a cup of coffee alone [in Srijem], never. Alright, I did work, but when I was at home, my female neighbors dropped in. When I came here, . . . I made coffee, but it didn't taste the same [drinking it alone]. It just did not work. Until I got used to it.

Certain traditions are added to the repertoire of distinctions setting apart the newcomers from the local population. For example, the newcomers claim that godparenthood in Srijem has been carried on from generation to generation, "always" between two families and/or households, while in the area of settlement the tradition is different. A young farmer, whom we came to know in chapter 3, attributes a mythical dimension to godparenthood in Srijem:

> We have one godparent for all occasions. The godparent was respected; it is said "First God, then the godparent." Here they have a hundred godparents. Here one has one godparent for marriage, another for baptism, yet another for confirmation. It was different at home. At home, there was one godparent for all occasions. And godparenthood was maintained for two, three hundred years, from generation to generation. We have always had a godparent from the same family since the foundation of our village. . . .

Further assertions on "big" distinctions between the two groups include the following, stated by an elderly farm woman concerning Christmas:

Woman: "We celebrate Christmas in our way, they in their way."
JČŽ: "What is the difference?"
Woman: "There's a big difference, a really big one. At home, a group of boys went around the houses singing on Christmas Eve.[12] You don't find that here. At home, if there are not ten different kinds of cake for Christmas, then it is not Christmas at all. Here they have only one kind, and it's a dry type at that. . . ."

The local population reportedly also view their customs with astonishment: "They consider it odd when we bring hay into the room—hay in the room was common at home for Christmas Eve, always. Here it's strange."

For the Croats from Srijem, those traditions represent "values" that the local population has lost or has never known. The locals are said not to recognize "the age" and "the value" of those traditions. To the contrary, they equate them with backwardness. The statements of a couple of teachers from Srijem sum up this view:

Wife: "We bring with us those values that have been lost here, but, as such, we are not accepted. They think that we are backward because of them. . . . They regard them as uncouth."

Husband: "How do the locals perceive us? They see us through those customs, through the lens of those old customs that we have kept. For example, hay at Christmastime, customs on Maundy Thursday—fires, remembering the Last Supper, roasting popcorn by the fire, etc., coming together, socializing . . . They see us as backward in a way, while at the same time we come from Srijem with qualifications that are higher, on average, than the average in this region of Croatia. We come with a much stronger material base [are financially better off], with a material base that is much greater than among the population here. And that's where the contradiction lies!"

The migrants interpret their own adherence to traditions as evidence of their Croatian identity: the traditions demonstrate their national affiliation, their Croatian ethnicity. Their perseverance in maintaining these customs is proof to them of their Croatian identity, not only under the new circumstances, but—even more importantly—in the context of socialist Yugoslavia. For example, Carnival, *mačkare,* in the village of Golubinci in Srijem is retrospectively interpreted as a symbol of the preservation of Croatian awareness among the Croats in Srijem. The migrants feel unable to communicate to their new neighbors the sacrifices they made in order to practice and preserve Croatian traditions under the former regime. They argue that they have kept them alive in spite of efforts of the Yugoslav Communist regime to eliminate them—the Communist regime which wanted to ban them. The conflict with the Communist regime is interpreted as expression and proof of belonging to the Croatian nation. According to a middle-aged veterinary surgeon:

I do not want to tell them [his new neighbors] anything, because I cannot explain to them what it meant in our village to follow the Carnival when the police were coming. But we went anyhow and they chased us. There were about five, six, ten policemen. At a certain point they realized that there was nothing they could do, and that even the Serbs had abandoned their Carnival and started participating in ours. But the police still came, and we tried to talk them round, and they kept silent.

I cannot explain to them what this meant. And now they [the locals] are telling me what it means to be a Croat.[13]

The *tamburitza* folk instrument is also presented as a marker of the Croatian identity of the Croats from Srijem. They claim it was an important part of their culture in the past. They comment with irony on the fact that that instrument was included in the list of Croatian symbols in Croatia only in the 1990s.[14] They find this act somewhat amusing, because the tamburitza has always had that symbolism for them. This way of thinking is underscored by the statement of a middle-aged veterinary surgeon from Srijem: "The *tambura* was something special. Whoever had money in Srijem hired tambura musicians to play at weddings. . . . My wish would be to hire tambura players and drive around in a cart pulled by horses 'till one could swoon with delight."

The lack of similar traditions among the locals or, as in the case of tamburitza, its reinvention, leads the migrants to doubt the identity of the local population. This was expressed by a teacher from Srijem: "We thought that we had come among Croats, but maybe we were wrong. . . . We had a mistaken expectation that the Croats here knew the traditions that we had there. . . . We thought that we would find them here—from the manner of greeting to customs—but that was not the case."

"Good" and "Bad" Croats or How to Measure Croatian-ness

The settlement of the Srijem Croats in Croatia was accompanied by positive expectations as to their future incorporation into Croatian society and acceptance by the local population. However, "homecoming" to the "ethnic homeland" entailed perception and construction of difference and strangeness vis-à-vis the local Croatian population. The most visibly distinctive characteristic of the population from Srijem is their Ekavian idiom, which, they argue, has been identified by the local Croats as a variant of Serbian.[15] It is only a step from that perception to identifying the new settlers as Serbs. According to the Croats from Srijem, immediately upon their settlement members of the local population said: "One kind of Serbs left, another lot has arrived. That comment was made because of our Ekavian." That identification was incomprehensible to the migrants, especially since it came during and after the war between the Croats and Serbs. My informants were more bewildered than offended by the insinuation.

The Srijem Croats were confronted with new neighbors—some "other kind" of Croats—in a context in which, as an immigrant population, they were "newcomers" (*došlje, dodoši*),[16] socially isolated, incompetent in the local culture, and sometimes perceived as the "new Serbs." Moreover, in the context of the Croatia of the early 1990s, in which the key social identity was ethnically (nationally) defined, the Croats from Srijem thought that they had to "prove" to their coethnic compatriots that they, too, were Croats. At the time of the migration and settlement of the Srijem Croats, which coincided with Serbian aggression on Croatia, national identification pushed aside other levels of identification (subnational, regional, local) and imposed itself as the dominant identifying marker of the majority of inhabitants. Simultaneously, encouraging homogenization and consensus among Croatian citizens, official Croatian policy promoted the nationalization of identity as part of the project for creation of the new nation state, presenting it as a necessary means in the struggle against Serbian hegemony and aggression. The following statement by a teacher from Srijem explains why it was necessary to spur on the Croatian identity of the migrants from Srijem:

> When our people came at the end of 1991, in the summer and autumn of 1991 and at the beginning of 1992, we had to create a picture of the people from Srijem as Croats. First to prove that he exists in Srijem and then to create a picture of him—how he thinks, which customs he has, which feelings he has! And, with all that, that he spoke in Srijem Ekavian. We had to prove things like that at that time.

The Communist Other, which was more or less identified with the Serbian Other and had served as an identification reference in the old home was not operable in the new situation. A new discursive strategy of identification was set in motion and built up on a whole series of differences that set the Srijem Croats apart from the locals. As we have seen in their comparisons, they perceive themselves as being generally superior to the local population. At the same time, the ostensible continuity of their traditions is taken as evidence of their ethnic quality and, by extension, of the settlers' own Croatian ethnicity.

The Srijem Croats define their Croatian-ness by a historical instance of culture, that is, by their historical traditions. Relying on the conception of culture as a distinctive set of traditions and values with clear-cut boundaries, that is, culture as a constant, as a lasting and unchangeable attribute of an ethnic group (or nation, or any other social entity), they espouse that culture is at the base of identifying an ethnic entity.

In such a conception, culture is reified into a set of characteristics and reduced to an immutable substance rooted in the ethnic group (Abu-Lughod 1991; Eriksen 1993). Cultural difference is treated as a defining and immutable characteristic of a group, the characteristic which defines its identity. This cultural logic presupposes that the ethnic or national community *is* its culture (Stolcke 1996). In this vein, culture and ethnic identity are treated as natural, static, and ascribed aspects of human groups.

However, historical processes and the experience of the Srijem Croats dispute cultural logic and speak about culture change and about cultural mixing that arise as a consequence of migration and resettlement (for example, in economic behavior) as well as about the openness and flexibility of identity. In the processes of cultural hybridization and reidentification induced by migration, an active and creative use of culture by the migrants is a key factor leading to reassessment of their own identity and that of the local Others. This chapter has analyzed those processes in the area of settlement (in Gradina and Virovitica), while the next chapter will take them up again from the perspective of an organized effort on the part of the migrant association to create a distinctive migrant identity.

The circumstances of settlement for the Srijem Croats have resulted in the ethnicization of their traditions. It is not clear whether the "traditions" that are today marked as important and which "testify" to the Croatian identity of the coethnic migrants were indeed maintained and practiced by all Croats in Srijem. The procession around the village on Christmas Eve (*betlemaši*) and at Carnival time seems to have been practiced in only some of the villages in Srijem, and Carnival seems to have lost its vigor in the 1980s. The settlement in Croatia actually brought about retraditionalization.[17] By transforming local traditions, which once demarcated individual Croatian villages in Srijem, into an identity feature of the entire migrant population, previously distinct local traditions of the Srijem Croats were reinvented as singular, regional—Srijem and ethnic (national)—Croatian traditions. This reinvention accompanied the process of identity reconstruction among the resettled population.

According to the Srijem Croats, the Croatian-ness of their traditions resides in their experience of having had to maintain them in a hostile Communist environment. As they put it, it was in resistance and opposition to the Communist regime, itself identified with the Serbian nation,[18] that a "true" Croat could be recognized. In other words, the "real" Croats are those who managed to preserve old Croatian traditions at the time when it was not desirable, and when it was even dangerous. The migrants contrast their own, subsequently inscribed, courage in maintaining their traditions with that of the Croats in Croatia: "There we were in Serbia, and yet we were *greater Croats,* we were *better Croats* than they were. We did not submit to the Serbs. The Croats here, they were in Croatia and the Serbs were their masters" (emphasis added by the author).

For the same reasons, an elderly farmer from Srijem expresses his doubts about the Croatian-ness of the locals: "Here they are not Croats to the extent that I expected. They are not. Those living around Đakovo [eastern Croatia] and thereabouts, that's OK, but the ones here are not real Croats."

Maintaining Croatian traditions—both folk and religious—is interpreted by the coethnic migrants as defiance and resistance to Communism and to the Serbs. From today's perspective, for a coethnic migrant to be a Croat under the Communist regime meant being in political opposition to, and thus resisting, Serbian hegemony. Today, these characteristics are testimony to the migrants' Croatian identity, which, from their point of view, is more accountable, or in their words "better" than that of the locals. Speaking of "better," "bigger" or "truer" Croats implies that the others are "worse" or "not good," or, as is heard in some statements, "not real Croats" or even "not Croats at all."

To what extent does this local stratification of Croats echo the state rhetoric of "divided nationhood" in the second half of the 1990s, in which the ruling party—the Croatian Democratic Union—kept dividing the Croats into "good" (those pro-ruling party and anti-Communist), and "bad" (those pro-[ex]Communist and allegedly pro-Yugoslavia)? It is more than probable that this influential official rhetoric could have been seeping into local discursive strategies, for, as we have seen, the opposition between the Communists and the Croats, which was promoted by the Croatian state in the 1990s, was also being reproduced locally by the Croats from Srijem.

The cultural logic that is at the base of the distinction between two different "kinds" of Croats is an integral part of a popular conception of ethnicity and belonging (cf. Fulbrook 1996). The popular conception of belonging is cultural: according to that conception, only culturally similar people are considered members of the we-group, all those that are perceived as culturally different are excluded from it. Cultural homogeneity is achieved by those who share common communication space and who, via direct contacts and interaction, create a community with rules of behavior and thinking that are recognizable and expected by its members. Consequently, it is obviously not possible for the Croats from Srijem, who have only recently settled in Croatia, to share a similar life style to that of the local population. The recent encounter between the locals and the newcomers might explain why neither group takes the other as belonging to the we-group, and this in spite of a common ethnicity. On the contrary, the construction of difference with regard to the other group leads to ethnicization of one's own traditions and to denial to the other group of the "good" Croatian identity.

Thus, ethnicity (nationality)[19] does not seem to be a determining principle of identity in a situation of coethnic migration. The idea of shared ethnic (national) identity is overlain by a restrictive cultural notion—by a popular conception of ethnicity and belonging—which excludes culturally different subgroups from the ethnic (national) group. For both migrants and locals, socialization and cultural similarity are much more important categories for defining the boundaries of the groups than common ethnic (national) belonging. In direct communication, real and perceived differences in sociocultural markers push aside national commonality. Therefore, on the micro-level, in spite of the rhetoric about the unity and homogeneity of culture and the nation which dominated the Croatian political scene in the mid 1990s, common national identity did not lessen the importance of perceived and imputed differences between the two groups. Because subjective ascription to the Croatian nation is unquestionable for both the local and the immigrant population, a means to cope with the situation—in which one is confronted within the emically ascribed national community with cultural heterogeneity—is found in stratifying one's own Croatian-ness and that of the other group, or even in denying it to the other group. This stratification is supported by the parallel rhetoric pertaining to the broader society, which divides citizens into "good" and "bad" Croats.

It follows from this analysis that ethnicity (nationality) inheres internal complexity, and that it does not serve as an all-encompassing unifying principle for construction of collective identity, not even when the latter is promoted by the general social context and political discourse. It is clear that ethnic homogenization of the national state does not strengthen national identity. Coethnic migration, as a special case of migration, homogenizes the nation state ethnically, but since it also enhances cultural differences it might lead to divisions within the nation built along the borderline between the immigrants and the local population.

About the Same Thing from the Other Side: Statements by the Local Population in Gradina

Greetings

JČŽ: "How do the locals greet one another?"

Interlocutor: "'*Bog, bog*' [God be with you],[20] and some say 'Good day,' 'Good morning,' most of them say 'Good morning' in the morning, and '*Bog, Bog*' later in the day."

JČŽ: "And the Croats from Srijem?"

Interlocutor: "'May the Lord and the Virgin be praised' [the man sang the greeting]. . . . Everyone says 'May the Lord and the Virgin be praised.' They greet each other politely. While that '*Bog*,' that's something that our people, these local old settler people have concocted as if they are some sort of . . . A grandmother from there [from Srijem] said: 'That's how we used to greet each other. We didn't use [the greeting] like you do here. You don't even say '*Bog*,' but '*Bok*' [pronouncing the word with the short 'o']. What sort of greeting is that, said that grandmother, the real Croatian greeting is 'May the Lord and the Virgin be praised,' or 'May the Lord be praised,' not '*Bok*' [short].' That really irritates me, my goodness, how that '*Bok*' irritates me."

A 50-year-old man, a public servant

Talking

Interlocutor: "Do you know what disturbs our inhabitants here the most? I know it, but it does not bother me. It bothers them that the Srijem Croats cannot unlearn speaking in Ekavian, saying *lebac*,[21] and such things. That irritates a lot [of these people] here. It does not bother me. But I know—we have had migrants from Zagorje here since World War I, they came even before Yugoslavia was established, and they still say *kaj*.[22] Or the Dalmatians, they still say *lipo, bilo* and call their mothers *mate*.[23] But some [local people]—there are bigoted people—they say, the Srijem people speak more in Ekavian than the Serbs who lived in Gradina ever did. Then I say, the Serbs also spoke Ekavian here. They did not speak it until before the war, and then just before the war they started saying '*bre*'[24] and using Ekavian and all that."

A 50-year-old man, a public servant

JČŽ: "Have you heard local persons say 'New Serbs have arrived'?"

Interlocutor A: "I haven't heard that, personally."

Interlocutor B: [laughter] "They haven't. But they [the locals] object that those from Srijem won't speak our language, but use more Ekavian. Ah, that was the only thing that irritated them."

JČŽ: "That is how they speak in Srijem."
Interlocutor B: "But they do not make an effort to change it."

> A man about 40 years old, a qualified worker and
> a woman about 70 years old, a farmer

Interlocutor: "There were no problems [with children at school]. There was no separation, no mocking. What surprised me was that the children rarely made a mistake and spoke in Ekavian. That was a rare case. They just normally switched to the Croatian standard language."

> A woman about 50 years old, a school teacher

Interlocutor: "Still today, people do not think about the fact that he [a person from Srijem] grew up speaking that way . . . They [the people from Srijem] try to change how they speak, but it is difficult for a man aged about fifty, or forty years . . . he can't . . . It doesn't bother me personally and many other people how they speak, but some people do not reflect about it, especially when they are drinking, and they criticize the people from Srijem."

> A man about 60 years old, a farmer

Traditions

JČŽ: "Have you introduced any topics at school regarding the multicultural society?"
Interlocutor: "I didn't think it was necessary. It wasn't necessary, because there were no differences among the children. So it wasn't necessary. We used to talk at the homeroom meeting about folk customs at Christmas, for example, or at Easter. They were different everywhere. There were similarities, but there were also differences, so that the children . . . I told them to ask their parents about those traditions, so that some interesting customs emerged . . . But, basically, it all came down to the same thing, naturally enough, to what is most important."
JČŽ: "Are there any older customs in Gradina?"
Interlocutor: "Yes. For example, characteristic old songs and dances are *Još Hrvatska nije propala* [Croatia has not yet perished], then *Sirota sam ja* [I'm a poor girl] and the *drmeš* dance. Those are songs, and the round-dances that are really danced. Even today. That is characteristic for Gradina." . . .
JČŽ: "Have the inhabitants in Gradina valued and maintained their traditions?"
Interlocutor: "Yes, they have valued them and maintained them. They loved them and they really have been maintained until today."

> A woman about 50 years old, a school teacher

Interlocutor: "For example, the old folk costume in Gradina—that is authentic. You have it in every house. The old costume, nothing which has been made, let's say, in the past ten years. Male costume is a bigger problem. They have ordinary long [loose] trousers and shirts, perhaps with a bit of embroidery on the front, but simple. The female costume is old. In every house, you have two or three old women who keep them for their grandchildren. My mother has about twenty sets of costume. They were handed down to the children from her grandmother and great-grandmother, and from her mother-in-law." . . .

Interlocutor: "Those Serbs who lived here [before] trained us well. Things were all which way."

JČŽ: "Has the Croatian character of Gradina disappeared?"

Interlocutor: "No, it hasn't. One kept it [alive] at home. Though one was not allowed to . . . Maybe, I don't agree with some older people who say that system forbade any display of Croatian-ness. Maybe it did not allow you to sing *Ban Jelačić*[25] or something like that. But it did not forbid you to put on your costume and to say that you were a Croat. Or to go to the church. I was an altar boy . . . The parish priest used to come to see us at my parents' house and nobody ever persecuted us for that. Never!" . . .

Interlocutor: "A die-hard region [Virovitica]! A Croatian region! That is indisputable. Regardless . . . It was only that people somehow put the breaks on their Croatian-ness. Maybe it was out of misery and powerlessness to do anything, when you saw that the other one, the Serb, lived a better, easier life. I'd say that he [the Croat here] was more dispirited than [anything else] . . . And then he simply . . . he did not want to put his hand to anything."

A 30-year-old man, a civil servant

JČŽ: "Are there any new customs in Gradina now that the Srijem Croats have settled here?"

Interlocutor A: "No, it is mostly the same now. There was something, in the first year after they came, there was something shown on TV. There were some customs that were different. . . . A custom was shown, how they make rounds of the houses at Christmas Eve . . . [the *betlemaši* custom]. But if they still do it, I don't know about it. I think it is over with that."

JČŽ: "The Srijem people only did this in the first year after settlement?"

Interlocutor A: "It is likely that it was staged because of television. It is very likely that it was done just because of television. It took place in Gradina."

JČŽ: "Do the people from Srijem still make the rounds of houses on Christmas Eve?"

Interlocutor A: "I haven't noticed that they do. I would have to ask."

Interlocutor B: "Maybe they do there [in the new part of the village]. If they do it, then it is only among themselves."

A man about 50 years old, a civil servant, and his
approximately 20-year-old daughter, a housewife

Interlocutor A: "We used to have benches, here and there in front of houses. But as soon as they [the Srijem migrants] came—they put a bench in front of every house! [laughter] . . . Everybody knows it: for example, in our street there are about five to six benches around which people gather, in front of somebody's house. . . . You have certain houses in front of which people sit and talk."

JČŽ: "The benches in Gradina used to be only in front of some of the houses, not all?"

Interlocutor B: "From time immemorial."

Interlocutor A: "There is a bench in front of the third house from ours. We sit there. Everybody—old and young."

A man about 30 years old, a qualified worker,
and a woman about 50 years old, a farmer

JČŽ: "Do the Srijem migrants differ from the locals?"

Interlocutor: "How, how? I do not see any big differences. I really don't. The way of life is the same."

JČŽ: "They live like you do?"

Interlocutor: "I'd say that we maintain the same customs—Catholic ones, and normal customs. They do nothing different from us."

JČŽ: "You haven't noticed any difference?"

Interlocutor: "I will tell you now that I have noticed that they have accustomed themselves a little to this area. This is how it should be."

JČŽ: "Why?"

Interlocutor: "Because they are Croats. It does not matter that this is the Podravina or Slavonia region, whatever we call it. But we are not going to get accustomed to them, they have to accustom themselves to this area. Not to me! Not to me! To the customs! . . . They celebrated St. Michael in Slankamen. Here they celebrate St. Elias [the Gradina patron saint] and that is great! I don't have to add anything else. What could I add? Isn't that so? That is how it should be. Celebrate where you are. I go to America, and, as a Croat, I have to salute the American flag or stand up when the American anthem is played—and that's it! The one who stayed in Slankamen [in Srijem], though he is a Croat, when the Serbian or Yugoslav anthem—whatever it is called today—is played, he has to get up and to adapt. That is his anthem over there."

JČŽ: "You are local people and in the majority, and they have come here. Is that important?"

Interlocutor: "It should be important, of course, of course it is. Why not? Well, now, it would be all upside down if we had to [change] . . . That I start talking in Ekavian and they start talking in Ijekavian."

JČŽ: "Shouldn't you also accommodate to them?"

Interlocutor: "Hmm? I could . . . You know, they maybe maintain their Croatian cultural heritage better than we do. On Christmas Eve, some things like that. . . . I tell you that they have maintained things . . . Look at their embroidery, on their folk costumes. OK, we, too, have our folk embroidery. Every region has its own—Slavonia, Podravina, Zagorje. We are all Croats. Every [region] has its embroidery and other things. Their embroidery is ornate. Look at their horses when they go to Đakovo Festival, and elsewhere, at the Vinkovci Autumn Festival and places like that. I mean, they maintain their Croatian-ness, very deep Croatian-ness!" . . .

JČŽ: "Do you think that they have preserved more customs than the local people?"

Interlocutor: "Yes, I do. You know, we have always celebrated Christmas, the *Kalends* [custom], the Christmas greetings custom. The *betlemaši* custom has been lost here—I do not remember it. But they [people from Srijem] still have it! I was surprised one night, sometime in 1993 or 1994, I do not know exactly . . . The *betlemaši* were coming to our place. What's this now? They were singing, *Oh Bethlehem, the famous town.* They offer wine and cakes, and there are children. You have to give the children something. That was the first time in my life. We had Christmas greetings customs in the morning, but only small children would go to offer Christmas greetings to their neighbors and relatives, and to those who lived nearby, and they would be given a little bit money. It was the same for Easter—a child was given an orange, and an Easter egg or two, and that was it! But they . . . they maintain the *betlemaši,* very much, it means a lot to them."

A man about 40 years old, a qualified worker

Making a Living

Interlocutor: "It is understandable that it was a great change for them when they settled here. It's a different clime, the people are different, the food is different, the life is different. This is a purely agricultural area. People till the land and our people have learnt to work, from dawn to dark they are out in the fields working. All they knew was how to sell their produce to the cooperative, and only a few of them went to the market in Virovitica and sold their produce there. They worked for themselves and to feed the small number of livestock they kept at home. But these people [from Srijem] have worked differently. They engaged more in the growing of vegetables and fruit, and it was normal for them to take their produce and sell it at the markets in the bigger towns. I have noticed that quite a number of the locals in Gradina have picked this up from them. Not so much in the production of fruit, but more in the production of vegetables. So I think that a certain pace of life and coexistence are possible and normal. Because some years have passed by since they came here and they have become accustomed to each other. I think that things are developing normally."

A woman about 50 years old, a school teacher

Interlocutor A: "Life is harder here. The land here is difficult to plough, over there they had fruit trees and you just pick the fruit. It was easier there, that's what I think. . . . You have to roll up your sleeves and really get your hands dirty here, you have to work harder here than they did there."

JČŽ: "Have they understood how one should work the fields here?"

Interlocutor A: "Yes, they have, they have."

JČŽ: "Have they asked for advice?"

Interlocutor A: "No, they haven't. Some have asked, those who want to make contact . . . Those younger people who made contact. They have got over this [resettlement] more easily than the older people. But among the older people, it's hopeless, there's nothing you can do. . . . I know, they brought us some innovations. . . . They brought some innovations—we have never grown watermelons. We would plant them sometimes in the garden, but they were no bigger than a fist. But now, Ž. [a man from Srijem] has grown a watermelon of 15 kilos."

JČŽ: "Have the locals managed to grow such big watermelons?"

Interlocutor A: "Yes, the locals have also grown them."

Interlocutor B: "You know how it is. Here we just buy a watermelon [laughter], we dry the seeds and we throw them out, and the watermelon starts growing immediately. [laughter] Their system is different. I have watched how it is done. I had an opportunity to see it at S.'s [a man from Srijem]. I have seen how they do it at his place: you need to have very fine stable manure—then you dig, and then you plant. The seedling is put in the ground later. Eh, and that's how you get a watermelon!" . . .

JČŽ: "Do you do have contact with the migrants when you need something? Do you ask them for advice?"

Interlocutor A: "Well, they are real masters at fruit growing. That's a fact . . . There's no doubt about it! That's how it is!"

JČŽ: "What have they taken over from you?"

Interlocutor A: "Now they plant green and red peppers [capsicums]. And especially beans . . . Here and there, because they brought some beans with them. . . . Some sort of green beans, they brought the seeds with them. Now our people have started planting them."

Two men about 50 and 30 years old,
a public servant and a qualified worker

Interlocutor: "In general, when I look around, they [people from Srijem] have found their feet very well. But then again, it depends, not all of them, you know. It has always been like that. You can put me—what can I say—in a rich flatland and give me machinery. But if I don't know how to work well and I don't know how to manage things, I won't prosper. And you can take someone else with less machinery and less land, and he knows how to manage and how to produce well and how to sell well. He will prosper. It has always been like that, it depends on how you shift for yourself. That's how it goes."

JČŽ: "Have the Srijem people here coped well?"

Interlocutor: "My personal opinion is that on average, on average, let's say about 80 percent are not doing so bad. It is good! They have managed well, on average, this is what I think. About 20 percent have not [have not managed well]. It is sad to see a family—there is one here, our neighbors, they have three degrees at home, and not one of them is working!"

Interlocutor: "They [people from Srijem] work, they work the land decently. They had more, I can tell you. On the whole, what those people had [in Srijem]—at least that's what I think, they had, for example, an acre or two of peaches, from early bearer to late bearer types. And every day, for example, when the season started, they went to market. It was a question of money. Then the grapes ripened, the first time, and then again, and they were handling ready cash all the time. But here, you deliver your wheat, and you wait for three months. Will you get your money? And then they pay you out in three instalments! You yourself know how it goes. There they handled ready cash!"

A man about 40 years old, a qualified worker

Interlocutor: "They [people from Srijem] only asked around a bit—they ask around a bit and think they know everything. But I told them: 'It's not the same, the climate is not the same.' In spring they tried to sow wheat followed by wheat [sowing wheat again on the same land in the following year]—but that does not work here. I tell them 'People, it's good here, you only have to do what we do!' And they take some of it in, some ask questions, some say nothing and watch wisely, but they change. They change! We can learn from them. . . . They are well ahead of us in fruit growing. They are stronger than us in fruit growing, there's no doubt about it. Where they are strong, they can endure more. Our man can rarely succeed in selling at the markets . . . , but they are merchants. That is what they miss the most. Whoever you talk to, that is what they lack the most—the vicinity of a big town, of big market places. This is what they lack the most! They need to adapt to a different way of life, let's say more a more modest life, simply with a lot of work. . . . But since these are times when you can't sell anything . . . That's what bothers them! Bothers them and bothers us, too! But it bothers us less, because we are used to not being able to sell [our produce]."

A man about 60 years old, a peasant farmer

About the Settlers From Srijem

Interlocutor: "People who are industrious, who work . . ."

> A woman about 50 years old, a school teacher

Interlocutor: "Cheerful people, good natured—with some exceptions. Hard working, hard working, they really work. Eh, that's my opinion of the people from Srijem."

> A man about 40 years old, a qualified worker

Interlocutor: "They have managed, they have got along. Quite well. They are sophisticated people. But you can see that they are suffering about something. All of them! Especially those from Slankamen. It seems to me that they lived better there than here. . . . Sometimes I ask these older women [from Srijem], 'Granny, tell me, would you return there?'—'Oh my, my son, straight away,' she says, 'straight away, my son.' I feel so sorry when I look at them. I think: 'Ah, so sad, she spent 70, or 65 years there. Imagine that you had to leave everything.' . . . We should not be surprised that some of them are withdrawn and do not mingle, and all that. They also suffer in a way. OK, young people adapt quickly, young people . . . I know many cases when a young person goes to Germany [to work], but he does not suffer, and he suffers even less here. The young do not have to think about things the way old people do."

> A man about 50 years old, a public servant

Interlocutor: "I have never asked them [women from Srijem] what sort of life they had there. They told me what their life was like. They had to come here, and the situation was such that they came here. And what it was like for them—only they know! I only know that when they came they were not badly received, they came and they were received as God commands, nobody maltreated them, nobody said anything against them. How could it be that man's fault if he had to leave there and came here? It's his [property]! What has is got to do with me? He didn't move onto my land. He moved to his own, the property he exchanged, and, as far as I'm concerned, that's all there is to it. I didn't have anything against it. I immediately got on with D. [her new neighbor from Srijem] the first day he came here, and also with his father. And with those grandmothers—there are two of them. But of course I did [get on with them] since I am already old myself. And so it's nice that we can get together and chat the way people do." . . .

Interlocutor: "They are good, hard working [people]. As a whole, they all like to work."

> A woman about 70 years old, a peasant farmer

Notes

1. "*Istjeraše s ognjišta me mog*" [They forced me out from my hearth] 1993, "*Jesu li zamijenili ili?*" [Have they exchanged or?] 1994, "*Novi dom*" [New home] 1994, "*Srijemske sudbine*" [Srijem destinies] 1995, "*Vrijeme teče*" [Time goes by] 1998, "*Sjećanje na Gibarac*" [Remembering Gibarac] 1998.
2. This method is used after the watermelon has been picked from the vine and is usually applied at markets to prove to prospective buyers that the fruit is ripe.
3. The local population in Gradina refers to all the resettled people from Srijem as *Slankamenci*, or people from Slankamen, because most migrants came from that village (see chapter 1).
4. According to the 1991 census, there were 3,555 inhabitants in Slankamen; 4,494 in Golubinci; 1,829 in Kukujevci; 6,169 in Beška, etc. Villages in the surroundings of Virovitica are much smaller: 233 inhabitants in Ada; 698 in Cabuna; 305 in Dijelka; 177 in Žlebina, etc. (*Popis stanovništva, domaćinstava, stanova i poljoprivrednih gazdinstava 31. mart. 1991. Prvi rezultati* [Census of the population, households and agricultural estates, March 31 1991. Preliminary results], *Statistički bilten* 206, 1991. Novi Sad: Pokrajinski zavod za statistiku; *Popis stanovništva 1991. Narodnosni sastav stanovništva Hrvatske po naseljima* [The population census 1991. Ethnic structure of the population of Croatia by localities], 1992, Zagreb: Republički zavod za statistiku.
5. This statement dates from 1996. I learnt only a year later in a conversation with the mayor of Gradina that the installation of gas and water supply systems were planned in all the villages of the Gradina district.
6. Compare the statement: "Do you remember our old house? In the old yard we had about seven to eight [sq] meters of concrete paving. And bricks where the carts went. Back at that time [in the 1960s]! Ey? You see!"
7. It is approximately in the 1960s and the beginning of the 1970s that the Srijem Croats locate important advances in the economy, the cleaning up of the villages and the appearance of the houses in their region. Until then, said a man, "We were quite backward, but what could we do? We were really backward, until the 1970s. Earlier, we were still more backward. Those were such times." His wife added: "It was rare that the floor in the house was paved. It was an earthen floor."
8. Settlers of German origin, who arrived in the eighteenth and nineteenth centuries.
9. Most villages of origin of the Srijem settlers were ethnically mixed.
10. They do acknowledge that in Church matters "everything is the same."
11. This refers to the fact that Croats in Croatia were not baptized "properly"—as infants—but are being baptized now, as grownups.
12. This is a custom known as *betlemaši* in which a group of children carrying nativity creches goes around the village visiting households and singing Christmas carols. A Croatian ethnologist, Milovan Gavazzi, described it as a custom which was "not so old," known by "Hungarians and Romanians and some other peoples in Europe" and brought to northern Croatian regions from the northwest (Gavazzi 1939: 47).
13. However, a statement by an elderly woman from Srijem speaks about fear at the mere expression of Croatian affiliation in Srijem during the era of socialist Yugoslavia: "I was always ashamed to say that I am a Croat. We have never had the courage. . . . We have always been afraid. We have never been as we should have, we Croats especially are that way. They [the Serbs] have always behaved more arrogantly." It may not be by chance that this was stated by a woman. As already indicated in the previous chapter, women have had a different standpoint about national belonging than men.

They paid less attention to nationality or, judging from the foregoing statement, they feared public expression of their affiliation.

14. Ruža Bonifačić has identified several periods in the history of Croatian people in which the *tamburitza* played an important symbolic role. In the most recent period, in the 1990s, we witnessed a revival of the *tamburitza* as a Croatian national instrument (Bonifačić 1998: 141). See also Bonifačić (1995).

15. Besides *Ekavian,* which is associated with the Serbian standard (in contrast to *Ijekavian* in the Croatian standard, for example, *mleko* vs. *mlijeko* [milk]), one word in everyday use—bread—in the migrants' variant *leb* or *lebac* (instead of *kruh* in standard Croatian) served as the basis for associating the migrants with the Serbs (see chapter 1, footnote 17). With regard to the attribution of a certain way of speaking to a particular ethnic group, it is notable that one Srijem Croat claimed that there was a difference in the Ekavian of the Serbs and Croats in Srijem: "Everybody in Golubinci who had a good ear . . . [although] both the Serbs and the Croats spoke Ekavian, anyone with good ear could tell from the way they spoke, according to how they drawled, who was a Croat and who was a Serb. If you knew how to, you could tell the difference."

16. They sometimes also use this term themselves.

17. This was temporary, for after initial reinvention of traditions, enthusiasm waned among the Srijem Croats for their performance. Retraditionalization of culture is a phenomenon that has been identified in other migrant groups (Schuladen 1994).

18. In the 1990s, it was commonly assumed, not only among Srijem Croats but among Croats in general, that the Communist Yugoslavia had received more support from its Serbian citizens than from its Croatian citizens. Therefore, the Croats tend to identify the Serbs, rather than themselves, as supporters of the Communist (and Yugoslav) regime.

19. Due to the fact that the Croatian state adopted the ethnic definition of the nation, the differentiation made by certain theoreticians between ethnicity and nationality, and ethnic group and nation, is not important in the context of this discussion.

20. Literally "Bog" means God. The greeting is probably a shortened form of the greeting "Bog s tobom" [God be with you]. Sometimes it is pronounced "Bok."

21. See footnote 15.

22. The Croatian language has three dialects that are distinguished by the pronoun "what"—*što, kaj, ča*—as Stokavian, Kajkavian and Chakavian, see chapter 1, footnote 17.

23. There are other subcharacteristics, e.g., a Chakavian speaker in Dalmatia using the Ikavian subdialect shortens the "ije" in the standard Croatian word for "white"—from *bijelo* to *bilo,* for "milk"—from *mlijeko* to *mliko,* and so on.

24. This is an interjectional propword, used only by Serbs, never by Croats.

25. A famous civil governor of Croatia in the nineteenth century, one of the icons of Croatian identity.

Chapter 6

Between Individual and Collective Integration into Croatian Society

Our tragedy was a tragedy until Vukovar started to burn. Only when all of Croatia was in flames, when Vukovar was about to fall, when people were left without their children, when their houses were seized, burnt down, demolished, their tractors and combine harvesters [driven away] . . . when their sons fell in battle. . . . How can I compare myself with a person from Vukovar, who has lost sons, tractors, his house, everything burnt down, destroyed, his family . . . How could I say that we are the same? I would feel ashamed to say that! In comparison with him I was lucky, it was a blessing in disguise. What we have lived through is overshadowed by what happened there. We have not tried to be lumped together with these people who have gone through a really catastrophic tragedy. That is why we have kept silent in a way and have not wanted to promote ourselves as displaced persons, as refugees.

A man about 50 years old, from Beška, a driver

The coethnic migration of the Croats from Srijem is approached here from the point of view of their association—the Community of Croatian Refugees and Internally Displaced Persons from Vojvodina (*Zajednica prognanih i izbjeglih Hrvata iz Vojvodine*)[1]—founded at the end of 1991 with the intention of promoting the interests of the migrants. I argue that the foundation and the activities of the migrant association in (re)presenting and incorporating the migrants could be viewed as a process of their constitution as a particular ethnic (or subnational) group within the Croatian national community. The migrants' constitution as a subnational community is the result of their social differentiation and boundary making vis-à-vis other social groups, with elements that are identical to those which occur in the process of ethnicization of a group into a community with particular ethnic markers. It was initiated by a group of about ten migrants—the leaders of the Community—who settled in Zagreb, Virovitica, and Split. Because the most prominent leaders originated from Srijem, the activities of the Community were mostly aimed at the creation and promotion of the Srijem—and not the Vojvodinian—identity of the migrants.

This interpretation is based on the interactionist approach, which defines ethnicity as a process of self-identification and identification by others in social interaction. As a specific form of social organization, ethnic groups are formed in contact with other groups on the basis of perceived cultural differences, the belief in common descent, and historical experiences. Ethnic incorporation is most frequently initiated by intellectuals whereby ethnic communities become participants in economic competition in modern societies (Eriksen 1993; Verdery 1996; Vermeulen and Govers 1996). Don Handelman analyzed ethnicity in terms of a four-fold continuum of organizational incorporation: it starts as an ethnic category, develops into an ethnic network, an ethnic association, and culminates as an ethnic community (Handelman 1977). The ethnic category merely labels members of a community—the name identifies them and establishes a boundary toward other social groups. The ethnic network sustains a consistent series of contacts among members along ethnic lines. Ethnic association points to an organizational apparatus that expresses and promotes the common ethnic interests of a group. The highest degree of ethnic incorporation is an ethnic community, which is a territorially based ethnic organization.

The activities of the migrant association will be analyzed precisely from the viewpoint of those different forms of ethnic incorporation. It can be argued that, at different periods between 1991 and 1998, the migrant association was promoting different degrees or forms of ethnic incorporation of the migrants. By its foundation in late 1991, it took a first step in that process—the step by which the migrants identified in a certain way and established common interests. Afterward, in expressing and promoting the interests of the population, which it purportedly represented, the association oscillated between various degrees of ethnic incorporation: from a mere ethnic categorization to a tight corporate group having its own territory. This chapter traces this development as it was influenced by social and political processes within Croatian society, and exemplified by the activities, programs, different documents, and publications of the migrant association, and in the interviews with the leading members of the Community.

At the Outset: Categorizing the Settlers

Leaders of the Democratic League of the Croats from Vojvodina political party, who resided in eastern Srijem and southern Bačka, were among the first Croats from Vojvodina to reach Croatia during 1991. At the very beginning, they acted as an informal group, spreading information about the violation of human and civil rights in Vojvodina (Bičanić 1994: 310). Among other activities, they met with the head of the European Union Observer Mission in Zagreb to appeal them to put a stop to "the terror against the Croats and other minority groups in Vojvodina."[2]

Confronted with ever increasing emigration from Vojvodina, but still not comprehending its dimensions, the leaders created an association at the end of 1991 founded under the name of Community of Croatian Refugees and Internally Displaced Persons from Vojvodina. The constituting of the migrants as an ethnic group begins with the foundation of their association and the invention of its name, which precisely and exclusively demarcates the population in question. Although it is stated in the name of the association that it represents Croats, who make up the majority of the settled population, the Statute posits that the Community is a "voluntary and non-party association of *citizens*" (emphasis added), which does not discriminate based on national affiliation, and welcomes Croats and other nationalities displaced from the territory of Vojvodina (Statut, Art. 1 1991).

Other elements in the name of the association require further explanation. It should be noted that the name contains the dichotomy between "refugee" and "internally displaced person," which was used by the Croatian state in the 1990s to differentiate population displaced from its own territory from that of neighboring countries. According to the United Nations Convention (1951), refugees are people who are forced to leave their country and find refuge outside its borders. However, in 1991, a large number of inhabitants in war-affected zones in Croatia were displaced and temporarily settled in other parts of Croatia. According to the international Convention, those people could not be considered refugees—*izbjeglice*[3]—but were called "internally displaced persons" or "internal refugees"—*prognanici*.

As explained by the migrant leaders, "refugees" in the title of the Community refers to settlers from the Bačka and Banat regions, while "internally displaced persons" refer to those from eastern Srijem. That distinction is legitimized by historical reasons (for two centuries eastern Srijem was part of Croatia, see chapter 1) and by a particular feeling

of belonging among the migrants from eastern Srijem. Regardless of
its current administrative incorporation into Vojvodina, that is, Serbia, the settlers, whether they are leaders or ordinary migrants, stress
that eastern Srijem belongs to Croatia. Srijem is spoken of as "Croatian territory," its inhabitants as "a branch of a Croatian tree," whose
"Croatian-ness has never been questioned." Let us look at some of the
migrants' statements:

JČŽ: "Do you want to say that you did not think that you lived in Serbia?"
Interlocutor A: "No, no . . . Every Christmas, every Easter, even on the 1 May
    we sang *Lijepa naša* [Our Beautiful Country—the Croatian national an-
    them] in Slankamen over the past 30 years. We always sang it at Church,
    in the Croatian Peasant Home. After singing the Yugoslav anthem *Hej
    Slaveni* [Greetings, You Slavs] at midnight, we sang *Lijepa naša*. Every-
    body came, young and old people, just to sing *Lijepa naša*. And that over
    the last 30 years. Next to the Communist Party flag, and the Yugoslav
    flag, the Croatian flag always hung on our Croatian Peasant Home, dur-
    ing the last 13 years." . . .
JČŽ: "In a way you considered Srijem to be a part of Croatia?"
Interlocutor A: "Yes, listen, we lived like Croats. We practiced our religion, we
    lived as Roman Catholics, we sang our songs, we went to our Church.[4]
    We lived in Yugoslavia, but we felt that we were Croats. We breathed
    Croatian, we thought Croatian, we prayed Croatian, Croatian . . ."
Interlocutor B: "*Bunjevci* [the Croats in northern Bačka] have been present
    in Zagreb much longer than the people from Srijem. . . . They were ori-
    ented toward Zagreb from a Diaspora, that means from a foreign coun-
    try, while the Croats in Srijem have clung to Srijem as to their own coun-
    try you know. . . . The Croats in Srijem have always had the feeling of
    belonging to the Croatian state and to the territory on which they lived,
    which is an integral part of Croatia, and, as such, they did not hanker
    after Zagreb."

As "autochthonous and nation-building Croats," the Croats from Srijem who lived in Vojvodina considered that Zagreb, the capital of the
Republic of Croatia, was also their capital: "Zagreb, not Belgrade, was
the capital city for me, even when there was Yugoslavia, although Belgrade was 40 km and Zagreb 400 km away [from my village]. Not only
for me, but for every Croat from Srijem."

As "autochthonous" Croats, "aware of their national identity, and of
their nation-building thought and consciousness," the Croats from Srijem do not consider that they came as exiled Diaspora: "We have never
been a Diaspora. The Diaspora are those across the Danube, those in
Bačka and Banat." Therefore, the migration to the Republic of Croatia

is not understood as a migration from a neighboring, "foreign" land, but as a migration within "state borders." Accordingly, the migrants from eastern Srijem refer to themselves as "internally displaced persons" (or internal refugees) and not as "refugees." In contrast, migrants from other regions of Vojvodina (from Bačka and Banat), which have never been part of Croatia—and who do not consider their territory to be part of Croatia—are called "refugees," since this term denotes people from another country who found refuge outside it. Self-identification of the people from Srijem as "internally displaced persons" points to the discrepancy between their basic feeling of national belonging and administrative and state realities.[5]

In 1998, the Community finally omitted the distinction between external and internal refugees from its name, formally renaming itself as the Association of Displaced Croats from Srijem, Bačka, and Banat (*Udruga protjeranih Hrvata iz Srijema, Bačke i Banata*).[6] This change reflects the mitigation of the refugee crisis in Croatia and the gradual return of both internal and external refugees. With the disappearance of the public interest in those groups, the Community judged that there was no more need for internal differentiation among migrants from Vojvodina.

It was not by chance that the term "Vojvodina" was included in the original name of the Community. It can be found in early documents and in the official name of the association. Besides its shortness, which makes it more economical, the leaders claim that its use was most determined by the fact that Vojvodina was politically and administratively a more readily recognizable and more relevant unit than its three constituent regions, at least in addressing an international public. However, since Vojvodina, as a political institution, was, according to some migrant leaders, "an artificial Serbian invention of the second half of the nineteenth century,"[7] the Community resorted to using the names of the three narrower regions within Vojvodina—Srijem, Bačka, and Banat—at first informally, and then formally from 1993 onward. That change coincided with a decrease in the Community's activities aimed at an international audience and its orientation toward the national audience. The change should also be understood in the light of the fact that most of the leaders of the Community originated from Srijem, a fact that they stressed in almost all of their public speeches.

In sum, the Community has unambiguously defined the population that it represents as Croatian. Stressing the forced migration as the constitutive element in its foundation, it has placed the settlers in the publicly well-known categories of "internal and external refugees." In the end, by abandoning the more encompassing name of Vojvodina in exchange for the three regional names, it has precisely defined the population by region.

Activities of the Migrant Association

The basic activities of the Community were defined in 1991 as "solving the existential problems" of the migrants, meaning "securing any kind of help necessary in such extraordinary and difficult circumstances of war as were those in Croatia" and "appealing for civil and national rights" for all citizens in Vojvodina (Statut, Art. 7 1991). All of the activities of the Community can be subsumed between these two goals, stated in the old and new versions of its Statute.

"The Programs of Activities" operationalize the goals into several concrete activities, four of which seem to have been prevalent between 1991 and 1998: 1) disseminating information about the province of emigration and the state of civil and minority rights within it; 2) solving the existential problems of the migrants; 3) preserving their cultural heritage; and 4) promoting the economic and political interests of the migrants. All four were subject to parallel engagement on the part of the Community, but there were periods in which some were given more attention than others.

Disseminating Information

In the first months after the Community's foundation, neither the proportions of the migration nor its irreversible character were yet known. During that period, the activities of the Community were largely directed toward attracting the attention of the domestic and international public (by appeals to the United Nations, the White House, the European Union, etc.) to the discrimination against non-Serbian populations in Vojvodina, to requests that refugees safely return to their homes, and to providing information about the "true" status of the abandoned territory.[8] Also during that period, the Community was primarily a kind of exile organization[9] of Croats and other nationalities from Vojvodina, and especially from Srijem, particularly interested in what was going on in the land of their origin.

The abandoned homeland of eastern Srijem was presented to the domestic public as "Croatian historical territory." This rhetoric appeared in public speeches given by the leaders, and culminated in a so-called "Declaration," which can be considered the key political document issued by the Community. It makes clear that Srijem, and not Vojvodina, lies at the center of the Community's interests. Preparation of the Declaration started at the very outset of the Community's activities, but it was finally formulated and published at the end of 1993. The Declaration asserts that eastern Srijem has been "a Croatian historical, ethnic, geographical and nation-building territory for more than 1,300 years." For two hundred years (approximately between 1718 and 1918) and in the period between 1941 and 1945, the territory had been under Croatian control, while after 1945, "against the will of the Croatian people, without a decision of the legally elected people's representatives and the legally constituted Croatian Parliament," it was annexed to Vojvodina. In 1988, after the abolishment of Vojvodinian autonomy within Serbia, "for the first time in its history, Vojvodina became a northern Serbian province." Though the Croats have been forced to leave the region, they do not accept their "extirpation" nor do they renounce their right to "Croatian Srijem, our autochthonous state territory, neither today, nor in 1,000 years" (Deklaracija 1995). To the contrary, they retain the hope that they will return to the region: "Persons and peoples can be forcefully scattered, but our right to our land, our home and our skyline cannot be taken away from us, nor our hope of return and coexistence with all those who long for peace and joint life in the region of Croatian Srijem" (Deklaracija 1995).

At the end of the document, the Croats from Vojvodina urge the United Nations and other international institutions to "liberate a part of Croatian Srijem from Serbian occupation."

The Declaration brings out three key terms related to eastern Srijem—occupation, forced expulsion, and the refusal to give up territory. Since the present Serbian governance over eastern Srijem is considered an occupation force in the region, its former inhabitants consider their emigration as forced. Not a single inhabitant would have left the region had s/he had a choice. Therefore, for the people of eastern Srijem, forced migration is just a necessary evil, an unacceptable yet expected method used by the "enemy who has occupied their country"—the Serbian government who abolished Vojvodinian autonomy. Departure does not mean giving up the territory, according to one of their leaders:

> We should view it as if the emigration has never occurred. We deem that Srijem is occupied, everything is to be expected under occupation. . . . Not a single Croat needs to be in Srijem! But this is cleansing of Croatian historical territory. Such a method is unacceptable as a *fait accompli* at the end of the second Millennium. Nobody needs to be there, but we can't accept that. That is not the reason to waive our claim to it.

Emigration is interpreted as a means of survival, which will ensure the survival of Croats from Srijem. The territorial loss of Srijem, one man said, "does not mean that we have to lose the People." Leaving is intended to save one's own life and the dignity of the Croats from Srijem. The president of the Community said:

> For those who wish to remain Croats, and Roman Catholics, for those who cannot stand everyday harassment, terror, slander of their nation on television, in the print media, in the workplace—if they still have it [a job]—for those who do not wish to assimilate, who wish to maintain their human and national dignity, who wish to have peace and freedom, who think about their children, who—when the time to marry approaches—think about whom their son or their daughter will marry, who think about the future and survival of the family—for all those I think it is best—the smartest thing is to leave while there is still time.[10]

The departure from Srijem is considered temporary, lasting until the moment when return will be ensured with the independence and democratization of Vojvodina. The idea of "return" is variously interpreted by the leaders of the Community. To some it means "political return" of eastern Srijem to Croatia: "The goal of the Community is to prepare itself for the moment when Srijem will be within the Croatian state, be it now or in 150 years," said the president of the Community. To others, it is more "a right to return" or "the return of Srijem into Croatian awareness," which would follow democratization and regionalization in Serbia, and its *rapprochement* with European integrative processes:

> Conditions will be created and politicians in Vojvodina will realize they [inhabitants in Vojvodina] pour money into the coffers in Belgrade, and that they are their servants. The salvation of Vojvodina lies in democratization. They will recall that they had Croats, that they have Hungarians and other nationalities, as well as those who came from Croatia and who are ethnic Croats. . . . They can have a link to the community of civilized nations only via Croatia. Here lies our chance, not for return, but for the return of Srijem into the awareness of Croats and the Croatian state. . . . The return of Srijem into awareness, but as an assumption, not as reality. Srijem need not be a part of Croatian territory, but it will be economically integrated—that will happen naturally.

Another leader speaks in the same vein, claiming that Croatian economic help to eastern Srijem, and to the entire province of Vojvodina, could provoke political divisions in Serbia:

> The Community needs to fight for the right to help Srijem. For the right!
> We should secure the right to help it. From the moment that they had
> our support, then one would see, figuratively, what conditions are like in
> that state [Croatia]—that, regardless of all difficulties, it is much differ-
> ent in this state than there [in Serbia]. . . . When it is realized that . . .
> Vojvodina and not Yugoslavia has the privilege to cooperate with Croatia,
> then Vojvodina will break away from Serbia.

Finally, the idea of return contained in the Declaration is understood by
some as a "false yet necessary hope," as a psychological support offered
to the migrants to help them cope with migration. One leader thinks
that nurturing the hope of return is necessary for the migrants to survive
in the new surroundings, since it gives hope that emigration was only
a temporary solution: "I am convinced that there is a large number of
persons who need to believe in return. But if they had a chance to return, only one percent would do so. They all want terribly what is over
there, it borders on fanaticism. But they would like to return to what it
was before."

Another leader is of a different opinion and considers nurturing the
hope of return a falsehood he strongly condemns: "The problem is not
that he thinks that way! But for a leader to . . . to launch such a *canard*
in public! What is the ordinary man to think . . . This is simply lying
about things, that is the Communist system."

The rhetoric of the hope of return was mentioned in the Community's
programs for the years 1996 to 1997, as well as in the opening speeches of
the members and non-members of the Community at its yearly convention in 1999 in Zagreb, where different speakers expressed various com-
prehensions of the return. There was mention of the economic, cultural,
and even physical return to Vojvodina and to eastern Srijem.

Regardless of those differences in conceptualizing the return, the
Declaration affirms that the territory of eastern Srijem is a basic symbolic feature of migrant identity. The territory is not just land; it is a part
of a symbolic model of the world (cf. Mach 1993: 174–175). For the
Croats from eastern Srijem, the abandoned territory is an inseparable
part of their national identity. In its characterization as "Croatian historical territory," it is "proof" of the indisputable adherence and loyalty
of the Croats from eastern Srijem to the Croatian people and Croatia, in
spite of current political and administrative circumstances, which have
left it outside Croatia. Therefore, the basic message of the Declaration
is that eastern Srijem—where everything testifies to Croatian *lieux de
mémoire*—is historically, geographically, ethnically, and culturally a part
of the Croatian lands. In the words of an eminent migrant: "Srijem is

full of Croatian culture, of the signs of the life of the Croats, full of churches. In Srijem, every step, everything speaks Croatian and is recognized as such."

The Declaration, the Community's most important political document, offered a statement about its current positions and a platform for future activities. In addition, it gave a strong statement about the Croatian identity of the migrant population. However, its role in the psychological adaptation of migrants cannot be overemphasized.

Solving Existential Problems

By the spring of 1992, about ten thousand migrants from Vojvodina had entered Croatia (Bičanić 1994: 324–326), forcing the Community to turn more to its practical aim—solving and alleviating the basic existential problems of the migrants. The problems arose as a result of the declaration of independence of Croatia (25 June 1991), by which act all immigrants to Croatia, regardless of their ethnicity, became foreign citizens. According to one migrant leader, the status of migrants from Vojvodina was entirely undefined at the very beginning: "We were nothing, not even foreigners, because we were coming from a state which did not have formal relations with Croatia." Since they could not be subsumed under any legal category designating foreign populations, in the first few months after arrival the migrants could not even get Croatian citizenship (Bičanić 1994: 327). In the spring of 1992, the then president of the Community negatively evaluated the possibilities that the migrants be incorporated into the legal order of the Republic of Croatia. Namely, although early on—already at the first meeting with the state president in 1992—it was agreed to confer upon the migrants all the rights enjoyed by refugees and internally displaced persons, and for the state to be cooperative in solving the migrants' difficulties, due to the non-existence of legal decrees that would clearly and without dilemmas solve their problems, the process of their legal incorporation ground to a halt (Bičanić 1994: 324–326).

When they were officially given the status of refugees and internally displaced persons in the spring of 1992, a problem arose because a majority of settlers refused to be treated as such:

> Many persons were coming and did not want to be called "refugees" so they went to live with their relatives—a brother or a sister, whoever was here, and they did not register [as refugees]. This was . . . It was shameful for a man from Srijem to be an incomer, with a plastic carry-bag.[11] To have the status of a refugee and to beg at Caritas [the Roman Catholic charity

organization]. Pride did not allow people to do that. Indeed, many did not have a need for that, because they had exchanged houses, legally exchanged their properties [with departing Serbs], and continued to work.[12]

Migrant problems were being solved by special decrees issued by the relevant ministries (of the Interior, of Justice, Social Care, Health, Education, etc.). They had the validity of law although they were not subject to customary legislative procedure. The omission of that procedure was intended to help the migrants in the most efficient and speedy way, those "people who needed everything," as one leader said:

> I think that the Community has done a lot. It may be difficult to explain this. The most was done immediately after the arrival of people, at that very first moment. You know, people had huge problems with respect to "papirology" [bureaucratic procedures], and all that. . . . I'd like to point out that the state has given us support. Ordinary people have supported us in everything. When I say in everything, I mean that we were a state on the move, we were a people who needed everything.[13]

The leaders assert that, regardless of their ethnic affiliation (Croats, Serbs, Hungarians, Slovaks, Roma, etc.), the migrants from Vojvodina were granted Croatian citizenship in about two to three weeks:

JČŽ: "Was this decreed by the government?"
Interlocutor: "Yes, yes, this was suggested from the very top, even by the president Tudman himself, that this be solved. . . . The Croats from Croatia could wait in line, but not the Croats from Vojvodina!"[14]

Other administrative problems had to be settled following the conferral of Croatian citizenship. First, the migrants became legal proprietors of the exchanged property. In addition, it was made possible for them to import their cars and agricultural implements, as well as other moveable property, to transfer their telephone lines from Vojvodina, to exchange drivers licenses, and enroll children at school, albeit temporarily, pending the validation of school certificates. Most of those measures for economic and social integration were carried out on the basis of specific ministerial decrees exempting the migrants from paying various taxes (for example, on property transactions, import of cars, agricultural implements, and moveable property, etc.).

During this second period of its activities, the Community was primarily acting as a mediator between the state and the migrants and, in a certain sense it took on the role of interpreter of migrant problems. The leaders estimate that about fifteen thousand migrants, or about one third of the resettled population, took advantage of the mediation of the Community. Others were directly contacting state offices and regulating their status and property rights individually, especially by the time that all the local offices received instructions on how to settle the migrants' requests.

The migrants generally judge that their problems "have been solved quite well and to general satisfaction." Therefore, it can be argued that, apart from the very first period in which there was a certain lack of orientation because the newcomers were outside the familiar legal framework, the state acted efficiently in solving the numerous problems of the migrant population, thereby showing support to the coethnic migration.[15] The leading migrants attribute the satisfactory action of the state to the understanding shown by certain individuals, who held high positions in the state apparatus. At the same time, they praise their own excellent self-organization and persuasiveness in explaining their problems to the bureaucracy.

The years 1992 and 1993 were devoted to providing practical help to the migrants. Later, as the migration slowed, the Community turned to cultural activities—organizing public lectures, publishing, and book presentations. The Community started publishing books within a special series, called "The Croat from Srijem" (there have been about 10 books published, mainly books of poetry or historical accounts), as well as a bulletin, "Zov Srijema" (The Call of Srijem). The first issue of the bulletin was published in April 1995 and there were 29 issues in total by spring 2001.

As stated by the editor of the bulletin,[16] its aim was:

> First of all, this bulletin should satisfy the needs of our displaced Srijem fellow, give him spiritual support and make common cause with him in all misfortunes that accompany him as a refugee, no matter to what extent his departure from his centuries-old Srijem hearth was "voluntary." In this way he nurtures his sense of community with the whole of the Croatian national body!
>
> Not only this! It is not enough to tell to our fellow that Srijem has always been Croatian! This needs to be proven, he needs to be given proof of this! This strengthens him in his suffering. This makes meaningful his grief over his place of birth, over the rich soil of Srijem. We have all of that in mind in this bulletin and want to realize it. We wish to show Croatia all the values, but also all the distinctive features of our Srijem fellow, in all spheres of activities, in all spheres of his life in the lowlands.

The thought that the migrants from Srijem needed to strengthen their own Croatian consciousness and to "prove" their Croatian-ness to the

Croatian public (see also chapter 5) was in the background of the cultural activities of the Community and the rhetoric of its leaders. They aimed at teaching the Croats in Croatia that the migrants from Srijem did not come from Serbia, and that they belonged to the same Croatian nation; in the words of one leader:

> To show to ordinary Croatian people here that we are one nation, that we have not arrived from some Serbia over there, that we belong to the same ethnic group. There is no difference between us and those from Slavonia [region in Croatia]. This had to be shown so that we could be accepted, which was really met with acceptance by the people here. Personally I no longer feel like a refugee.

Migrant leaders thought that they needed to "prove" both to the inhabitants of Croatia and to the Croats from Vojvodina, especially to those from Srijem, that they were ethnic Croats—to the first group, because the Croats from Vojvodina came from a territory which is administratively a part of Serbia, that is, Yugoslavia; to both the first and the second because, in most places of settlement, the incomers and the native population were confronted with mutual cultural and linguistic differences which caused misperceptions, making migrant integration difficult, and resulting in social separation between the two groups (see chapter 5). By emphasizing, by "proving" their Croatian-ness, the migrants hoped to be accepted in their new settlements. Such a state of affairs explains why one of the goals of the Community has been to foster patriotic feelings among the migrant Croats and to present their cultural heritage to the population in Croatia. What the resettled group with its highly developed Croatian awareness regarded as paradoxical at first glance is, in fact, necessary, as one of the migrant leaders explained, so as to avoid isolation: "We knew who we were and what we were. Now we have become newcomers, something we have never wanted to be. We do not know who we are, what we are, what our status is. We have to elevate our patriotism in order not to land in depression, in order not to have to migrate again."

By strengthening patriotism, the Community wants to attenuate antagonistic situations in the places of settlement. It is hard to tell to what extent it has actually worked in that sense. The research in Gradina, for example, does not point to the success of that endeavor.

The strengthening of patriotism implies a certain education of the population, that is, the spread of the idea of intra-national multiculturalism among the Croats and the compatibility of that fact with the feeling of belonging to the Croatian nation. As a counterpoint to the cultural logic of belonging and ethnicity expressed by "ordinary" migrants (see chapter 5), most of the leaders of the Community have noticed that the Croats are a culturally heterogenous community. However, they do not think that cultural differences lessen their national awareness nor should they cause divisions among the Croats. The Community leaders stress that all Croats, regardless of the differences of their cultural heritage, belong to the national community:

> I have frequently said: "People, why are you so much against the Srijem Ekavian? Well? How does a fellow from Slavonia resemble someone from Dubrovnik? Is there anything that they share except for the feeling of belonging to the Croatian nation? Nothing, nothing else! Well? Then why are we [from Srijem] different?" . . . The most important thing is what a man thinks and carries in his heart and in his soul, etc. The language that he speaks is not important.

"The beauty lies in the variety," claimed another leader. A third stressed that the arrival of the migrants from Vojvodina was an enrichment of the Croatian nation, which might also bring the renewal of Croatia, similar to that which was attributed to German coethnic migrants after World War II:

> This is exactly what I believe to be the wealth of Croatia: that this culture, this culture of work, these habits be amalgamated . . . A friend from Germany, a *Volksdeutcher*, a Danube *Švaba* told me something interesting thirty years ago. He says, when the [ethnic] Germans from Vojvodina and Romania, and from all the Danubian countries, came to Germany, they were *Ausländer*, foreigners, for the local German people. For the locals, they were unwanted children for a very long, long time. They had to prove themselves for a long time . . . And this friend is one of them. He says, "For a long time we had to prove ourselves and, while doing so, we had in fact built up this modern Germany. We are the creators of this contemporary, this so modern Germany." Then I understood: that's exactly what we are—not only those of us from Srijem, but also the Croats from Janjevo [a village in Kosovo], even the Croats from Herzegovina or Boka Kotorska,[17] who come with those differences and with those regional cultures—we should represent the wealth of rich variety of this Croatia.

As much as there are regional cultural differences, which are not incompatible with belonging to the same nation, there are also cultural differences within the regions: there exist a number of narrower cultural identities ("micro-identities") within the shared Srijem identity. They should also, claim the leaders, be nurtured: "This is not wiping out of our identity, it is enrichment through differences."

So-called "homeland clubs" have been mentioned since 1995 as frameworks for nurturing narrower, local cultural identities. In distinction to the branches of the Community, which had been organized based on the current place of residence of the migrants, homeland clubs are founded based on the previous place of settlement in Vojvodina. Up until 2000, five homeland clubs from five settlements in eastern Srijem had been founded (Gibarac, Beška, Kukujevci, Hrtkovci, and Slankamen). Their members gather once a year on the patron-saint day of their original settlement. They engage in certain public projects (building of necessary infrastructure in places of settlement, financing the building of churches, etc.) and are especially eager to preserve the folklore and traditions of the "old land" and to pass them on to the younger generation.

Some migrant leaders claim that homeland clubs currently implement the most important goal of the Community—the preservation of migrant cultural identity. It is not a matter of preservation of a more encompassing Srijem or Vojvodinian identity—my interlocutors have difficulties in defining the first and, even more, the second—but of preservation of local micro- identities, of cultural heritage brought over from the places of origin.[18] Regarding such reorientation in its activities, some migrant leaders predict that the Community will slowly cease to exist. The Community's original basic interest—solving the administrative problems of the migrant population—which brought together the inhabitants of mutually insufficiently familiar regions and localities in Srijem, is more or less waning today and, in some opinions, can now yield its place to the activities of the homeland clubs. One of the leaders explains that this is not a development that is generally understood:

> Every village has its customs, in distinction to those in another village. This is what the homeland club is all about! But some people started [to ask]: "Why should we fall apart now, why should we atomize?" They do not understand that this is inevitable because Beška and Golubinci, Hrtkovci or Slankamen, or—what can I say—Surčin or Kukujevci [all villages in eastern Srijem], cannot have the same micro-culture, so to speak. Each village has something specific.

However, some leaders deem that the Community might survive as an "umbrella organization" for homeland clubs, whose work it will coordinate, for, in the words of one leader: "We nurture particularities, but we are happy altogether." If that plan were to be implemented, the Community would be reduced to coordinating the work of homeland clubs and to organizing the yearly meeting of migrants.

Political Activities

It is regarding the very question of the Community's future, through which the future presentation of the resettled population could be channelled, that the migrant leaders have split, to the extent that some of them have withdrawn from the Community's work. Some migrant leaders strongly oppose the development of the Community into a loose "umbrella organization" overarching individual home-land clubs, and argue for a better and tighter integration of the entire migrant population and its political activity. They believe that this should be achieved via conceptually clear and systematically planned activities. In their view, the alternative to carefully thought out activities encompassing the entire group is assimilation of the migrant population: "Either we will exist as a Community or we won't exist at all—we shall be drowned in the Croatian entity—those here in the Slavonian entity, the ones over there in the Zadar entity, Zagreb . . . We live all over [Croatia]. We shall lose our identity as such." The leader quoted here sees only two possibilities: assimilation into the Croatian nation or stronger incorporation and the preservation of the migrant identity via political activities and the redefinition of the program of the Community.

One way to achieve a stronger incorporation of migrants would be the appointment of a migrant representative, either in the Croatian Parliament or in some other governmental institution. That person would be expected to represent the interests of the migrant population, contributing to their better organization and improvement of their status as a specific sub-group in Croatian society. One leader compared a potential Srijem representative with representatives of ethnic minorities in the Croatian Parliament, by which he explicitly equalized the migrant population with ethnic minorities in Croatia: "If those minorities or ethnic groups—whatever they are called—have their own representative, why shouldn't we have ours?"

However, plans to have a representative in the state apparatus have failed. It is hard to say why this happened. The leaders contend that it is partly due to the fact that the Community did not become sufficiently engaged in promoting the project. The failure might also have been caused by the unwillingness of the state to grant the migrants such a representative.

In 1995, the leading migrants came up with another proposal that they thought would strengthen their organization and contribute to their better integration into Croatian society. The proposal is known as the "pilot project" for resettling the Croatian territories which, after a five-year Serbian occupation, were regained and reincorporated into the Croatian state after a military campaign that took place in August 1995. Referred to by the Serbs who controlled them between 1991 and 1995 as the "Krajina" (the Borderland), those territories were almost completely abandoned by the Serbian population during the afore-mentioned campaign.[19]

In early October 1995, the Community wrote a Letter of Intent to the state authorities presenting its proposal for settling the former "Krajina," specifically the regions of the Plitvice Lakes and Ravni Kotari (in the hinterland of Zadar) with the migrants from Srijem, Bačka, and Banat, which were reportedly prepared to undertake yet another resettlement. The Community claimed that it could organize everyday life in those areas in all of its aspects—from the economic to cultural—relying on its own human resources. The letter enumerated economic assets that the Community wanted to "take over," either by buying or renting them (cattle farms, agricultural areas, hotels and shops, small factories, etc.).

The project was actually a response to the call by the state to resettle the reincorporated areas. To this effect, the state issued the "Act on Temporary Take-over and Administration of Certain Property" (enacted on 27 September 1995[20]). The Act stipulated that all real estate and moveable property of persons[21] who had left Croatia after 17 August 1995 would be brought under temporary state management. It could be given into the "possession and usufruct" of refugees, internally displaced persons, returnees,[22] and other special categories of the population, under the condition that it not be alienated. The Act anticipated the possibility for its exchange between the Serbs who left the "Krajina" with the Croats forced to leave the territory of Yugoslavia.[23]

Even before the enactment of this law, the Community had informed state institutions that it was interested in the liberated areas. It had organized visits to the area and engaged professionals of various profiles to undertake an assessment of the state of affairs and opportunities to renew economic infrastructure in the proposed area of resettlement. It was said that the migrant leaders had even attracted the attention of foreign investors for the project. Those leaders of the Community who were most eager to see the implementation of the project argued that it was well planned and that it could bring certain strategic and economic advantages to the state. By populating a deserted border area and reviving economic activity, the Community deemed that it would be bringing the area back "to life": in the military sense (this is a border area that would be inhabited by Croatian population); the demographic sense (the area was practically uninhabited after the departure of the Serbs); and the economic sense (economic infrastructure was entirely or partially devastated). They believed that they would develop the area into a model economic region. One leader assured me: "I guarantee them [the state] that they will not recognize Korenica [a township in the vicinity of Plitvice Lakes] in three years' time. Just let the Srijem Croats go there! No one who goes through Korenica will ever forget the place!"

Some migrant leaders wanted to realize their political ambitions with this project. They expected that they would take over political functions in the settled areas. Others explained that a more compact settlement of migrants sharing origins, mentality, and destiny, would enable the restoration of situations and relations previously enjoyed in the region of origin:

Interlocutor A: "We thought we would again bring together those people so they could be 'their own masters on their own piece of land,'[24] because they are scattered now. His house is here, but what's his is over there. When we have time, we see each other. If we were together, we would see each other every day, every moment. That would mean a lot for the old generation."

Interlocutor B: "That Korenica—I was worried about winter there. But, I thought, we would all come together there. We would build [something]! It's all new! From the beginning. Then, Plitvice Lakes[25]—you have jobs there for everybody, for the children, for everybody. Look, damn it all, we would learn! Just like I learnt to live in Virovitica, they [the children] would learn to live in Korenica and at the Plitvice Lakes!"

The project had an economic, demographic, territorial, political, and cultural dimension. They would all lead toward a restoration of the community of life of the migrant population, or at least that part of it that would decide to reemigrate. The project would also lead to their constitution as a specific subgroup of the population, a subnational group within the Croatian ethno-national community.

A government official, the state representative in the negotiations with the migrants regarding the plan of resettlement, said that it was "an attractive but unfeasible project."[26] He suggested that several reasons prevented its implementation: unresolved legal issues regarding real estate in the reincorporated territories; too many individuals showing interest in them; authoritarian local "chiefs" unwilling to see a large incoming population settling in the area; unreasonable requests by the Community with regard to the "take-over" of economic assets; the impossibility that the Community became the legal owner of property, etc.

It is difficult to state with certainty why the project failed. It was a delicate matter of which the participants—as much as the state representative—were unwilling to talk and had intensely polarized opinions, not least within the Community itself. Some migrant leaders attribute its failure to "higher political interests," to local "powerful men" who wanted to control the region themselves, and to its "unsound financial basis":

Interlocutor: "I think that the project was unrealistic, without an economic base. When you do not have an economic foundation, it does not work, all of it was pure fantasy."

JČŽ: "Would you say that this was the main reason why the program was not implemented?"

Interlocutor: "Exactly, exactly. Those were negotiations, some agreements in principle. But when we were about to do something concrete, then we got stuck How? Let's now resettle ten families! With what? How? You need . . . First of all this costs money! A man can live with less money in his house, but if he goes somewhere else, to another house—the house needs to be made usable, put in order, you need to go and start working. With what? How? I think that this was very unrealistic, all very unrealistically planned."

Some see a basic mistake in the offer of the state to allocate, albeit for temporary use, the property of the exiled Serbian population to various categories of war-afflicted people. According to them, no person from Srijem could conceive of settling in somebody else's house:

Interlocutor A: "Land deeds are the law. . . . The president of the state can tell me that this is mine. But it is all in vain when I know that it is not mine."

Interlocutor B: "This is a question of morality."

In the end, only a few families from Srijem did resettle there, not under the auspices of the Community, but in direct contact with and the approval of the Croatian Ministry of Renewal and Development.

Some migrant leaders thought the state would unambiguously and clearly show its care for the migrant population as a whole by giving its support to the project, and, at least in the economic sense, compensate them for the losses endured as a result of the migration. The expectation that the state ought to do something for the migrants is linked to their self-perception as victims: "The greatest loser is the one who lost a member of the family. We are the second greatest losers, for I always say that I would be happy if I were returning to my ruins to build them again," explained a prominent leader.

The leaders (as well as the migrants in general) have a similar perception of the "tragedy" that struck "our people," but they do not agree on whether it should be used as a basis for claiming special status and privileges for the migrants. Some think it has not been and should not be used in such a way and proudly assert that, "Croatia does not take enough care about us. We have survived here in a high percentage on our own." Other leading migrants think that the entire group "deserves" recompensation. They have not claimed it so far, ostensibly because the state has had other priorities, especially when dealing with other war-afflicted persons. In 1998 and 1999, they thought that the time had come to openly express their requests: "We want our tragedy to be publicly acknowledged!"

They believe that everything circumvented them, that their tragedy was not "acknowledged," and that the public was not acquainted with the true picture of their sufferings.[27] They especially want to be given economic support, for example, through preferential treatment in the allocation of credits.

Some leaders think that it is the task of the Community to ensure that the migrants are helped economically. To achieve that end, it should propose to the state a "new systematic plan of action," similar to the "pilot project," and stop "wandering without a clear conception of what should be done."

The leaders consider that it might already be too late to do anything on behalf of the entire migrant population. Too many years have passed and it is difficult to mobilize the group for a common goal that would be based on its shared destiny—forced migration and the tragedy that it brought about in an economic, social, and psychological sense (material loss, loss of security, unfamiliar surroundings that do not accept them, loss of social capital, and the like). The leaders are aware that they have not succeeded in turning the common tragedy into a positive development. Their destiny as forced migrants could have played an important role in their better organization and incorporation in the new settlement: the role that common origin plays in the constitution of ethnic groups (Eriksen 1993; Smith 1986). The Community did not succeed in incorporating the migrants into a subnational community based on common origin. On the one hand, the state did not provide support for such an endeavor. State support to the migrants failed to go beyond giving them citizenship rights. As much as such rights were a basic prerogative for participation and integration into Croatian society, they did not meet the expectations of some of the leaders. On the other hand, the reason for the failure of subnational ethnic incorporation of the migrants also lies with the Community: some leaders say that the failure is partly due to its "own lack of aggressiveness, lack of entrepreneurial spirit and inventiveness," and partly to the more pressing problems with which the state was confronted, such as the refugee population amounting to 12 percent of the entire population in Croatia in 1992 (cf. Čapo Žmegač 1996).

The failure to develop into a corporate subgroup, a kind of subnational ethnic community within the Croatian nation, is also due to the divisive nature of the leaders' dilemma: should they have insisted on the special status of the migrants which would be legitimized by the shared experience of forced migration? Or, should they have been satisfied with the entitlement to individual civil rights and renounced a tighter and more effective form of organization of the migrant population? In other words, the dilemma is whether the migrants—*qua* Croatian citizens—should ask for special status. Should they integrate into the Croatian society as individual citizens, or collectively as a particular subnational group? The majority of leaders sharing this dilemma are actually inconsistent because they argue that they are, and they do not want to be other than, Croatian citizens enjoying the same rights as other citizens; and yet, they simultaneously require special rights for the migrant population. A former leader is aware that coupling civic equality on the one hand, and a particular social status on the other, is illogical:

> Above all, I do not want now to be a refugee any more. I am a Croat in Croatia, a Croatian citizen, according to my nationality and religion. I have my house and my family. Why would I now be some sort of refugee and associated to refugee status at all? I do not want that any more. I do not want to burden either myself or my offspring with that. I am a Croat in Croatia and this is my state.

This man no longer wants to identify with his emigration and his refugee story, nor does he want to ask for specific rights for himself and for the entire migrant population based on the refugee identity. He distances himself from the migrant identity, leaving it to the decision of each individual as a Croatian citizen how s/he should identify herself/himself. Another leader has come to the same conclusion:

> What can the Community do for our children? We have already gone through what we have gone through, our children do not need special status. Our children will secure for themselves [what they need] better than

we have done. It should be made possible for them to integrate as soon as possible, in a way that they do not forget where they came from and . . . what can I say? All that is important is that the tradition be [maintained].

The introduction of homeland clubs as one of aims of the Community, and the assumption that its future role will be their coordination, shows that the Community as an institution is even further renouncing a tighter form of migrant organization. Let us recapitulate in the conclusion the genesis of this effort and the dilemma which has caused its failure.

The Leaders' Dilemma:
Equal Citizens or a "Sect of Srijem Croats"

The founding of the Community of Croatian Refugees and Internally Displaced Persons from Vojvodina in 1991 was the first step in creating an organization which was to lead toward the subnational incorporation of the migrant population. It was a measure for ascribing a certain ethnic category to the migrants—Croatian Refugees and Internally Displaced Persons from Vojvodina—and in establishing a formal association, which would purportedly represent their interests in the social and political arena. By its choice of attributes in denoting the migrants as refugees and internally displaced people, the Community has offered the Croatian public a recognizable frame for its own social legitimization, while at the same time attempting to confer a kind of social identity on the population that it represented. As already mentioned, this identification was not acknowledged by the migrant population itself, which was unwilling to accept it. The founding myth of the group—the forced migration from Vojvodina—had a dual function in that first phase of the activities of the Community: it brought the migrants together into a particular interest group, and, at the same time, it set them apart from all other inhabitants of Croatia.

At its inception, the Community was predominantly an association with a practical aim: alleviating and mediating the regulation of citizenship and property rights for the migrants, and helping in other situations in which they found themselves as "foreigners" in the Croatian state. Practically without exception, the migrants were conferred Croatian citizenship within the shortest possible period of time. In solving their problems, either with the formal or informal support of the authorities, the Community achieved significant success in the civil affirmation of the migrants.

During the subsequent period, several interest groups formed within the Community had differing conceptions for its continual existence, many of these being related to ideas about the most favorable way of presenting and maintaining the identity of the migrants. A number of migrant leaders supported the plan for the territorialization of the migrant population. Besides the economic and identity component, another major element was the expectation that territorialization would ensure political self-government, psychosocial security, and preservation of the migrant identity.

The question of territory has been present in the activities of the Community in various ways. In the first phase, the Community expressed concern for the territory the migrants had left behind under the political and nationalistic pressure of the Serbian and Yugoslav authorities and of the Serbs who moved from Croatia. During that period, territory as an idea about land "plays an important role in shaping cultural identity" (Mach 1993: 173). To the population from Srijem, the lost land became a part of a collective memory and identity; from a concrete land of settlement it grew into a symbolic image, a mythologized landscape. Just as with any group deprived of its land, "this image and its emotional associations become a basis for the ideology of return to the land or to regain sovereignty over it" (Ibid.). The meaning of the Declaration, the most important political document issued by the Community, is best understood in this light: it is an ideological text intended to nurture the hope of return to the abandoned homeland and to lay claim to regaining its sovereignty. The biblical metaphors used by some leaders: "Do you know how the Jews greet one another? 'Next year in Jerusalem.' We should be saying 'Next year in Srijem,'" or 'Adam always wants to return to heaven,'" express the deep symbolism the migrants attach to the lost land.

Since, with time, the prospect of a return to Srijem was becoming increasingly unrealistic, rumination over the old territory was replaced with ideas about resettlement of a new one. Rather than concentrating on return to their own territory, as if tacitly recognizing the role of the territory in forming and maintaining the identity of the group, a number of leaders proposed a plan for settlement of new land. By taking economic, cultural, and political possession of it, the expectation was that the migrants would appropriate it as their own. By the same token, they would ensure their own survival as a group with a separate identity within Croatian society. The new territory, so they claimed, would simultaneously fulfill two functions: as a secure shelter and as a springboard of economic opportunity (cf. Mach 1993: 175). Some leaders had political intentions with regard to the new territory, demanding an exclusive, sovereign right over it, which is a request typical for the relations between a group and its land (Ibid., 174).

In sum, the leaders seem to have identified the importance that territory has in the formation of the feeling of belonging and identification of the group: in the Declaration, when they demanded a return of the lost territory as a non-exchangeable part of their identity; and in the plan for the establishment on a new territory, when they hoped to avoid assimilation and maintain the separate identity of the migrants from Srijem.

The Community's orientation toward the ethnicization of the migrant group is best manifested in the plan for resettlement. By economic, symbolic, and political appropriation of new territory, the Community would have taken a step toward stronger incorporation of an ethnic type: constituted until then as a subnational category and association, the migrants would have evolved into a subnational community: "The distinction between an ethnic association and an ethnic community is that, in the latter, members concentrate their corporate holdings in a fixed space, which they recognise as an ethnic unit existing within comparatively permanent territorial boundaries" (Handelman 1977: 197).

However, the attempt at establishing the territorial subnational community failed, for neither would the state give it support nor was the Community successful in convincing the state of the advantages of that project. Legal matters are most frequently invoked to explain the non-implementation of the project. However, I argue that there are ideological reasons, both on the part of the state and the migrant leaders, that might explicate its failure.

The Croatian state is constituted as a monoethnic nation in which common Croatian origin is the basis for membership in the nation. This ideology is correlated to the assumption about cultural homogeneity of a supposedly "monolithic" Croatian nation. This assumption reflects the imperative of a sovereign state in-the-making to ensure a nationally bounded and unified population by stressing the uniqueness of its culture and history. The national closure of citizenship is achieved "by attributing some distinctiveness—'shared' values, language, blood, history or culture to the collective citizenry" (Soysal 1996: 17). By accentuating its uniqueness and cultivating its particularity, the Croatian state was creating identity within its borders; while by attributing differences to its neighbors, it was constructing its Others (cf. Ibid., 26). In other words, the rhetoric of an emergent nation state is homogenizing (Williams, quoted in Verdery 1996: 43–47). This rhetoric works against the constitution and strengthening of narrower regional, subnational or cultural identities in its midst, and in favor of a uniform cultural system, which is backed up by pronounced political and economic centralization. The state could easily recognize in the plan for resettlement the intention to found a separate—cultural and subnational—identity of the migrant population. It is arguable that this was an important, although unexpressed, reason for the state not having given the plan its support.

On the other hand, the leaders of the Community were not unanimously in favor of the plan: as we have seen, some had reservations of a political and moral nature, while for some, it intensified the dilemma regarding the definition of the migrants' status and the way of their integration into Croatian society—as individual citizens with similar rights and duties as other citizens, or as a collective with a particular culture, history, and destiny. This was clearly expressed by some leaders as a conflict between their unquestionable national allegiance to the Croatian nation and a wish to promote a separate ethnocultural identity of the migrants. A former leader said that the insistence on special status and particular identity of the Croats from Srijem was a sort of "ambush,"[28] which "almost reminds one of a state within the state" and points to the existence of a "sect of the Srijem Croats." That leader detected a politically unacceptable meaning which the ethnicization of the migrants would have had for the nascent Croatian nation state. A former leader and his wife thought the same:

Husband: "We are Croats. We have come to Croatia. What would we want now? We have solved our problems, we manage, we have integrated. What do we want now?"

Wife: "This is it. It is not our goal to be set apart from our own people."

It may be hypothesized that it is under the influence of the state national rhetoric about the ethnically and culturally homogenous Croatian nation, that caused some leaders to step back from the effort to constitute the migrants from Srijem as a subnational community. Their attitude has led to discussions within the Community and to conflict with the more pragmatic members who have not seen any ideologically "dangerous" signs in the plan for resettlement of the liberated territories. The consequence was the demise of some of the leaders and further turmoil in the Community. Simultaneously, the state gave no support to the plan for resettlement and the Community narrowed its activities to the cultural plane. At the end of the 1990s, the Community was developing into a cultural organization whose aim was limited to preserving local, micro-cultural heritage via homeland clubs. By this turning point, as one of the leaders ironically commented, the Community is reduced to "a folklore association of sorts." The end result is a loose type of migrant association whose main aim is the maintenance of cultural differences at the level of localities of origin. At the same time, this is an abdication of any pretence at creating a subnational community of the Srijem Croats.

Notes

1. Hereafter, I shall refer to it as the Community. See footnote 6.
2. "Počeci organiziranja u ZIPHV" [The beginning of organizing in the ZIPHV], *Zov Srijema* III (17), 1997: 4.
3. The Croatian term for a refugee, *izbjeglica,* is derived from the word escape and not from the word refuge as in English. Therefore, it had negative connotations and people were reluctant to accept it as a designation of their status.
4. "Our" here infers in contrast to the Serbian, meaning that the Serbs had Serbian songs, and went to the Serbian Orthodox Church.
5. See chapter 3 for statements on the return and the extension of the Croatian border toward Zemun, today part of Belgrade.
6. According to the new state law on associations, the original name, Community, was changed to Association. Because my interlocutors kept on using the old name even after the official name change I shall continue to refer to it as the Community.
7. As a province, Vojvodina was first established during political turmoil in the Austro-Hungarian Monarchy in 1848, when it was, albeit only for a decade, formally recognized as a province (*Enciklopedija Leksikografskog zavoda,* vol. 7, 1964, Zagreb: Leksikografski zavod, headword "The Serbs"). Its foundation was the result of the Serbian national movement, which, from the perspective of the leaders of contemporary Croatian migrants from Srijem, dismisses it as a reference point in their identification.
8. See Bičanić (1994: 318–320). Leaders of the Community vary in their estimation of the success achieved in attracting media interest and in the internationalization of the "Vojvodinian case." Some argue that they have managed to present "the tragedy and the meaning" of their situation both to domestic and outside audiences. Those who are disappointed with the Community claim that "our tragedy was not covered enough, nor was it attributed the same political importance as the Bosnian case." Still others plead for calm and thoughtful activities, and emphasize their satisfaction with previous and contemporary coverage by the media.
9. This is evident from the proposal of the first president of the Community to establish the National Croatian Council in Exile (Bičanić 1994).
10. Orlović, Franjo: "Ostati ili otići?" [To remain or to leave?], *Zov Srijema* I (6), 1995: 20. As far as I could ascertain, this was the first written statement by a Community leader, its president in this case, in which it is publicly stated that emigration from Srijem was the most reasonable solution for the Croats still living there. It was written in the period after the liberation of Croatian territories and the flight of the Serbs into Serbia in the summer of 1995.
11. See chapter 4, footnote 12.

12. Many non-leader migrants confirmed this statement from a migrant leader. Their refusal to be identified with internally displaced persons from Croatia and refugees from Bosnia-Herzegovina runs counter to the identification attributed to the migrants by the founders of the Community. Many migrants were deterred from asking help from the Community because they disliked being called a "refugee" or an "internally displaced person." However, in the eyes of their leaders, those terms were instrumental and necessary in turning the attention of Croatian society to the plight of the settlers from Vojvodina.

13. There is also the following opinion: "Those decrees induced us to migrate. Had it been more difficult [to obtain legal status], many of us would not have come . . . Therefore, I say, that all of this was in a certain way organized with the aim that we come and fill in the places of the Serbs. Had it not been so easy, we would have never exchanged."

14. Indeed, for ethnic Croats who lived in Croatia prior and during the 1991 to 1992 war years, but were not born in Croatia, the process of acquiring Croatian citizenship lasted on average six months, while it took Croats from Vojvodina about three weeks.

15. It should be mentioned, however, that until 2001, a fundamental problem had not yet been solved. Migrants' pensions were not revaluated in keeping with pensions in Croatia and were extremely low.

16. Lončarević, Juraj: "Tisak i izdavačka djelatnost o Hrvatima u Srijemu nakon Drugog svjetskog rata" [Printing and publishing activities about Croats in Srijem after World War II], *Zov Srijema* III (15), 1997: 19.

17. After the proclamation of independence of the Republic of Croatia, groups of Croats—in Janjevo in Kosovo, in Bosnia-Herzegovina, and Boka Kotorska in Montenegro—were left outside Croatian borders, in the new Yugoslavia. To a lesser or greater extent, those from Kosovo and Bosnia were moving to Croatia.

18. Preserving a more encompassing identity would have been a more difficult task because, as mentioned in chapter 1, the migrants are in many ways a heterogenous group of people. It is therefore not surprising that the current attempts at preserving the migrants' identity are restricted to maintaining local, village identities, and that there are no attempts at the creation of a wider regional identity. The heterogeneity of the migrants can also help explain why the founding myth of the migrant community had to be searched for in their shared destiny of forced migration, and not in their joint cultural or regional identity.

19. The Croatian territories liberated from Serbian occupation in August 1995 are northern Dalmatia, eastern Lika, Kordun, and Banovina (see map 2). The guarantees given by the Croatian state to the Serbian population regarding their security notwithstanding, the Serbs started leaving those territories as soon as it was clear that the Croatian military campaign was successful. During the campaign itself, the behavior of the Croatian military to Serbian civilian population was correct. In the immediate aftermath, however, cases of plunder and even murder have been reported.

20. The act was rescinded in 1998.

21. Mainly, these were Serbs who left Croatia during the aforementioned military campaign, which took place in August 1995.

22. The military campaign of 1995 made possible the return of internally displaced persons—the Croats—who were granted the status of "returnees."

23. Jurić, Mato: "Zakon o privremenom preuzimanju i upravljanju određenom imovinom" [Act on Temporary Take-over and Administration of Certain Property], *Zov Srijema* I (4), 1995: 7.

24. "*Svoji na svome.*" This was a ubiquitous slogan, very popular in the early days of the independence movement in Croatia in the 1990s.
25. Plitvice Lakes are a famous tourist resort in Croatia, see map 2.
26. I spoke to this person only once, very briefly over the telephone. Further attempts to set a meeting were unsuccessful. See Epilogue.
27. See the statement: 'Frequently, you find malevolent people. It is often said that we have come here because of I don't know what or why, but that's how it is. In the end, not everybody is pleased with our coming here."
28. Ambush here alludes to treason.

Chapter 7

Community, Identification, Interaction

But, look here, it's—I said it just now—it's the problem of all major migrations. They all involve the same problem—barriers, non-acceptance
on the part of the domestic population of the one who comes there.
However, what would Zagreb [the capital of Croatia] be today if people
hadn't moved there? . . . There wouldn't be anything anywhere. Every
new arrival of a certain number of people brings some innovations with
it. For example, it was a [new] concept in Virovitica when the people
from Slankamen planted the first watermelons. These locals in Virovitica
laughed, but, today, more of them are planting watermelons than the migrants from Slankamen. And it's probably part of human nature to find
it difficult to accept something [new], especially if someone turns up on
your doorstep with some advanced ideas . . .

> A man about 50 years old, from Slankamen, holds a degree

So far I have analyzed the notions that the Srijem Croats hold about
themselves and about their neighbors, the old residents in the surroundings of Virovitica. Along with treating, in each chapter, some of the particular theoretical themes in the field of studying migration and ethnicity (the relationship between ethnicity and culture, the cultural logic of
identity, integration into the host society), I have discussed the processes
of individual and collective identification of the newly settled Srijem
Croats at the local and at the broader social level.

In chapter 3, I discussed the identification strategies of the Srijem
settlers in Gradina by establishing the multiplicity of individual identifications and the plurality of the strategies of adaptation and integration. They varied, from emphasis on belonging to the imaginary Srijem

community and verbal rejection of incorporation in the new community, to suppression of Srijem identity in the private sphere and emphasis on pragmatic identity as the basis for integration. A third group of people chose to present their identity as reflected by their descendants. Consequently, it was shown that Srijem identity is a symbol with varying meanings among the migrants.

In chapter 4, I dealt in more detail with the older generation's strategy by which personal identity relies on descendants. In chapter 5, attention was focused on those settlers who build their collective identity on their actual and perceived cultural differences in comparison with the local population in the locality of resettlement. An integral part of that attempt of the construction of Srijem identity is the ascription of negative identity to the local population.

The perspective in chapter 6 was macro-analytical and institutional. The formation of Srijem identity was observed from the aspect of the representatives of the settlers from Srijem active in the core migrant association. The activities of the Community were analyzed as an attempt at construction of a collective Srijem identity according to the model of construction of ethnic communities.

In this chapter, I shall round out the interpretation of the previous ones, in an effort to answer some questions put in chapter 1: What was the social context in which the described notions of the Srijem Croats about themselves and their neighbors emerged? Why is it that, even several years after resettlement, the division between the local population and the new settlers is being maintained, with mutually simplified and, sometimes, also with negative representations? Finally, in order to answer the question about the extent to which the collective notion of the Other informs the behavior of the individual in interaction with a member of the other group, I am relocating the analysis from the level of discursive practice to the area of interaction between the locals and the newcomers. In an attempt to answer those questions, I shall have recourse to the notion of the community.

Collective identity was defined in chapter 1 as a symbolic construct by which a group of people express their sameness. The notion of sameness contains the relational idea and includes a subjective expression of difference from the Other, by setting up a barrier against other identities. For its part, the barrier at which one identity ends and the other begins, although potentially unclear, defines the contours of the community. Consequently, the formation of community is the direct result of the identification process, by which groups, demarcating themselves from their neighbors, postulate their own unity. As with identity, community is a symbolic construct, an imaginary entity bounded by the perception if its boundaries; since it is defined by a feeling of belonging, the community is, similarly to identity, a subjective category (Cohen 1985: 9–15).

Antagonism between "The Established" and "The Outsiders"

In their study aptly titled, *The Established and the Outsiders* (1965), Norbert Elias and John Scotson posited that there are regularities in relations inside communities whose fundamental configuration is the result of the process of migration, in the course of which two formerly independent groups become interdependent as neighbors. They argued that any resettlement of an ethnically, culturally or racially different group of people, in itself more or less homogenous, which is being studied under such varied headings—as ethnic, immigration or racial studies—is only an instance of a basic social configuration that results from mobility and the encounter of the local population with the newcomers. The social separation between them, they argued, could not be explained as a function of national differences, ethnic origins or race differentials between the old and the new settlers. Neither could it be explained by structural factors, for in socioeconomic terms, there were hardly any differences between the populations they studied: both groups held similar factory jobs, and had similar salaries and education. According to the authors, sociological oldness in the area was the decisive factor in the formation of the gap between the old and the new inhabitants. The old inhabitants had had time to develop "a fairly set communal life, a parochial tradition of their own." The newcomers were felt as a threat to the order established by the local population, with its power differentials and an entrenched position of the leading families in the old part of the settlement. They felt that any close contact with the newcomers "would lower their own standing, . . . that it would impair the prestige of their neighbourhood" (Ibid., 149). The migrants were expected to adapt to the role of "newcomers." They were cast into the role of *outsiders* with respect to the *established* and more powerful old inhabitants. By keeping the newcomers at a distance, by rejecting them or assigning them a lower status, the established inhabitants preserved their status and entrenched power positions. While the established were bent on maintaining their position, the newcomers were bent on improving theirs.

Srijem Croats were precisely the outsiders described by Elias and Scotson, seeking entry and acknowledgement in the communities that had established traditions of their own. From the viewpoint of the established population, they were intruders upon an already existing social structure and social positions, and, by this very fact, a disruptive element in the existing structure. From their own standpoint, the Srijem Croats merely engaged in reformulation of their identities in order to situate and establish themselves in the new community. Redefining their identity was part of the process of incorporation, of finding a place for themselves, and of gaining a position in the new social environment, both locally and in the society at large. By closing their ranks, the established population opened the gate to the formation of a separate migrant identity.

However, there is a peculiarity with regard to outsiders in the case under examination here. The coethnic migrants from Srijem did not accept the role of outsiders ascribed to them by the established population. Rather, they rejected the symbolic code by which they were cast into an outsider position and replaced it with their own code, which stressed the superiority of their own group. It was thus the newcomers, rather than the established population, who attributed negative identity to the other group, or, put more precisely, the process worked in both directions. Some specific characteristics can explain the rejection of the stigma by the coethnic migrants from Srijem.

The coethnic migrants came with a well-developed sense of their own identity, defined by the multiethnic context in which they had lived and also by the superior—real or perceived—position they held in their former society. These people, forced out of the social configuration in which they had been established and having held a particular and, sometimes, respected place in society, which they achieved through their own efforts and the prominence of foregoing generations, knew "who and what they were" in their own locality. They came from an environment where they managed very well and knew everyone and, as they themselves said, were "their own masters on their own piece of land." According to one of the settlers, that loss of social capital, perhaps imperceptible at first glance, has been irretrievable for them:

> In Slankamen, N.N. was . . . Those people who were something there will never be that again. As far as they're concerned, it's finished . . . almost finished! Look, it takes a generation for a man to develop into something in a particular environment, to become some sort of personality. . . . When someone returns to his own place, he is once again what he was. We will never again be what we were!

In their new environment, they lack social connections, acquaintanceship and friendship, which they regard as being essential for life in any milieu. Being used to a certain position and social prestige, they aspire to them in their new surroundings but, at least in the early period after their arrival, they are unattainable, because "the locals hold everything in their hands": "Fair enough, we Srijem Croats are a bit . . . how should I put it . . . a bit pushy, materially well-off, very industrious and they [people from Srijem] expect everyone to make way so that they can move forward. But that's not possible at this moment. Since the locals hold everything in their hands."

When exchanging their properties with the Croatian Serbs, they expected that the entrenched population in Croatia would accept them because of their Croatian identity, and that they would speedily regain their lost social status. In the encounter and confrontation with their apparently proximate Other—their Croatian co-citizens—a process of mutual discovery and redefinition was set in motion. It was a painful process in which they found, on the one hand, that they were ignored, neglected or even discriminated against by the locals and, on the other, that they had a specific historical experience which made them different and somehow "better" than their coethnic neighbors. They became aware that common ethnic affiliation was not a sufficient reason for their being incorporated into the existing social order: in the perception of the local population, their national affiliation was less important than the fact that they were new settlers.[1] Therefore, the Srijem Croats themselves experienced a situation similar to that encountered by ethnic Croatian settlers from Bosnia-Herzegovina in Srijem villages during the 1940s (see chapter 1); those same people that they had then derogatively referred to as *dodoši* and *došlje* (newcomers) and whom, despite the fact that they were Croats, they had not accepted as members of their communities in Srijem, were now migrating to Croatia together with them:

> There were Bosnians [ethnic Croatian settlers from Bosnia] living in Slankamen. . . . They came after that war [World War II]. They were Croats. For example, one of them was a friend of mine. A very good friend. My grandmother always used to say: "Why do you hang around with that Bosnian?," even though thirty years or more had passed [since his family's resettlement in Slankamen]. Now we are those Bosnians who have come here, although we came in a different way: they came with nothing, but were given everything. We left something behind but we were given something here. That's normal, I have realized that we are now the ones who have come [we are the newcomers]. We have to work, and to prove ourselves.

An important element in the efforts of part of the Srijem Croats to establish themselves socially in the place of resettlement is their self-awareness and self-respect, this self-awareness having already been formed in the old homeland in the interaction with the Serbs, within what was one of the most developed regions in the former Yugoslavia. They have a high opinion of the standards, norms, and way of life that they had in Srijem and of their own economic strength. Their assessments were reinforced in the new environment in which they fed on the processes of remembering, by which the things abandoned took on magnified, mythic, and irreplaceable contours, incomparable to anything that was encountered in the new surroundings. The abandoned locality, house, land, and property were unattainable and unforgettable assets that could have no adequate replacement in the new environment: one dreams of the place of birth, calls it "home," becomes tearful at its very mention, and regards it as a significant part of one's own being, as shown by the migrants' statements in chapter 2. To those largely rich and self-aware peasants and farmers, the marginal regions of Croatia in which they settled apparently offered little compared to the wealth of their homeland. As we have seen in chapter 5, perceptions of difference, moreover of superior distinctiveness, lead them to set the hierarchy of their own Croatian-ness and that of others. Their discourse of superiority should not be understood as mere belittling of the established population, but primarily as a means by which they construct their identity in the new surroundings.[2] As they themselves say, talk of superiority is their way of "proving themselves" to their new neighbors; this is their means of establishing themselves in the existing status order. By ascribing negative identity to the entrenched population, they are, in fact, trying to secure (high) status for themselves in their new environment.

Other coethnic migrants mentioned in chapter 1 also nurtured a superior stance toward the local established population among whom they made their new home. For example, Asia Minor Greeks kept the conviction of the excellence of their ways through many hardships (Hirschon 1989: 13). Thirty years after the migration, the Algerian French considered themselves "more French than the French" (Baussant 2002: 371), while the Russian Jews in Israel cherish what they believe to be their superior cultural and linguistic heritage (Remennick 2003).

In this particular respect, all of those cases of coethnic migration—in spite of a difference in the timing and the particular wider context of each of them—diverge from the general sociological model proposed by Elias and Scotson, thus providing insight into ways in which politically uprooted people—victims of the dissolution of multinational state structures and concomitant national homogenization of new nation states—cope with the challenges of survival and with the issue of identity after resettlement in their "ethnic homeland." Indeed, it may be that the coethnic encounter is a limiting case of Elias's and Scotson's paradigmatic encounter between the established and the outsider populations, in which the newcomers overthrow the inferior position imposed upon them by the locals (cf. Čapo Žmegač 2005).

The Srijem Croats construct a simplified image of the local population on the basis of perceived cultural diversity and on a negative evaluation of the communal amenities in the places to which they have migrated. However, my Srijem interlocutors in Gradina and Virovitica did not move into places without water supply systems, sewage, churches, public health stations, post offices and telephones. That notwithstanding, their perception of the local reality, which was also influenced by the documentaries about the resettled Srijem Croats shown on Croatian television, are based on places in the Virovitica area that lack these facilities, which they regard as the basic indicators of the urban development of a township or village. Their image of the local population is built up on a simplified perception of reality, stemming from the negative characteristics of neighboring places.[3] Once formed, the stereotype of the region of settlement is perpetuated, so that one young female migrant, addressing her Srijem collocutors, who were expressing only the negative aspects of their settlement in Gradina, protested: "You also have some advantages here. Don't talk only about the shortcomings!"

For the Srijem Croats, disparagement of the locals is a means of the evaluation and legitimation of their own identity (cf. Lipiansky 1998), to which they resort in order to attain social status and, along with that, identity in the local community. This serves as a recompense for loss of status and dignity, for the pain and suffering they have endured because of the forced expulsion from their home regions, and for the impossibility of their taking (dominant) positions in the local hierarchy immediately upon their arrival; it is also a source of comfort and a means of survival in the changed environment, among unknown people with unfamiliar mores, and opposition to what they see as their undesirable image among the locals—that of displaced persons and refugees. "But we are not carpet-baggers, we are semi-trailer people, because we came with semi-trailers, not carpet-bags," said one Srijem Croat (quoted in chapter 5), alluding to the fact that the local population expected the arrival of displaced people with all that they owned packed into a couple of suitcases. This expectation arose according to the ever-present picture from the early 1990s of refugees carrying plastic bags containing all the property they had managed to throw together before they fled. In stark contrast to that image of the refugees, the Srijem Croats arrived with heavy transport trucks, and it is as semi-trailer people that they want to confirm themselves in their new community.

However, as the years have passed from the time of settlement, some of the Srijem Croats have taken a critical look at their own stance immediately after they moved there, toward the local population and toward their new environment. It seems to at least some of them that "those great differences" they saw early on either did not exist or have disappeared, and that there was no real foundation for their negative evaluation of the new community. Over the two year period from my first conversation with one young migrant, she has practically completely changed her attitudes and now speaks (self)critically about the Srijem Croats, claiming that they exaggerated in emphasizing their self-awareness and superiority in relation to the Gradina community:

> They [the local population] have brought us somewhat down to earth. We are not some sort of quality of inestimable worth. You know, there are other good and wise people on different sides. Perhaps even wiser than we are! For example, we now see that there are *gazde* [well-to-do farmers] in this village [Gradina], too, isn't that so, and not as we thought that we were the main ones . . . [We now see] that some people have perhaps more than we do. And that means that they [the local population] also have some qualities. . . . While now, here, they also see that we are worth something, and we see that they are worth something, isn't that so? They are all fascinated with our watermelons and fruit, right? It's all still an attraction. [laughter] And they are still trying, you know, to do it [plant] the way we do, but it's not really working. . . . But there are some things we can't know better than they do. We won't ever be able to raise tobacco the way they do, right?

The Local Population's Perspective

The views of the local population concerning the new situation have been partly presented in chapter 5, juxtaposed with the views of the migrants, but without analysis since I wanted to make it possible for readers to compare the statements of both sides and to create for themselves a certain notion about the coethnic encounter. With the aid of those statements and others on the part of members of the local population, I shall try here to reconstruct their side of the "story," aiming at a better understanding of the reasons for their reserved and passive attitude toward their new neighbors, the Croats from Srijem.

With their resettlement in the area around Virovitica, the Srijem Croats were moving into a migratory and multiethnic region. Statistics show that, during the 1920s and the 1960s, Gradina had the highest rate of immigrant inflow, primarily from other parts of Croatia, and also from Bosnia-Herzegovina (Sivački et al. 1986). Although these immigrants were not only ethnic Serbs from Croatia or from Bosnia (since they also included ethnic Croats from Croatian Zagorje and Dalmatia), the ethnic Serbs from Herzegovina and Dalmatia were in the forefront of the perception of the migrants among the entrenched inhabitants of Gradina. The Serbian settlers, made mostly of veterans of World War I, *solunci* (see chapter 1), settled in Gradina during the 1920s, creating the so-called New Gradina (the newer part of the village) into which the Srijem Croats have now moved, following the departure of Gradina's ethnic Serbian population to Serbia.

When the established inhabitants of Gradina speak of the history of their relations with the ethnic Serbian inhabitants, from the perspective of the 1990s and the political upheavals that they brought, they speak largely of the decades of rivalry and struggle for local positions and economic prosperity in which, in their estimation, "they [the established Croatian population] got the short end of the stick." The old settler interlocutors claim that, thanks to the fact that Serbian war veterans were granted land and were exempt from taxes in Yugoslavia in the period between the two world wars and were protected employees in the former local agricultural combine in socialist Yugoslavia, they got ahead and were in a better financial position than the Croatian inhabitants in the old part of the village. An evident sign of their prosperity were the houses in the new part of the village which, as the Gradina inhabitants agree, were until recently newer and better than the houses in the old part of the village:

JČŽ: "Did the economic status of the people grow at an equal pace in the old and the new parts of the village?"

Interlocutor: "Yes, equally, in one and the other, although I think that those in New Gradina had a greater number of well-off families, because they did not have to pay taxes or anything when they moved here, so they did better than those who had to take care of those payment obligations, and settle them. I remember the time when they [tax collectors] used to come, and take the horses, the hogs, lard, meat, everything, just everything that there was, whatever it was . . . They—the tax collectors picked up everything, confiscated everything and took it away—so life was hard. And so it was normal that the life of the old settlers here, and those who did not have to pay [was different]—they [the Serbian settlers in the new part of the village] really got ahead."

JČŽ: "Are there more multi-storey houses and new houses in the new part of the village?"

Interlocutor: "They're newer because they were built later, yes, the houses are newer. However, here in Gradina [the older part of the village] now, there are old houses but also newer ones, I would say thanks to *Viržinija*" [the tobacco processing plant in Virovitica].

Apart from the privileges they had, such as tax exemption, my interlocutors deem that the Serbs' loudness, obtrusiveness, and pushiness[4] also made it possible for the Serbs to do better in economic terms. Allegedly, they also had political influence, which was largely due to the ethnic Serbian Buha family whose young member had been a Partisan hero,[5] and could thus set the orientation of the village's development, such as when the location of certain key public institutions was in question. They were located between the old and the new parts of the village, more distant from the center of the old part which, in the view of its inhabitants, was impractical and unjust. Although the inhabitants in the old part of the village constituted the majority of the population of the village, they were now obliged to walk a long distance to reach these institutions. In the symbolic sense, it was made clear that the old part of the village was no longer its central focus:

Interlocutor A: "This [old part of] the village hasn't had anything new in fifty years. Blueprints were drawn up for a building here across the road [in the center of the old part], a business building for a new shop, and so on, in the 1960s. It was never built because the Serbs would not permit it. It was planned to build the public health station here, where that kiosk stands [in the old part of the village], and then one of the . . . Serbs said 'If it's not built up there, there near my house [in the new part of the village], it won't be built anywhere.' So, naturally enough, people said all right, let it be a kilometer away, at least we'll have a health station in Gradina. That's what's important. And a school was planned for the old part of the village. But no! It had to go up there, nearer to the Serbian part of the village."

Interlocutor B: "So we were always at loggerheads with those Serbs: this is the center, Gradina spread out from here, this is where the first houses were, and so on. Everything that was being moved away from here created some sort of fear among the local people that the center of the village would lose its significance, and be moved up there among the Serbs."

The old inhabitants of Gradina have extended to the Srijem migrants their stance toward the Serbian immigrants. In the early days after the arrival of the Srijem migrants, they may have expected the situation to be different because the migrants were Croats, but they soon started to experience the newcomers as a threat, as people who would try to impose themselves, and "draw away" the core local institutions into their part of the village, just as the Serbs had done in the past:

> And now, despite the fact that those who came are Croats, our people, there was still a lot of apprehension during those 1990s. Now they are . . . New people have again arrived. It does not matter now whether they are Serbs or Croats, they are new people and will now . . . Once again, things [the communal facilities] will move up there to them. We will turn out the losers. Perhaps it's . . . That was the biggest problem, perhaps, in their being accepted or not accepted, in the attitude to those people who arrived.

I do not know what relations between the established and new settlers in Gradina were actually like immediately after the arrival of the latter, since I started my research several years after they came there. Local people who held important local positions when the Srijem Croats arrived, claimed they were pleased that the Croatian migrants replaced the Serbs, and that, initially, they were accommodating and helpful,[6] not only because it was expected of them because of their public functions, but also because they sympathized with them. They say they were aware the situation could lead to social problems and the isolation of the newcomers, and they hoped to speed up their integration into the local community with their friendliness and readiness to help. However, it seems their authority was not sufficient enough to prevent the isolation of the Srijem Croats in the new part of the village, or to develop non-institutional mechanisms aimed at better links between the established population and the newcomers.

Why did the old local population see a threat in the newcomers from Srijem and the possibility that the new settlers would eclipse them both socially and economically? Why did they transfer their notion of their structurally inferior position in comparison with their former ethnic Serb neighbors to the Croatian migrants from Srijem?

According to the local population, the basic difference between themselves and the newcomers lies in their economic philosophy. Not only are the Srijem Croats hard working and diligent, but their attitude toward labor is characterized by an entrepreneurial spirit, which the people of Gradina evaluate positively, praising their merchant and business undertakings, even to the extent that a local man commented that the Srijem Croats were "men of the world." They believe that, first and foremost, the Srijem Croats seek out their economic advantage and aim not only to ensure their basic existence, but also to make an extra profit. For their part, speaking about themselves, the Croats believe that they, too, are hard working, but have never learned to trade or had an opportunity to sell their own produce, instead having done business exclusively with the former socially owned combine, working enough to fulfill their own needs, but not much more than that. According to one young man from Gradina, who also tills the land, the philosophy of the old local population is: "He does what he wants. What do I care. [I have] a Slavonian soul, a broad Slavonian soul. If it works, it works, if it doesn't, it doesn't, and I don't worry very much either way." The Srijem Croats are said to be different. Let us look at the statements of two people from Gradina:

JČŽ: "Are the Srijem Croats different from the people here?"

Interlocutor A: "I don't know how to answer that. They differ in that they have—how should I put it: if he has his objective and some angle of his own, that's all that concerns him. If it's to their advantage, that's what they concentrate on. They don't care about anyone else around them. And that's good. . . . They have learnt all about trading. With apples, with peaches, with foodstuffs, with anything, with that fruit."

JČŽ: "In the beginning, what was the most obvious difference between the established and the migrants?"

Interlocutor B: "In my opinion, there was none. One thing . . . well all right, perhaps that mentality of theirs. . . . They are better economists than the local folk. When they arrived, they immediately showed that they were interested in working and making money, not just in working for work's sake. While people here, let's say, our people are mainly . . . I plant maize, and wheat, and I have less work to do. And the fact that I don't make a profit on it, it's not important! But not to this one. The Srijem Croat says, 'I won't plant maize because it's not worth it, I will plant watermelons.' And they taught us a thing or two with those watermelons."

Thus, on the whole, that basic difference of work values perceived with respect to the newcomers is exceptionally highly valued by the established population. However, they are averse to it when the Srijem Croats (who have noticed the same thing, see chapter 5) translate this characteristic into depreciating comments about the domestic population, which the latter, naturally enough, find offensive. I was only able to hear the following regarding the depreciatory comments in question:

> Perhaps there were some problems at the beginning, but they were largely [brought about] by people who in some way . . . I don't know what they expected to be given here when they arrived, so that they offended the

local population with some of their expressions, and words. But we have moved on.

According to the same woman from Gradina, a television program[7] in which it was reportedly said "that these [the people from Srijem] are real Croats and they should mix with the Croats here; in some way theirs is Croatian blue blood," provoked resentment among the old local population. I watched a tape of that broadcast and found what was actually in question was the awkward statement of a local man, a doctor, who performed important local political functions during the early 1990s. Speaking in the eugenic sense, he said the Srijem Croats would introduce "some fresh blood" among the established population, and the Croats would become "one of the healthiest peoples in the world" [*sic*] in the twenty-first century. In the memory of this Gradina woman, his statement remained as a stumbling block in the relations between the old inhabitants and the new settlers, despite the fact that it did not originate from the Srijem migrants.

The old inhabitants of Gradina believe the migrants have no understanding of the old locals' former position with respect to the Serbs, or of the consequences this had for their economic status. They think the migrants should understand their economic circumstances and that they should not be belittled.

According to what I was told by a prominent man of the older generation, the reserve of the local population toward the Srijem Croats has other causes—the stronger economic position of the migrants:

Interlocutor: "Slowly, let's say, as we are gaining a similar economic position, so we are understanding each other better. . . . People are people. They [the Srijem Croats] sometimes offended some individuals." . . .

JČŽ: "So the Srijem Croats offended the local people?"

Interlocutor: "Yes, they sometimes belittled the local man. But he [the Srijem Croat] did not know what I know. . . . He didn't know how hard it was for that man to get ahead here, how he was subordinate [to the Serbs], much worse than they [the Srijem Croats] were there [in Serbia]. They were a Croatian village there [Slankamen in Srijem], but we had [Serbian] national heroes here, who beat their chest at every turn."

The Srijem Croats reportedly behave in a superior fashion in relation to their new community, which additionally burdens their relations with the established population. "Only they are more inclined to swell up with their own importance than we are. They want a lot, would like to have even more, and complain about things . . . ," said a man from Gradina.

All of this causes negative reactions among the entrenched local population, who experience the self-awareness of the Srijem Croats and their superior status ideology, which lies at the core of the settlers' identity-building strategy in the new environment, as a threat to their own identity and a potential danger for the development of a situation in which they could, once again, find themselves on an unequal footing with their fellow inhabitants, as they were when Serbs lived in the village. By their wary stance toward the newcomers, and their categorization of them as Others, or as people similar in some characteristics to the Serbs, the established, too, contribute to the drawing of boundaries and the mutual exclusion of the two groups.

In the reported statement of some of the local inhabitants: "Slankamen people, they are other Serbs"—which my interlocutor disavowed—there is explicit identification of the Srijem Croats as "the new Serbs":

> You know, in these other villages they say: "My goodness, the Slankamen people, they are other Serbs." Don't say that, people, they are not other Serbs. They had to flee from Serbia, and now to say that they are Serbs, that's out of the question! But there are people like that [who say so] . . .

Identifying the Srijem Croats as Serbs is not exclusively linked to their Ekavian organic idiom (see chapter 1, footnote 17), but, as we have seen, also to the perception of the local population regarding their economic strength, their mentality and way of life, and particularly with their being seen as possibly playing a *déjà vu* social and political role in the life of Gradina.

Name-giving is an act of categorization, and categorization is a simplification of reality that does not allow the use of the sum of the diverse characteristics of a group and the individuals who make up the group. Limitation to one feature—whether real or perceived—is regarded as sufficient for identification of the group (Bausinger 1988: 16). Thus, the established population views the newcomers as Serbs. By that attribution, they are not denoting the essence of the migrant Srijem Croats but rather speaking of their stance toward them (cf. Bilefeld 1998: 131). Since the established have fresh memories of their historical experience, they feel threatened that the migrants, despite the fact they are largely Croats, will take the former position of the Serbs in the social hierarchy. Therefore, by analogy, they call them the "new" or "other" Serbs. That categorization does not speak about the ontological status of the migrants; rather, it speaks about the attitude of the locals toward the new settlers, which is defined by what they perceive as the ontological migration configuration. This is exceptionally well illustrated by the following statement:

> When a new group of people arrives, as with the Srijem migrants, some sort of fear develops—not repugnance toward them—but fear of those people. Someone will now push us aside again. They [the Serbs] did . . . Whoever has ever come here, surpassed us from the very beginning. Now, someone else is coming who will [leave us out of the running] . . .

This is basically a description of the tense migration situation, which arises in the encounter between the established and the outsider population, as Elias and Scotson would put it. The common ethnicity or nationality of the established population and the newcomers does not lessen its effects. The researched situation in Gradina also has certain specific features: the newcomers do not interiorize the identity ascribed to them by the local population; indeed, in the process of re-identification and establishment in the new community, they create a negative image of the old local population. It conflicts with the efforts of the entrenched population in the newly arisen social configuration to free themselves of their own negative image, of the stigma interiorized (cf. Cohen 1985) during life under socialism in a village with a numerically small, but economically and politically stronger, ethnic Serbian population.

The idea of their own inferiority in relation to the strangers who are arriving in their region is a component of the self-identification of the old inhabitants of Gradina. By holding such a self-perception, it is understandable why they are unable to develop an ideology that would emphasize their superiority and establish them as a self-confident community. They expected the familiar scenario to repeat itself with the arrival of the Srijem Croats: they expected that the newcomers, as victims of the war, would receive special treatment from the Croatian state, just as the former Yugoslav state had extended special care to the Serbian settlers in the past. In other words, they feared the newcomers would be privileged in relation to the entrenched population, which would enable their speedy economic advancement and taking over of the leading roles in the village. A particular interpretation of history and the notion of its repetition led the old local inhabitants to transfer to the new migrants their fear of newcomers in general and, as a preventive measure, they closed their ranks. Their encounter with the self-aware "semi-trailer people" contributed even more to the tensions between them and their wariness of their new neighbors.

Their perception of the situation also caused their passivity regarding promotion of the Srijem migrants' integration. The local population expected the newcomers would adapt to life in the village: "Our people expect . . . we expect them [the Srijem Croats] [to adapt] to us, and they expect us to [adapt to them]. Now you don't know who [should adapt] to whom!"

The established population expected the migrants would take the initiative and become active in the social, political, and religious institutions in the village: in the local district authority and the administration of the village, the soccer club, the hunting and volunteer fire brigade, the church, and so forth. In their opinion, the migrants are not on the whole active in the village organizations, although they do provide them with funding support.

However, the old locals' view does not seem to me to be well-founded since several of the Srijem Croats participated in local politics and organizations immediately after their arrival; they registered their names on the voting rolls, and several of them took part in filling posts in the local associations. It would seem that, if the newcomers did not personally take the initiative, the established population did not prompt them to become active in the local organizations. The above quoted Gradina man, who held a position in the local district authority, explained why he preferred the individual activism of the Srijem Croats:

> I won't go begging anyone to do anything. That's for sure! You [they] came here to us. You will get everything you need, but I won't ask you for anything. How should I put it . . . after all, I'm the one who is at home here and, and how can I put it . . . I am a *gazda* [a well-off farmer], or call it what you will. Which means, if you come to me, we will shake hands, no problem. We had the Serbs, and whoever came here, we had to tremble, and beg, and, I don't know . . . dance around them. In the end, they all left us behind and then, finally, we had to beg them—again. Now we are [all] Croats, we are all our own people. There is no need for divisions between us, but . . . F. V. [a Srijem Croat] came to me. "Listen," he said, "I used to be active in folklore [activities], it's something I know. If you can do this, and this, and that for me, set up the conditions," he says, "I guarantee that you will have the best folklore [group] all the way from Osijek to Zagreb." . . . I said. "No problem, man, if you know how to, we will do it." . . . F. really did take the reins into his hand, and it's super! . . . In other words, he said "I want to work"—so, there you are. The lad's working. Some of them came down here, they played soccer in Slankamen. "Can they play?"—"Yes, no problem." Whoever wants to, can, but we won't allow anyone to sit at home and criticize [us, saying] that nothing is as

it should be, that I did not accept him. Look, I won't accept you if you are sitting there on your land. What do I care about how you live at home! But, if something is in the interest of village and if you want to do it, then do it.

The above quote makes it obvious that this man, himself a representative of the local district authority, prefers the new settlers to become active in the interests of the village as a whole, and not merely in their own interest. This statement, unlike some of those cited previously, puts more emphasis on the common ethnicity of the old inhabitants and new settlers than on opposition which could arise because of the relationship between established and newcomers: since they are all Croats, he does not expect the migrants to have any special needs and rights. Consequently, in the context of this statement, the same ethnicity plays an important role in the stance toward the newcomers, while it is ignored in others. For this local official, their common ethnicity serves as justification for the participation of the Srijem Croats in local life. He prefers individual, personal involvement in the community, because he thinks it will prevent the collective public declaration of the newcomers and the possibility of their seeking special rights for their own group. This statement should be placed in the context of the fear among the established inhabitants that, by the collective activity and demands of the new settlers, they could become "the new Serbs." In order to prevent that, he offers them individual participation in the existing village associations, but also lays at their door the fault for the relatively poor communication between the two groups:

I would prefer to draw a parallel on how much those people who came here accepted us. That was the bigger question, with a lot of dilemmas. In my opinion, we held out our hand to all of them—to be here, to come and to feel welcome. I'm not sure, but we could have done all sorts of things—to these people from Srijem—to make it hard for them, for it to be even more difficult for them in the misfortune of their having been forced to move, if we had not wanted to accept them. We were led by the idea that these were our people; they were Croats!

The Stereotyped Rhetoric of Difference

Neither the reaction of the migrants nor the reactions of the old population were planned or characteristic to either of the groups. Mutual stereotyping by the groups is the result of the described social configuration and the encounter between the two populations, each with its own specific experience and interpretation of its past and present. And while the diversity of their cultural systems provides material for the creation of stereotyped images about the other group, the formulae for expressing differences and setting the boundaries are influenced by a certain genre (cf. McDonald 1993: 228), derived from the social rhetoric of difference in the Croatia of the 1990s. It sets the formula for the stereotyped expression of difference and boundary making between the groups.

During the 1990s, the following were the fundamental opposing categories, which helped the Croats present themselves and upon which they built up their diversity from the Other: traditional/modern; uncivilized/civilized; rural/urban; Balkan/European; Eastern/Western; and, Serbian/Croatian. In the first half of the 1990s, marked by the conflict with the Serbs—at the time the main negative mirror against which they tried to present themselves—the Croats identified themselves with the second category in that series of binary oppositions and ascribed the Serbs the characteristics of the first. As I showed in analysis of the discussion that accompanied the ritual slaying of an ox on the island of Korčula in 1999, those oppositions dominated the language of the public media (Čapo Žmegač 2001a). They are also present in the mutual attributions of the local and the migrant population in the Virovitica area: the new settlers perceive themselves as advanced, modern, and urban, while they regard the old local population as backward, traditional, and rural. At the same time, the latter call some of the new neighbors' characteristics "Eastern and Serbian."

The mutual attributions of the old inhabitants and the migrants perhaps indicate another social rhetoric of difference present in Croatia from around the second half of the 1990s. It is located within the national context and "divides" the nation into "good" and "bad" Croats; the "bad Croats" having acquired the characteristics which are imputed to the Serbs.[8] In their efforts to emphasize their own identity and establish their social position in the new environment, it seems this rhetoric was also used by some of the Srijem Croats—when they attributed "less Croatian-ness" to the old population in Gradina and even expressed doubts about their having "Croatian spirit" at all, as shown in chapter 5.

These were two basically contradictory discourses in use in the Croatia of the 1990s, which influenced the discursive strategies of the established population and the migrants: one was unitary and ethnonational and, being in the service of the struggle against Serbian aggression, it promoted the nationalization of identity and prompted the domination of the national over other collective identifications; the other, contrary to the first in that it was divisive, categorized the nation into "good" and "bad" members. The first discourse, based on the ideology of cultural and national unity, was particularly present in the first half of the 1990s; the second discourse, based on internal political divisions, although it did not fully force out the first discourse, was dominant in the second half of the 1990s. The participants in the newly created social configuration in Gradina make use of both discourses, depending on which suits them best in the particular context. Both the discourse on the unity of "the Croatian corpus" and the one on its dichotomy function according to the needs of the situation for explaining the notions and behavior of both groups. It is said that the Srijem Croats, just *because they are Croats,* will integrate quickly and without problems and become part of the local community, but situations do arise in which the fact that they are new settlers, some *different sort of Croats,* perhaps with doubtful Croatian characteristics, is more important than the fact of their common national affiliation with the locals. The reverse also holds, when the migrants are speaking about the established inhabitants.

Talk of "a divided nation" falls on responsive ears in Gradina and in the Virovitica area because of the specific features of the local social situation, created by the geographic and social dislocation of the Srijem Croats and resettlement; the reaction to the forced displacement; the loss of social status and economic and political power; the specifically segregated settlement of the migrants in the new environment among unknown people with their own established standards and traditions, and the interiorized stigma about their own identity; and, finally, but no less importantly, the broad economic circumstances in the country during the second half of the 1990s, which made it harder for both the Srijem and local farmers to prosper. All of these are factors contributing to the demarcation between the migrants and the established group. Spurred on by talk of a "divided nation," these factors continue to perpetuate mutual stereotyping between them, even six to seven years after resettlement.

Stereotyping and Individualization

Stereotyping is attribution of identical characteristics to each individual in a group, notwithstanding actual variations in the group (Cashmore 1996). Comments on the industrious and pushy nature of the Srijem

Croats are also stereotypes, just as are the notions about the economic
disinterestedness and "lesser Croatian-ness" of the established inhabitants: not all Srijem Croats are hard working, nor do all the local inhabitants lack interest in making a profit from tilling their land in addition to
the minimum necessary to ensure their existence.

A large number of my interlocutors from both "sides" spoke simultaneously in stereotypes while also individualizing the members of the
other group. Some of them rejected the use of simplified images of the
other group. When asked if he could remember any problems with the
local population, one young Srijem Croat responded by differentiating
individuals within the local group: "But I can't say . . . if I see a drunken
person I can't say that everybody is drunk" (quoted in chapter 3).

In the same way, the established interlocutors differentiate the migrants, sometimes attributing stereotypes to neighboring places or other
people in Gradina. Below are some statements that illustrate this point,
along with those already quoted: "On many occasions it has become the
conventional wisdom in these parts that if anyone has done anything
bad, it must have been someone from Slankamen. But I said from the
first day, from the very first day, speak up with his name and his surname
if he is not as he should be!"

The same elderly inhabitant of Gradina relativized both the material
strength and characteristics of the Srijem Croats, and their internal unity:

> But there are good and bad [persons] everywhere, just everywhere. And
> they found all sorts among us, but I say that they found us as an [integral]
> group—we have all lived here, but I am convinced that they left behind
> part of the poorest and worst [among them], the ones who did not have
> the wherewithal [to move], who had no possibility to come here. While
> those who are here, they came . . . came from one place [or] from differ-
> ent places. However, there is already a lot of disagreement among them.
> And you also have it that someone becomes offended because the other
> one defames him. Puts him to shame!

Stereotypes are maintained due to homogeneity and firm bonding between the members of the group that create them, to conformism, and
social control of the community. If the community is not firmly knit
and if it does not force individuals to reconcile with the community's
stance toward its neighbors, the stereotype will shatter. Or, as the situation is here, it will coexist with individualized evaluations of the members of the other group.

Neither the local nor the Srijem community in Gradina is firm: the
former because of the interiorized stigma about its identity, and the latter

because it is in the process of being formed. The Srijem community is not strong enough to be able to maintain awareness of its existence and effectively separate itself from its neighbors by manipulating the symbols of the community and supporting the stereotypes about the old inhabitants. During the research period, Srijem community spirit relied on the stereotyping of its neighbors, but not on rituals which would have brought together all Srijem Croats and indicated, through the use of symbols, their Otherness from the local population. During the first few years after they settled in Gradina, the Srijem Croats tried to gather around the *betlemaši* and *mačkare* customs (see chapter 5). However, when I was doing my research, they had already abandoned the *betlemaši* procession, and were no longer organizing Carnival festivities separately from the domestic population.

Their heterogeneity is a contributing factor to the poor cohesion of the Srijem settlers in Gradina. Although some of its members would like to present them as a homogenous group, the picture of a unitary, homogenous community of Srijem Croats is not confirmed in reality. That is only their public face (cf. Cohen 1985: 74ff.), the face they want to present to their new neighbors (and perhaps to the researcher). The group's public face they want to present is uniform and "made-up," a face to be shown off, without blemishes, a face which presents the group as a community of people who think the same and have the same status. However, this image exists only in representation for it is necessary in the process of intentional demarcation toward its neighbors: each differentiation in relation to its neighbors ignores the internal differentiation of its members—in age, gender, status, economic circumstances, origins, personal experience, and so forth.

The Srijem Croats who have settled in the surroundings of Virovitica do not make up a homogenous group from the aspects of origins, speech or culture. They come from various places in Srijem; as well as Croats, there is also a certain minor number of members of other nations. And they differ in origins: some of them have lived in Srijem for generations while others became inhabitants of Srijem only a few decades ago, moving there as children or as adults from Bosnia-Herzegovina, or from underdeveloped regions in Croatia (as has already been discussed in chapters 1 and 6). The latter, being less bonded with "Srijem soil," found their feet more easily in this new exodus because, in the opinion of one man from Srijem:

> They had less ties with that soil. They were less [emotionally] encumbered with it. They had a different mentality. They were less sentimental.

They were more prepared to come to grips with something different . . .
They were not so tied to the land. One of our problems is that we are
so tied to it. It's probably because of being brought up that way. And it's
probably still there in our subconscious: land means some sort of security, the land, that agriculture in fact. So people there became bonded to
it more and more [to the land they left behind in Srijem] and found it
harder to cope here.

There are also economic differences between the migrant Srijem Croats from the various Srijem villages, differences which have come about
due to micro-pedological factors and the origins of the population. The
Srijem Croats explain the differences in the mentalities and customs of
the people from Golubinci and Slankamen, as mentioned in chapter 5,
by historical events, the time at which their villages were established,
and their location in the central or outlying part of Srijem. In addition, the Srijem migrants who have moved to Gradina from the villages
of Slankamen, Kukujevci, Golubinci, Indija, and Vajska mostly do not
know each other. Sometimes, it is not easy for them to establish mutual
relations, since there was no social contact between them when they
were living in Srijem, and the villagers do not know the people or anything about the events from other villages:

Interlocutor A: "But we are scattered all over here. We cannot fit in with the
people from Slankamen, nor they with us. It's different here. It's as if we
feel foreign. We like our people from Golubinci. It's all fine with them
[people from Slankamen], but it's . . ."

Interlocutor B: "There's nothing [for us] to talk about, they [people from other
Srijem villages] have their own [lives]. It's just like I told you—an empty
record. He says so-and-so died, so-and-so got married . . . 'Who? What?'
[We don't know them.]"

However, some people find it easier in their new environment to get to
know the strangers among the Srijem Croats,[9] and distant relatives with
whom they had practically no contacts in Srijem. This was testified to
with humor by a young woman speaking about her husband's kinsman,
whom she knew only by sight in Srijem and with whom they became
close only after migrating to the same place in Croatia:

I knew him [only] like that, by sight. "That's my uncle," says D. [her
husband]. "He is," he says, "some sort of uncle of mine." That's the way
he said it. Later, that "some sort of uncle" became the main uncle here!
[laughter] . . . I knew he was some sort of uncle. And then, he [turns out
to be] a real relative! Now I even know how he likes his coffee. [laughter]

The primary identities of the migrants are connected with the localities from which they have come. Despite mobility connected with trading activities, localities are the areas of primary socialization and enculturation of these people, and, in that way, of their identification. Consequently, creating a spirit of community among the newcomers is not an easy process—the Srijem Croats who have settled in Gradina are connected by only two characteristics: largely Croatian national affiliation and the forced exodus from Srijem. Although there have been attempts to create a social boundary against the local population and to bring together the Srijem Croats into a community, these attempts on the local level have not been of an organized nature. They have remained only as individual discursive strategies of identification, which have not been accepted by all members of the group. Not all the migrants in Gradina accept the idea of creating and utilizing migrant identity as the foundation for integration in the new environment. In other words, some people have refused to meld in their individual identity in a collective Srijem identity, instead making efforts to incorporate themselves in the new environment by a "civic" strategy of incorporation—as individuals, and not as members of the Srijem Croat group (see chapter 3).

I showed in the previous chapter that the same ambivalence regarding selection of the presentation strategy of the displaced population is repeated on the macro-level. There is division among the leaders of the Community of Croatian Refugees and Internally Displaced Persons from Srijem, Bačka, and Banat into those who want to stimulate the process of ethnicization: the shaping of a separate Srijem identity within the Croatian nation, and those who do not regard such collectivization as being necessary. The latter legitimate their stance by citing the common national affiliation of all Croats, in the light of which the constituting of a subnational community appears to be a subversive act. Thereby, either consciously or unconsciously, intentionally or unintentionally, they support the rhetoric of national and cultural unity that opposes differentiation within Croatian identity, and they see the possibility of "national treason" (cf. Bilefeld 1998) in the ethnicization of separate Srijem identity. For their part, the supporters of the idea of formation and maintenance of separate Srijem identity do not see such activity as an ethno-national matter. They regard their membership in the "Croatian corpus" as being unquestionable, and see an exclusively pragmatic drive toward achieving economic objectives (and perhaps, also personal ones) in the attempt to constitute themselves as a separate group within Croatian society, along with the pay-off of indemnity to the displaced Srijem Croats for the damage they have suffered in their forced migration from Srijem.

Both the migrants who reject activities as a group and the stereo-typed conceptions about the local population, and those with an eth-nocentric stance to their hosts and the place in which they have settled, individualize the local population and have excellent relations with them. It is not easy to explain this apparent contradiction within the framework of earlier contact theories and the theories of social iden-tity, which postulate that individual interactions will be informed by collective notions about neighbors, meaning that people who identify with their own group will communicate with members of the other group in the stereotyped manner defined by the notions of the group (Forbes 1997).

Based on some insights from social psychology, particularly on the reappraisal of contact theory by Hugh D. Forbes (1997), I propose to explain the apparent contradiction with the hypothesis of two levels of reality: one level pertains to mutual images and representations of the groups in contacts, the other pertains to the interactive practice on the level of the individual. Discursive strategies of identification on both sides produce simplified representations of the social reality, an image of the other group as "a black and white design" (Elias and Scotson 1965: 81), which does not leave room for differentiation among group members. The shared representation is not just a sum of individual experiences and points of view; rather, it is a result of a particular social configuration which came into being in the en-counter of the locals with the newcomers. Insofar as it is a social and not an individual fact, it is not sufficient that for it to be changed the relations between individual members of each group change, or that the number of individual interactions rises (cf. Forbes 1997). In other words, the existence of tensions and value judgments at the level of the migrant and established population in Gradina cannot be explained by individual experiences but exclusively by group relations and the social configuration which comes about in their encounter, as has been described on the foregoing pages.

Analysis of the interaction between the newcomers and the estab-lished population opens up a new level for researching reality—the reality of behavior—showing how the individual can reject the society of reception and harbor a poor opinion of it, while at the same time participate in and maintain active contacts with neighbors, creating an intensive area of interaction.

The Ease of Person-to-Person Interaction

Interaction between the newcomers and the members of the established population shows culture to be a permanent process of creation and negotiation of meaning between people (Baumann 1996; Cohen 1985). Culture in their interactions is a process of creating and recreating a collective sense in an altered social situation: the participants in the interaction cross over and examine the collective boundary between the "us" and "them" groups, relativizing and exposing to ridicule the actual and perceived differences that separate them, and agreeing on the common semantic fields in which they feel at home and understand each other well.

As I have already mentioned, the lack of correspondence between the conceptions about Others and the interaction between individuals in the newly arisen social situation in Gradina can be explained by more recent sociopsychological theories, which differentiate individual from group reality. Mutual group perceptions are collective and cannot be interpreted by individual conflicts. They are the result of social processes in which there is a positive correlation between maintaining the stereotypes and the number of inter-group contacts: a large number of inter-group contacts only confirm and strengthen the existing stereotypes. On the individual level, for its part, in personal contact between individuals, the sign of correlation between the number of contacts and the stereotypes is altered, so that persons who have many contacts can easily correct mutual stereotypes (Forbes 1997; McDonald 1993). In other words, mutual negative perceptions of neighboring groups will not be reduced by a large number of individual contacts of members of the two groups—they will help to correct only personal stereotypes. Interaction will support such effects when it takes place between people of equal status, in situations in which they depend on cooperation, and are supported by politics.

The new and old inhabitants of Gradina enjoy very good personal relations on the individual level. I shall try to describe one situation of interaction between members of the local and the migrant population, which testifies to this in a convincing way. It arose in the summer of 1997 in a house in Gradina that was owned by a family who, although they had moved there only in the 1960s, were established inhabitants in relation to the Srijem Croats who came in the 1990s. Present at the encounter were the host's family (mother and son, and, intermittently, the son's wife and children), and members of two Srijem families (an older woman and a younger man). It would be difficult to recount the entire conversation since it took place simultaneously between several participants, so that some parts of the audio recording cannot be understood. The collocutors were teasing each other about the differences in the idiom of the Srijem Croats. Members of the established group and the Srijem migrants were talking about the misunderstandings that had arisen in initial conversations because of unfamiliar words used respectively by both groups, which were not understood by the other side.[10] It is not possible to conjure up the intonations, gestures, laughter, interjections, the facial expressions, and the enjoyment seen in the communication between all the participants in the conversation. This was indicated by the older Gradina woman, who at the end said that my question on the relations between the established inhabitants and the migrants from Srijem had been answered in the most convincing way: "There, you see, that is what it's like when we meet. Do you see! There are no dilemmas here, there is really nothing more that needs to be said." During the entire conversation, and when it was coming to an end, I had the impression that I was present at an "authentic" unstaged situation in which the participants soon paid no attention to the fact that it was being recorded and conducted in the presence of a stranger. This encounter and other similar ones solved many dilemmas and cleared up my ideas about the impossibility of communication between the newcomers and the established population arrived at on the basis of discursive analysis.

In the mentioned conversation, the difference in the idiom used by the Srijem Croats appears in quite a different function than in the mutual attributions of the old inhabitants and the migrants. In this case, idiom is the focus of a friendly discussion, which demonstrates the familiarity of these people with the numerous variants within the Croatian language, making it impossible on the basis of organic idiom to determine a person's national identity. In contrast, we saw that idiom has the function of demarcation of neighbors as part of the discursive strategy of identification, and can become a marker of national affiliation, in this case with the attribution of Serbian identity to the newcomer Croats from Srijem whose idiom is perceived as the Serbian standard language (see chapter 5).

The interaction between the members of the entrenched and migrant populations takes place on the principles of territorial proximity and mutual interest. In the first case, direct neighbors communicate regardless whether they are established or migrant population. They are drawn together by their territorial proximity and the same occupation (farming), and, in some types of interaction, by similar age: "I go out to these women—they sit in the street [on benches placed on the pavement in front of the houses]. [laughter] I have fitted in well. It's mostly women of my age who have come [to Gradina]." Then, there is *komšiluk* (neighborly) cooperation prompted by mutual need: "I need him, and he needs me," said a woman from Gradina whose house is in the "new" part of the village, when speaking about her Srijem Croat neighbor and the mutual help they give each other during spring and autumn agricultural activities:

> Well, we cooperate with them and they cooperate with us. With D. [man from Srijem]. What I mean is, he [cooperates] with us and we with him. And in general, with all of them here. . . . Yes, it's like this, yes, if he needs me or if I need him—no problem. We are . . . And they accepted us immediately and we accepted them when they came [laughter] so that they fitted in and had no worries. With all these neighbors of mine here . . . Well, all right, those further up there, they have their neighbors on that side, and we have our neighborhood, there are six or seven of us here. No problem . . . We help each other out whenever anything is needed.

Interaction to mutual advantage is usually economic in nature ("People largely become involved now from pure self-interest. I need you—so I do business with you. I don't need him—what do I care about him!"), as when an established inhabitant hires a newcomer to harvest his wheat, slaughter livestock, prune the fruit-trees, or fix the tractor. In such situations, self-interest and the capability of the person hired to do the job well is more important than kinship or friendship bonds, or the fact that someone is a migrant, because "business is business!"

The participation of individual Srijem Croats in local interest associations is another type of interaction between the migrants and the established, which to me, in contrast to the evaluation of some members of both groups, does not seem to be a rarity. Some have enrolled in the soccer club, some have become members of the hunting club, while others have promoted the renewal of the horse breeding or the folklore society in Gradina. In the two latter cases, Srijem Croats have been the initiators of these social activities. Some of the migrants joined in the local volunteer drive to refurbish the church immediately after their arrival, or joined the local political parties and took part in the local elections, either as candidates or as members of the electoral committees. Some never miss attending local district meetings, at which, together with the established population, they try to influence the decisions of the local administrative body regarding the improvement of Gradina's infrastructure. There was evidence of this at the meeting held in the summer of 1997, which was commented on by a public servant (contradicting the customary statement of Gradina people about the Srijem Croats failing to take part in local events):

For example, last night's town meeting: of the one hundred or so people who came, almost 50 percent were Srijem Croats! That shows that they are interested in what happens in the village, isn't that so? And there were several good suggestions from their side, and requests and questions. None [of the local people] said "What are you going on about now?," or "Who's asking you anything? You have [just] arrived, so what right do you have?" No, they are here! That [initial] period of those five years [of tense relations] is already behind us.

Moreover, Srijem women who had cleaned and maintained the church in Srijem have volunteered their services to the parish priest, and, since the reported appearance of the Virgin Mary in Gradina on 13 July 1997, they take part in the prayer meetings at the site or in the homes of local people. Several established godfather/godmother relationships and marriages, and friendships between the young members of the local and the migrant population can be added to this list of modes of interaction between the two groups.

Even when they are listing the numerous circumstances of interaction in which they themselves participate, the old and new inhabitants of Gradina do not notice that they are being contradictory when they state that there are no mutual communications, or that they are weak. This can be partly explained by the different levels of the statements—one is the level of the representation of the migrant Croats and their Gradina counterparts, and the other is the level of actual behavior. Part of the explanation also lies in the generalized image of the "new" village as the ghettoized part of the village. It supports the representation of the isolation of its inhabitants and of an absence of socializing with the inhabitants in the "old" village. It can also be explained by the large number of elderly people among the Srijem Croats who, because of their age and overall passivity, have less contact with the established population.

Conclusions

I have dealt in this chapter with the mutual representations of the established population and the newcomers, and with the interactions between the members of both groups. These two levels of reality are an artifact of two analytical procedures—one analyzes identity making with the help of discourse and representations of the self and the Other, and is based on what people tell the researcher; the other analyses people's actions and interactions in a particular sociocultural context, being based on the researcher's observation and participation in interactive situations.

The first is a discourse analysis, the second is the analysis of behavior and interaction.

While the discursive strategies of self-identification by the entrenched inhabitants—and that of the Srijem Croats, for that matter—actualize and immobilize the culture and identity of their own and of the other group, interaction points to the process-like and dynamic nature of culture and identity, and to the active role of people in that process. As is clearly shown by the statements that document them, Others in interactions are no longer what "we" are not, Others are what "we" make of them in "mutual adaptation," said one young woman from Srijem, in a tolerant negotiation and agreement on a new, perhaps even richer sense. Members of the entrenched population, the old inhabitants of Gradina, underscored the need for that process and the faith in its successful outcome:

Interlocutor A: "Let's reeducate the children, take what's worthwhile from one environment, and what's worthwhile from the other. Let's create something even richer!"

Interlocutor B: "It will all . . . all of it will come about with time—one generation has to [pass], then everything will be one."

Srijem Croats, too, testifying to the already well developed undertakings between the newcomers and the established population, say:

Interlocutor A: "But they have influenced us, and we have influenced them. They have accepted some of our ways and become brisker, and we have taken a page from their book and don't become so very upset when we don't succeed in something. That's what has happened, and that's how it is. [laughter] And that means, there may be some golden mean [auspicious balance] in the end with our children."

Interlocutor B: "But I think that this will remain as a lasting treasure for Croatia, our coming here and the exchange of cultural assets and the experience of life as a whole."

Interlocutor C: "Listen, these are the same people that we are with all their qualities. . . . Then somehow I simply saw that there is a great deal of good in all this [settling in Gradina]. And that one should take advantage of it as one does with all the good things in life, you know. Because if a man always looks on the bad side, nothing good can come of it."

These two levels of analysis are complementary because they speak in different ways about the social realities, which are the outcome of the coethnic and, according to Elias and Scotson, of any kind of encounter between the established and the newcomers. The reality of interaction is no more "true" than the one to which discourses and narrations testify, but it is different. Both are social facts. In the ethnographic study of coethnic encounter and the ensuing conflict that I have presented in this book, the discursive level has been given more attention, which can be explained by the type of fieldwork done (with the interview prevailing over other research techniques) and by the timing of the research (several years after the resettlement). However, since every conversation with interlocutors is the instance of their identification, meaning the discursive constitution of the interlocutor's identity, the representations—about oneself and others—presented in the conversations do not necessarily correspond with their behavior in concrete interaction. Indeed, they can be quite contradictory to them. As such, they need to be contrasted and complemented by the observation of processes of identification as actually lived in everyday actions and interactions. Indeed, as was suggested by Lila Abu-Lughod (1991: 147ff.), and shown in my research, drawing on the joint study of practice and discourse emphasizes contradictions and misunderstandings, strategies and interests, and the play of shifting and competing statements with practical implications.

Through observation, I have established the limitations of narrative sources in studying the process of identification. In order to counteract "the one-sided focus in identity studies on discourse and representation," this study joins Ton Otto and Henk Driessen (2000) in their request for studying identification as experienced in sociocultural contexts. Identities that are analyzed on the basis of discursive practice, or narrative sources, are more than mere artifacts of the method of research (interviewing): at a certain level, they are no less real than the identities uncovered in concrete interactions between established inhabitants and their migrant neighbors. However, they are not the only reality to which the ethnologist/anthropologist should devote attention: as this research shows, analysis of identity and processes of identification exclusively as discursive constructs remains one-sided and incomplete. It foresees a parallel reality—the reality of interaction, which does not have to correspond to the reality of narration (discourse).

I am making a case for complementing the study of discursive texts with the study of experience, which is informed by words, textual explanations, and the context. This combination of methodologies might be particularly important in the studies of identification, for, as this case study shows, the discourses on identity are only one particular locus of identity making; in order to understand them in their complexity and contradictions, we need to be informed about identities as lived (cf.

Frykman and Gilje 2003: 9ff) in the particular sociocultural environments and contexts in which they are deployed in (inter)action.

Another argument made in this chapter and in the book as a whole is that the treatment, acceptance, and incorporation of coethnic immigrants in their ethnic homelands is an instance of a more broadly relevant sociological configuration in which the intrusion of any migrant group, coethnic or not, sets the stage for cultural differentiation and symbolic (sometimes also real) conflict between the established and the newcomer population. This conflict does not build upon irreducible cultural differences; rather, it is inherently social in nature, the consequence of the social configuration that exposed the locals to meeting with the newcomers. Bent on preserving their status and power, the entrenched population close their ranks and refuse to reposition themselves with respect to the newcomers. This is done with the aim of defending the established social order. The migrants are expected to adapt to the role of newcomers' and are cast into the role of outsiders with respect to the established and locally more powerful old inhabitants.

However, the particular case under examination here, as well as other coethnic cases mentioned in chapter 1 (see also Čapo Žmegač 2005), diverges from the general model proposed by Elias and Scotson. A feature that sets apart the cases of incorporation of coethnic migrants into their ethnic homelands is the rejection, indeed, the reversal of the stigma cast upon them by the established population. The coethnic migrants develop a discourse of their own superior identity, which they buttress by real or perceived cultural differences. Both processes—the closure of the entrenched population and identity building among the migrants—lead to mutual construction of the symbolic boundary, with the end result that a subnational identity might emerge among the coethnic migrants. In the constitution of a separate migrant identity, we have a limiting case of ethnicity that emerges within full-fledged nations (cf. Hirschon 1989), because the common nationality was an insufficient common denominator to stop the local inhabitants from treating the newcomers as strangers and the newcomers from treating the locals as some "inferior nationals."

This analysis vividly shows that the resettlement problem, despite its specificities—whether it unfolds as an encounter between culturally, ethnically, religiously, linguistically, or otherwise diverse or similar groups—has the potential to evolve into a social and sociological problem because the participant groups in the encounter have conflicting intentions. The fact that the encounter takes place within a national community in no way reduces its potential virulence, nor does it alter the pattern in which it unfolds. This insight provides a motive for sensitive treatment of migration and resettlement, even within the national arena. Rather than assuming that due to the common ethnicity the co-ethnic migrants will easily integrate, in order to alleviate potential social problems, we need to develop and spread familiarity with the underlying mechanism of the encounter between the locally established and migrant populations (Čapo Žmegač 2005).

Notes

1. Some of my interlocutors, members of the local population of Gradina, nonetheless believe that the "old" and "new" settlers will manage to build a common future, thanks to their common ethnicity. "For instance, it will be solved much more easily and better than it would be with them [with the Serbs], because these are our people! Without exception!" There will be more on this point at the end of the chapter.
2. In one of my conversations with several Srijem Croats, who held university degrees, I told them directly that I had the impression they were taking a superior stance toward their new environment in their desire to impose themselves upon it. I received the following response: "It is inevitable that our story gives rise to a question like that. However, one couldn't, we couldn't put it like that. I think that our intention is not directed toward superiority. Our wish is directed to the level of life that we had at home—material, first and foremost—what we lost in these exchanges. So that is one of the elements. And further, we loved our region and want to continue its traditions."
3. In Winston Parva, analyzed by Elias and Scotson, ascription of identity acts similarly, but in the reverse direction: on the basis of the characteristics of a minority of the migrant settlers, the local population ascribes negative identity to the entire group (Elias and Scotson 1965).
4. "And while he is persistent, persistent and noisy, he gets what he wants by making a lot of fuss. Whether it was a loan, or anything else, he had to get it. That's what they were like."
5. In socialist Yugoslavia, the title of National Hero was awarded to Partisan fighters who distinguished themselves "above and beyond the call of duty" during World War II. It ensured the hero/ine (and the members of his/her family and the local community from which he/she came) considerable material and social privileges.
6. This is confirmed by the statements of Srijem Croats, see chapter 5.
7. "Novi dom" [New Home], scenario by Stjepan Kolak, Croatian Television, 1994.
8. Some political indicators are also added (opposition to the authorities, a pro-Yugoslav attitude and Communism). See chapter 5.
9. According to one young woman I spoke with, it is easier to make friends with other people from Srijem than with members of the established population in Gradina. One can have correct relations with the latter, but real friends are made with other people from Srijem: "Listen to this, I have some [female] friends [among the old inhabitants] who can come for a coffee, and we can talk about this and that connected with this place here. But we don't have anything deeper, any more serious conversations which would bring us closer together. And what has surprised me is that I have

made new, real friends with people from other places in Srijem, from Kukujevci for example. I didn't know these people before, just as I didn't know the people here. We had never met, but it's as though we have known each other—for a hundred years, as they say! [laughter] Somehow, we have become terribly close. I can't describe it. Something bonds us, we have a great deal of things in common."

10. It is not possible adequately to translate into English the transcript of that conversation since it was largely centered on linguistic misunderstandings between people who speak basically the same language, but in sufficiently different organic idioms, that caused misinterpretations in communication between them.

Epilogue:
Ethnologist and Her/His Public

Discussions about the reception of ethnographic work and writing are not numerous in anthropological literature (but see, e.g., the collection edited by Brettell 1993), and are practically nonexistent in Croatian ethnology. However, in European ethnologies that deal with their respective societies, the reception of ethnographic texts—primarily by the group researched, but also by society at large—becomes a significant issue. There seems to be a crucial reason why this is so: writing about Others proximate in several respects (geographically, socially, culturally, etc.) European ethnologists publish in the language they share with the researched group and the general public (cf. Čapo Žmegač, Gulin Zrnić, and Šantek 2006). There is yet another reason why a discussion of its reception is important for the present study: it is the result of a collaborative constitution of the research topic between the researcher and the subjects of the research, whom, while writing, I have had in mind as its most interested readers. Therefore, this epilogue is dedicated to the reflexivity of the other pole of the ethnographic cooperative enterprise—to those who were first given the role of co-creators in my fieldwork, and who later became the readers and evaluators of my ethnographic products.

Reflexivity in ethnology/anthropology implies, among others, that the production of knowledge has consequences, which are neither neutral nor necessarily desirable (Hammersley and Atkinson 1995: 16–17). I am especially interested in the consequences that the ethnological production of knowledge might have on the researched group. Assuming that our work—by which I mean the choice of a research topic, the research itself, and the publications about it—is neither socially nor politically neutral, I further ask what the impact is of ethnological research and writing on the relationship that an ethnologist establishes with the subjects of her/his research (during and after the fieldwork and publication of results), with her/his society, and her/his academic community. My research and writing on the coethnic migration of the Srijem Croats will be the basis for this inquiry into the ethical dilemmas and concrete decisions I had to make as a practitioner of "anthropology at home" (Jackson 1987). My dilemmas were made even more acute because of the fact that I was dealing with a topic in which both the actors and the society were passionately involved, and the entire situation was potentially saturated with political meanings.

Having embarked on this research, one of the first decisions I had to make was whether or not to take the standpoint of the research subjects in my publications and public presentations.

To Take the Standpoint of the Research Subjects or Not?

The ways in which ethnologists and anthropologists undertake research, whether they have studied geographically distant or proximate worlds related to research situations linked to politically sensitive topics, are different. Croatian ethnologists who have written about the 1991 to 1995 War disclosed that they were not neutral observers of everyday life, but politically and humanly engaged intellectuals who had adopted the standpoint of the historical events of their anthropological subjects (Čale Feldman 1995; Povrzanović 1993, 1995, 2000; Rihtman-Auguštin 2004).

It was sometimes difficult or even impossible for researchers of distant social spaces, who were confronted with a war or worked in situations that were extreme in some other way, not to take the position of the subjects of their research. Scheper-Hughes (1995) is one of the most vociferous advocates of a politically committed and morally engaged anthropological study in extreme situations. When he found himself in the midst of events that shattered the Chinese state and its citizens in the 1980s, Frank N. Pieke, an anthropologist, decided to adopt the perspective of those with whom he gathered his experience: "I cannot but write from the perspective of the people with whom I experienced it" (Pieke 1995: 78). In the conflict between the Chinese regime and the students, he chose the side of the latter. Without pretending to take an omniscient position, he chose the perspective that was dictated by his situation. From being an observer he became a participant: "I was no longer an observer. The catastrophe that was about to happen changed me into a participant. Although undeniably a foreigner, the threat of violence from a common enemy made me part of the people I had come to understand and respect during my seven months of fieldwork" (Ibid., 72).

It has not been unusual for anthropologists who have done research during a major crisis or conflict situation to take the stand of the research subjects. According to Antonius Robben's (1995: 83) somewhat ironic dictum, those anthropologists were "engrossed in ethnographic seduction." Christian Giordano goes so far as to argue (1998: 36) that ethnologists tend to study collective entities for which they feel a certain emotional involvement, such as the poor, the weak, the dominated, the exploited, the marginalized (women, homosexuals) etc., whom they end up presenting as "innocent victims." According to the same author, this tendency among ethnologists to study defavored social actors leads to the neglect of the "'unpleasant,' if not outright 'repugnant' part of society" (Ibid.). Questioning the "sense of justice" and the wish of the anthropologist to give a voice to social victims rather than to those empowered or to social manipulators, and, simultaneously, to reject the principles of empathy, dialogue, and polyphony in ethnographic research and writing, Giordano stated: "I can describe those I don't like better than those I do."

Robben (1995) studied contested historical reconstruction of the political violence of Argentina in the 1970s. Analyzing adversary interpretations of various participants in the events, the anthropologist discovered, to his surprise, that he was "seduced by bad guys" no less than by victims—the "bad guys" being generals indicted for ordering the disappearance of Argentine citizens. This experience has led him to warn ethnologists against "ethnographic seduction":

> The ethnographic seduction trades our critical stance as observers for an illusion of congeniality with cultural insiders. [footnote omitted] We no longer seek to grasp the native's point of view, but we believe, at least for the duration of the meeting, that we have become natives ourselves. We have become so enwrapped in the ethnographic encounter that we are led astray from our research objectives. . . . (Robben 1995: 85)

In my research into the forced migration of Srijem Croats and their integration in Croatian society, I was confronted with a dilemma on whether or not to commit myself to my interlocutors, and aware of the consequences that taking up one or the other stand might have for the research and writing. My dilemmas revolved around accountabilities, obligations, and loyalties held by the researcher—on the one hand, toward the milieu of research; on the other, toward the academic community to which s/he belongs and toward the (changing) canons of the discipline;

and, from a third aspect, toward the broader social community in which the anthropologist lives (which is shared with the research subjects). Not only were those accountabilities manifold, but they were also in conflict: the answerability toward the researched group could bring into question the obligation that a researcher has toward the academic community (which assesses the validity of her/his writing), and the obligation of the researcher as citizen toward her/his society. Depending on the position taken by the researcher, s/he gives precedence to one of the accountabilities. Namely, the choice of the role of an advocate or that of an analyst (cf. Ginsburg 1992: 137) of the research subjects defines in different ways the anthropologist's relations with the subjects, as well as the reception of research results. In this research, I have not decided to "lend" my voice to the research subjects, but have opted rather for the role of an ethnologist-analyst who has her own standpoint, which does not necessarily correspond to that, or, more precisely, to those of my interlocutors. In Scheper-Hughes's words (1995), then, I was a spectator (observer), and not a witness (cf. also Rihtman-Auguštin 2004).

Having decided to do this research, I did not anticipate that it would force me to reflect on its social and political implications, on the consequences that the publication of my writings might have for the researched group (both the migrants and the local population) and my future relations with them, and, last but not least, for myself. It became clear that reflexivity will be an uncontournable and important part of the research process at the very beginning of the fieldwork, when a group of the better educated migrants with leading positions in the migrant association wanted to assign me the role of their advocate, as an agent of sorts for their case. They tried to entrust me with this role due to two factors. First, I was myself a Croat, which for them was very important for they were forced to leave Srijem because they were Croats. Moreover, at the time of research, public opinion blamed the Serbs for starting the war and instigating their migration. Second, I am a close relative of a prominent migrant. These two characteristics would have made me a perfect defender of their cause, a mediator who would be able to transmit to the public both their victimization and their requests. Can there be a better situation than to have a spokesperson who is outside the group that s/he represents, while s/he enjoys the group's trust? Seen from the outside, it was precisely the fact of externality with regard to the subjects of research that would give credibility and persuasiveness to the anthropologist's discourse. Some migrants thus expected that my writings about them would serve to legitimate the evolving narration about the forced migration from Srijem and the victimization of the Srijem Croats. They went a step further, and warned me that they wanted to control what my collaborators[1] would publish in their texts.

It seems to me today that those unexpected requests on the part of the researched group have led me to devote rather extensive attention in the later phases of the research process to my relationship toward the research subjects and to the reflection about the reception of my writings. This was further prompted by the realization during the writing process that I wanted to keep the distance from the research subjects, no matter how deeply I sympathized with them during the fieldwork itself.

The fact that I assumed the role of an analyst was contrary to the expectations of some of the migrants. This option, therefore, implied several ethical dilemmas. Have I not in a certain way "betrayed" the trust of those who have confided in me their life stories?[2] In what ways will my choice impact the reactions of my interlocutors to my writings? After the publication of my research, would I be able to return among them, without feeling uneasy? Would I be able to explain my standpoint to them and continue my research in the same locality?

The question of accountability toward the researched group was made more complex when I realized that the gathered material contains information about conflicts between the migrant and local population. I feared that the publication of that material might have negative consequences for their already tense relations. The complexity of the entire problem was enhanced by the highly politicized nature of the research topic and its direct involvement with the social and political context in Croatia in the second half of the 1990s. The political and societal institutions of power of the period demanded (or even imposed) a certain image of a homogenous and unitary Croatian nation. As the research progressed, it became clear that the results of the research were not in tune with the propagated image of a unitary and non-conflictual society. I was worried that the publication of their statements might harm the researched group and negatively impact their public reputation. Because the research was for the larger part funded by state institutions,[3] and its results were not in tune with their discourse, I also discerned possible difficulties for myself. Finally, in the process of research and the writing of my findings, I have also started to reflect on the third type of audience—the academic one. The accountability that I primarily felt toward the research subjects, in the sense that I wanted to avoid possible harmful effects of this research for them, defined the ways in which I presented and restituted the research.

Reactions to the Restitution of the Research

The most general meaning of "restitution" as "a giving back to the rightful owner of something that has been lost or taken away; restoration" (Webster's New World Dictionary 1984: 1212) best depicts the concept of restitution that I want to use in this text. In ethnological/anthropological research, restitution of our research implies submitting our interpretations to the inspection of the people who participated in the research and to society at large. Françoise Zonabend, a French ethnologist, defines restitution as an *a posteriori* control of research. For her, restitution is the acquaintance with the impact that our observations and analyses have on the researched group, to whom this objectification of themselves is directed (Zonabend 1994: 4).

Reactions from my interlocutors to the Croatian edition of my book (Čapo Žmegač 2002b) devoted to their forced migration from Srijem and settlement in Croatia were quite different. Some have referred to it with praise, some with criticism. However, I have not studied their reactions systematically. The examples that follow were obtained as feedback during the presentation of the book in Virovitica on 26 May 2003, in individual conversations with some research subjects on this and on other occasions, and from a letter that was sent to me after the book was published. The subjects of the research who have approved of the book were satisfied with the way I depicted events in which they had taken part and how I recounted the interviews that we had had. My favorite is the praise voiced by a migrant from Srijem, a prominent migrant leader and a poet, that I "have written the best book about the Srijem settlers so far," and that, therefore, it would be superfluous for him to write one himself. Some were particularly impressed when they recognized their own statements, which I had quoted in even larger portions than in the English edition.

Such was the reaction of my close relative, himself a migrant, to whom I had given the manuscript before publication. He bore several important roles in this research: himself an interlocutor, but also my host in the locality of research; a mediator in the first toddling steps taken in the fieldwork. He was in a way the gatekeeper. To my great surprise, he reacted succinctly and clearly to the text about discursive strategies of identification (see chapter 5): "That's it. Everything is exact!" It seemed to me that he did not quite understand the analytical part of the chapter, in which perceived differences were treated as discursive strategies of identification. His reaction to another text (see chapter 6) was reserved: "Now, I do understand, this is how you want it, objectively.

You don't want to show it the way we do." A long explanation of his own viewpoint followed this statement, though it was already incorporated in the text. To me, his restraint actually meant acknowledgment of my work: it seemed to me that his comment acknowledged that I had succeeded in my intention to present various opinions and still give my own interpretation. The third text (chapter 7) had a similar destiny: my relative understood that my role was different from the one that the migrants wanted to assign me, but he was not offended by my refusal to assume it.

By exposing the manuscripts to the research subjects (even if only to individuals), I aimed to elicit possible reactions from them. The result was encouraging: my interpretations, expressed in the technical language of ethnic and identity studies, seemed not to have offended (at least) one of my interlocutors. However, the idea that I had still disappointed my relative, as well as many other settlers, because I adopted the position of the observer and analyst, did not disappear completely and cast a shadow over the relief brought about by his reactions.

Disappointed or perhaps unsatisfied readers were present at the presentation of the Croatian edition of the book in Virovitica, when a prominent migrant leader, himself one of research subjects, was invited to address the audience as a part of the book presentation, and asserted, that due to "scientific authority" and the "generation gap," I had given "an objective and distanced view" in the book. Therefore, as a "witness" of the events, he felt a need to complement it. This judgment served as a preamble to his long testimony in which he criticized Serbian politics and the year long preparation of the exodus of the Croats from Srijem. He also took a look back at the dynamics of interactions between the migrants and the locals in the new Croatian environment—from very good relations at the beginning, they went through a phase of "friction," and ended up in a "satisfactory state" twelve years after settlement.[4] The man finished his exposé with optimism, announcing that there would be many more books on the same topic, some academic, but also "other ones."

It is rather clear from this man's statement that he was not satisfied with my interpretation of the events. He criticized my "scientific objectivity," and, in opposition to my ostensible "view from a distance," he put forward his testimony, by which he gave the latter a higher epistemological status.

I could not witness the migration from Srijem and settlement in Croatia because I started the research five to six years after those constitutive events took place in the recent history of the Srijem Croats. Besides, as already mentioned, I assumed the position of an observer and analyst in this research, which, however, did not exclude recording emic perspectives. The presentation of subjects' accounts in the book is organized in such a way that the subjects themselves bear witness to the migration and the events following settlement. Although my interpretation runs through all the chapters, offering—as in any anthropological interpretation—a highly subjective and partial record of the subjects' lives (cf. Scheper-Hughes 1995), I did not leave the subjects voiceless. On the contrary, their voices dominate, sometimes "uncontrolled" by my comments and interpretations (compare chapters 2 and 5). I have given the research subjects a special place in the book—the place that belongs to them—because they led me into the basic themes of the research. It is based on their statements that I constructed my own interpretations (the process of which is always selective). By the chosen textual strategies, I also wanted to show empathy with my interlocutors and to enable their voices to be directly heard.[5]

The basic misunderstanding between myself and the critical migrant quoted above can be accounted for by the epistemological standpoint that I had taken, which is that truth cannot be declined in the singular. At this point, it is important to mention that it is precisely this migrant and his friends who wanted to assign to me the role of their advocate. This was done in an effort to build into my text one view—their own—of the events. However, I did not think that there was only one truth, for example, about the reasons for and circumstances of leaving Srijem (see chapter 4), nor about the differences between the area of origin and the area of settlement (see chapter 5).

I have treated all that was regarded as *the* truth about the migration and settlement by my interlocutors as their personal truths, even as a discourse, by which they tried to organize the memory of emigration, constructed the story on exile, and laid the foundations of their new identity. The assertion that "[i]nformants think in terms of truth, we do not" (Robben 1995: 96), to which one should add that they think their particular truth is the right one, has been confirmed by this research. The research subjects expect our texts to transcribe the truth, precisely the truth that they think they have conveyed to us during research (Zonabend 1994: 9). In this research into the integration of the Srijem settlers in Croatian society, truths have necessarily been plural and heterogenous. This is the reason for which personal truths or different viewpoints have been given so much space in the book, in direct and sometimes contesting quotes. But that was not a reason for me to abstain from giving my own interpretation of the events, my own partial and fragmentary truth, based on conversations with different persons, selected on the ground of their statements, the truth that to me seemed acceptable from an analytical, etic standpoint.

Another man, an inhabitant in the locality of research, but not my interlocutor during the research period, who legitimized himself with an almost quarter century of knowledge of local circumstances, reacted rather sharply in a letter he sent to me after the publication of the Croatian edition of the book. He took my interpretation to be literally *the* truth and thought I had given precedence to some truths over others. He did not understand that each interpretation is a certain construction of the researcher's "truth," which to her/him seems to be the most persuasive and the most logical explanation of what s/he has seen, experienced, and learnt in interactions with the researched group. By extensively mentioning details of local migration history, this local critic has unintentionally confirmed my basic hypothesis that each newcomer population goes through a shorter or longer period of friction, and possibly conflict, with the locally established population. This is due to an effort by the established to preserve their positions and social hierarchy and a converse endeavor on the part of the newcomers to become a part of the existing social structure. Since that critic did not understand my epistemological foundation, he reacted in a habitual way (cf. Zonabend 1994: 10), venturing the opinion that "my study would have been more complete," and the "conclusions different," had I mentioned the data of which he disposed.

What this man considers to be "data" are actually the interpretations he reads into them, for:

> Culture is interpretation. The "facts" of anthropology, the material which the anthropologist has gone to the field to find, are already themselves interpretations. The baseline data is already culturally mediated by the people whose culture we, as anthropologists, have come to explore. Facts are made—the word comes from the Latin factum, "made"—and the facts we interpret are made and remade. Therefore they cannot be collected as if they were rocks, picked up and put into cartons and shipped home to be analyzed in the laboratory (Rabinow 1977: 150).

"Data" can be interpreted in many ways by both anthropologists and the research subjects. Therefore, there is no privileged position nor absolute perspective in anthropological research, while ethnographic fieldwork is the intersubjective construction of knowledge in an encounter between the researcher and the research subjects (Ibid., 154ff.). This book is precisely such an attempt at interpreting a specific social situation.

Further Unwanted Consequences of Restitution

Thus far, I have presented the reactions of the research subjects to my writing. I envisaged other consequences that might appear after the research was published.

For example, I had misgivings regarding the publication of the migrants' perceptions of the locals and of the local standard of life (see chapter 5), for they did not, to use a euphemism, speak in flattering terms about their new neighbors. Although the reality of perceived differences was not decisive in my analysis, and although the function of perceived differences was to attribute Otherness to the locals and superiority to the migrants, I delayed the publication of this material, fearing that it might cause additional problems between the migrants and the locals. In the end, this material was published in a partly censored form.

Another difficulty lay in the circumstance that my data largely expressed the viewpoints of the migrants, and less those of the locals, who were reluctant to speak about the newcomers. The somewhat limited participation of the locals might be explained by the fact that a migrant had introduced me to the village and that I had therefore started the research by talking to migrants. This might have caused caution among the locals. Sometimes they refused to meet me, sometimes they were not willing to discuss their relations with the migrants, or they expressed the "official" view about good relations between the two groups.[6]

I also considered the possible consequences that the restitution of the research might have in society at large, particularly since the topic of the research was politicized and the research was taking place during the highly politicized time of the late 1990s. This was a moment in which those in power emphasized national unity and proclaimed the homogeneity of national identity, assessing that the recognition of any internal differentiation within the Croatian nation would lead to the weakening and division of the nation, which was not sufficiently integrated and had barely emerged from the war. At the same time, the results of this research were "dividing" the Croatian society according to the cultural and ethnic lines drawn by my interlocutors. While local and central centers of power were supporting the rhetoric of national unity, the demonstration that social integration of coethnic migrants according to the formula of a unified nation was not self-evident and was problematic, could have been interpreted as unacceptable, even as a critique of national ideology, which made me sensitive to the restitution of my research, not only locally—in the locality of research—but also in society at large.

In the research, I also came across an unpleasant topic to those in power. I am referring here to the "Act on Temporary Take-over and Administration of Certain Property," by which the state intended to reallocate the property of the Serbs who had left Croatia to the administration by various categories of the Croatian population (see chapter 6). In order to obtain a better picture of that failed project, I contacted a government official in charge of its implementation, but he refused to cooperate. It is clear that at the time of my inquiry—1998, which was also the year of the revocation of the Act due to international pressure—the official evaded engaging himself in a conversation on a politically awkward topic. However, I decided to refer to this in one of my texts, although such a decision could have had an inconvenient effect on the migrants, because, by disclosing the plan of resettlement of liberated territories, I was revealing an attempt on the part of the migrants to take part in a then legal but morally questionable endeavor,[7] to become administrators of the property of exiled Serbs. I presumed that this revelation could contribute to negative evaluation of migrants in the public eye. In this particular aspect of the research, it was therefore necessary to protect the people studied and to not harm them by exposing them to public scrutiny. Having addressed a politically awkward topic, I wondered whether I also needed protection (cf. Robben and Nordstrom 1995: 4). To protect the research subjects this incident was described in a longer text, in which the contested plan of resettlement and the dilemmas that it provoked did not come to the fore (see chapter 6). Having chosen an observer position, I attempted to present and not to judge the behavior and attitudes of the people and institutions involved, by which I have unintentionally protected myself.

My unease concerning the publication of the research results about this and other topics proved to be unfounded. Neither did my texts negatively influence the image of migrants in the public, nor did they, as far as I know, negatively impact the relations between the migrants and the locals in the area of resettlement, nor were there any echoes to my analyses in the non-academic audience.

How to Protect the Research Subjects

In order to reduce the possible difficulties that I assumed could eventuate from the restitution of my analyses in public, I developed a number of strategies. I have already mentioned one way by which I tried to protect the research subjects from harmful effects of the publication of the materials: possibly harmful parts of the analysis are incorporated into a much larger and different topic, and therefore rather unnoticeable. Postponing the publication was a strategy used at the beginning of the research. When I decided to publish, an important strategy employed—a strategy that is well known in anthropological literature—was the concealment of the identity of individual subjects.[8]

At a certain phase of the research, I took part at several international conferences where I presented the research. Presenting and publishing in foreign languages has opened up the possibilities of exposing materials and interpretations with less concern over whether the data will harm the people in the locality of research or whether they will be satisfied with my interpretion and the way I have presented them.

Potential difficulties linked to the restitution of research are quite different for an anthropologist who is an outsider in the society being researched. This is true even in a case when an anthropologist, such as Peter Loizos, while coming from the outside, can trace his roots in that society. In spite of his Greek origin, that British anthropologist who studied in Cyprus is only a visitor in the village of research. He lives in another country and he writes in a language which is generally unknown to his Greek interlocutors (Loizos 1994). However, the situation of an ethnologist who lives in the same society as her/his subjects, and shares their language—her/his main means of expression—is more vulnerable, especially when the research topic is contemporary and imbued with political implications or the probing of human intimacy. S/he must be ready to confront the consequences her/his publications might have for her/him and the research subjects. In distinction to Loizos (1994), I—or any other researcher at home—cannot simply leave my country only to return to it ten years after the research has been carried out, as was done by Loizos, because my country is my fieldwork location. My presence in the society of research is permanent and I cannot divide my identities between two localities and two states (Okely 1996: 26).

Writing in a foreign language, however, opens up a new aspect of restitution to which I want to bring the reader's attention. Even if we disregard the power relations in the international academic community (cf. Rihtman-Auguštin 2004), the question remains as to whether we can successfully present our research to colleagues who come from different ethnological/anthropological traditions. In spite of a growing number of encounters among scholars, understanding within the international academic community is not guaranteed. An example related to the research presented here confirms this argument. After having presented to her my research project on the integration of coethnic migrants, a

French sociologist, Brigitte Fichet, (1996) commented that it was "an interesting and actual [project] for Croatia, but was entirely foreign to a French reader, because, in distinction from the Anglo-Saxon mindset, the French reader was not used to speaking in terms of ethnic groups. Only recently has the usage of this term been spreading among the public and in scholarly literature" (translated from French by the author). Different disciplinary traditions and societal demands and expectations, homonymous concepts with unexpected semantic differences in various languages, and implicit ideologies and differential positioning of actors sometimes make international ethnological/anthropological dialogue rather difficult. When translating her/his texts into a foreign language, an ethnologist must choose her/his terms and expressions very carefully. S/he must adapt her/his writing to professional rules and the history of the discipline in the country of the language chosen (especially when it is a matter of a linguistically closed academic community, which to a large extent relies on the literature in its own language). An ethnologist does this so that colleagues in other countries will not take her/him for a simple native without professional qualifications (cf. Povrzanovi 1995, 2000), so that her/his objectivity and conclusions will not be questioned and the credibility of her/his interpretations discredited.

Writing and publishing in foreign languages, however, can be only one of the possibilities by which an anthropologist at home attempts to evade harmful effects for her/his research subjects, or, as in Loizos's case, for the relationship between the researcher and the researched group. Another more frequent strategy for an ethnologist aware of the accountability toward the researched group, when publishing in the country of research, is the censorship of the gathered material.

In the End:
The Distinct Position of an Ethnologist at Home

An ethnologist has the right and duty to offer her/his own vision of the society studied. That particular vision might cause misunderstanding with the research subjects (and, as shown here, it does). Caution with regard to restitution is part of a new relationship of the contemporary researcher with regard to the research at home, especially when one studies politically implicated topics in a conflict-ridden or authoritarian political situation. When a Croatian ethnologist no longer does research into folklore and neutral, depersonalized topics of the so-called material culture, when s/he does not do research into peasants in the past but into her/his contemporaries, describing their strategies and secrets, when s/he includes the state and various social manipulators in the project, when s/he studies the war and its consequences for various social strata, and the debates revolving around the definition of national identity, etc., her/his research problems are distinct from those encountered by ethnologists/anthropologists of distant worlds, distant both in the sense of space and time. That ethnologist is here, does research now, and writes here and now. When people with whom an ethnologist shares the wider social arena are encompassed by the research, which deals, for example, with their choices, ideas, and political activities, they will closely monitor the ethnologist's research and judge it, without perhaps understanding it in its entirety.

Five years ago when a first version of this reflexion was written[9] and the book was not yet written, I was inclined to pay much attention to the restitution and obligations that it brings about with regard to the subjects of research and the society in general.[10] Today, with a distance from the research and from the period in which it was conducted, it seems to me that I thought along those lines because of the exceedingly sensitive political and social context of Croatia in the 1990s, a context in which all relations were strained and standpoints constantly polarized, with all events, including those connected with ethnological work, charged with high emotional intensity. It was difficult in such a context to avoid tensions being inscribed in all phases of ethnological study. In other words, ethnological work did not merely consist of a scholarly contribution, but was also a direct political contribution (cf. Rihtman-Auguštin 2004), exposed to value judgments, pressures and attacks from all sides, with the ethnologist seeking her/his autonomy and place in their midst. That research context, undermined by political events, brought me face-to-face with unease and dilemmas, mostly with regard to possible harm to the research subjects, and to a lesser extent, to the researcher.

Today, I am more inclined to think that concern about restitution of one's own research is not self-explanatory. After the reaction to my writings, I am no longer convinced that ethnologists have to restitute their research primarily to the groups they research. On the one hand, restitution unavoidably leads to misunderstandings for the very reason that the type of objectification we practice is either incomprehensible or unacceptable to the research subjects, or because they reject it in favor of their own truths. On the other hand, we often overestimate our influence on society and the consequences that our scholarly texts can have upon it (and upon ourselves). This seems to be especially true in Croatia where ethnology is a marginal discipline. The ethnologist can rely on the comforting thought that the social marginality of her/his discipline will enable her/his publications to remain more or less unnoticed. For these reasons, today I would say that the ethnologist is primarily accountable to the (changeable) standards of her/his discipline and to her/himself. However, reflecting on restitution remains important in one sphere: ethnologists should not in any way do harm in their writings to their research subjects. For its part, that can mean that the ethnologist sometimes cannot speak of everything that s/he has seen or heard.

Notes

1. Aleksandra Muraj and Jadranka Grbić from the Institute of Ethnology and Folklore Research in Zagreb participated in the fieldwork research and each subsequently published an essay (Muraj 2002; Grbić 2002).
2. In any case, these were people who did not ask to be the subject matter of research and did not fully understand what I was actually aiming at in this research. Several younger migrants suggested that I talk to their parents, who would ostensibly be able to tell me much better than they, how they lived before their exile. They thought that I had interest primarily in the "traditional way of life" in Srijem. Somewhat mistrustful about my questions, another migrant inquired about my research topic several times. Finally, he suggested that I was a "sociologist of the contemporary moment" of sorts. After having placed me into a familiar category, he finally became more open toward my research. This testifies to an inability of research subjects in Croatia to recognize ethnology as a discipline that studies everyday life of our contemporaries. They still mainly recognize it as a study of the peasant way of life in the past. This tendency to misidentify ethnology might be even more pronounced now than fifteen years ago, when Lydia Sklevicky diagnosed the unrecognizability of ethnologists and their discipline within wider society (Sklevicky 1991).
3. The Croatian Ministry of Science and Technology was the main sponsor of my research. The Open Society Institute Croatia supported it in a very small percentage.
4. Having come to the locality of research several years after the settlement, I could not observe and study the first allegedly friendly phase in the relationship between the locals and the migrants.
5. This was also a means to avoid the reduction of the complexity of individual human experiences into impenetrable anthropological prose. Long quotations had the specificity of being written in the language of everyday life, which I wanted to preserve, particularly in the book, in the vein of fieldwork-based writing (cf. Abu-Lughod 1991: 151ff.). This, so I thought, would make it more accessible to the people that I purported to represent.
6. Hesitation of the locals to engage in research might testify to their strained or at least ambivalent stance toward newcomers. However, it might also be, at least in part, an artefact of the method of research, which was a compromise between a long-term immersion into the life of the locality of research, and occasional—shorter but more frequent—stays in the locality.

7. Indeed, some migrants have distanced themselves from the project, considering that it was unacceptable to settle in somebody else's house and to make use of somebody else's property (see chapter 6).

8. Actually anonymity is false, for if the text is given to the subjects of research they are bound to recognise themselves and their neighbors. As far as I know, this strategy, together with the concealment of the name of the research locality, was inagurated in Croatian ethnology in the 1980s, but it did not have a lasting impact on my colleagues, who, for the most part, continue to append the list of informants to their texts.

9. The text is drawn from my article "Faire de l'ethnologie en Croatie dans les années quatre-vingt-dix" (Čapo Žmegač 2001b). It has been significantly updated and expanded.

10. That is precisely why, in order to make my writing accessible to the subjects, I have weaved so many direct statements into the book.

Bibliography

Abu-Lughod, Lila. 1991. "Writing against Culture." In *Recapturing Anthropology. Working in the Present,* ed. Richard G. Fox. Santa Fe, New Mexico: School of American Research Press.

Aktar, Ayhan T. 1998. "Homogenizing the Nation, Turkifying the Economy: Turkish Experience of Population Exchange Reconsidered." Paper presented at the conference *The Compulsory Exchange of Populations between Greece and Turkey: Assessment of the Consequences of the Treaty of Lausanne 1923 Turko-Greek Exchange, 75th Anniversary* of the Refugee Studies Programme, University of Oxford at Wadham College, 17–20 September 1998.

Althabe, Gérard. 1996. "Construction de l'étranger dans la France urbaine d'aujourd'hui." In *L'Europe entre cultures et nations,* ed. Daniel Fabre. Paris: Editions de la Maison des sciences de l'homme.

Attias-Donfut, Claudine, and Martine Segalen. 1998. *Grands-parents. La famille à travers les générations.* Paris: Editions Odile Jacob.

Barth, Fredrik. 1969. *Ethnic groups and boundaries: the social organization of culture difference.* Boston: Little, Brown.

Baumann, Gerd. 1996. *Contesting culture. Discourses of identity in multi-ethnic London.* Cambridge: Cambridge University Press.

Bausinger, Hermann. 1988. "Name und Stereotyp." In *Stereotypvorstellungen im Alltagsleben. Beiträge zum Themenkreis Fremdbilder—Selbstbilder—Identität.* Festschrift für Georg R. Schroubek zum 65. Geburtstag, ed. Helge Gerndt. München: Münchner Vereinigung für Volkskunde.

Baussant, Michèle. 1998. "Territoires 'pieds-noirs,' ou de l'Algérie à la France, le pèlerinage à Notre-Dame-du-Salut." In *Le Voyage inachevé. . . à Joël Bonnemaison,* ed. Dominique Guillaud et al. Paris: Editions de l'Orstom, Prodig.

———. 1999. "Paradis perdus: la France et l'Algérie à travers le mariage des Européens catholiques d'Algérie." Vol 1 of *Les territoires de l'identité de Joël Bonnemaison. Le territoire, lien ou frontière?,* ed. Luc Cambrézy and Laurence Quinty-Bourgeois. Paris: L'Harmattan.

———. 2000. "Récit d'un pèlerin néophyte. Autour de la description du quartier du Mas-de-Mingue, à Nîmes, et de son sanctuaire." *Atelier* 19: 145–156.

————. 2002. *Pieds-noirs. Memoires d'exil.* Paris: Stock.

Benz, Wolfgang. 1992. "Fremde in der Heimat: Flucht-Vertreibung-Integration." In *Deutsche im Ausland—Fremde in Deutschland: Migration in Geschichte und Gegenwart,* ed. K. Bade. München: Beck.

Bernardi, Bernardo. 1994. "Il fattore etnico: dall'etnia all'etnocentrismo." *Ossimori. Periodico di antropologia e scienze umane* 4: 13–20.

Bičanić, Milan. 1994. *Srijem—krvavo krilo Hrvatske. Dokumenti i svjedočenja.* Zagreb: Mladost.

————. 1999. *Srijem—krvavo krilo Hrvatske. Dokumenti i svjedočenja.* 2nd ed. Osijek: Kelemen.

Bilefeld, Ulrih (Bielefeld, Urlich). 1998. *Stranci: prijatelji ili neprijatelji.* Beograd: Biblioteka XX. vek.

Blok, Anton. 2000. "Relatives and Rivals: The Narcissism of Minor Differences." In *Perplexities of Identification. Anthropological Studies in Cultural Differentiation and the Use of Resources,* ed. Henk Driessen and Ton Otto. Aarhus: Aarhus University Press.

Bonifačić, Ruža. 1995. "Changing of Symbols: the Folk Instrument *Tamburica* as a Political and Cultural Phenomenon." *Collegium Antropologicum* 19, no. 1: 65–77.

————. 1998. "Regional and National Aspects of Tamburica Tradition: The Case of the Zlatni Dukati Neotraditional Ensemble." In *Music, Politics, and War. Views from Croatia,* ed. Svanibor Pettan. Zagreb: Institute of Ethnology and Folklore Research.

Bourdieu, Pierre et al. 2002. "Eine sichere Geldanlage für die Familie. Das Einfamilienhaus: Produktspezifik und Logik des Produktionsfeldes." In *Der Einzige und sein Eigenheim,* Pierre Bourdieu et al. Hamburg: VSA-Verlag.

Brettell, Caroline B., ed. 1993. *When they read what we write: the politics of ethnography.* Westport, CT.-London: Bergin & Garvey.

Brubaker, Rogers. 1995. "Aftermaths of Empire and the unmixing of peoples: historical and comparative perspectives." *Ethnic and Racial Studies* 18, no. 2: 189–215.

————. 1998. "Migrations of Ethnic Unmixing in the 'New Europe.'" *International Migration Review* 32, no. 4: 1047–1065.

Camilleri, Carmel. 1998. "Les stratégies identitaires des immigrés." In *L'identité. L'individu, le groupe, la société.* Auxerre: Éditions Sciences humaines.

Cashmore, Ellis. 1996. "Prejudice." In *Dictionary of Race and Ethnic Relations,* Ellis Cashmore et al. London-New York: Routledge-Kegan Paul.

Clifford, James. 1983. "On Ethnographic Authority." *Representations* 1, no. 2: 118–146.

Cohen, Anthony. 1985. *The symbolic construction of community.* London-New York: Routledge.

Crkvenčić, Ivan, and Dragutin Feletar. 1986. "Neka obilježja suvremenih demografskih kretanja u općini Virovitica." In *Virovitički zbornik 1234–1984.* Virovitica: HAZU.

Čale Feldman, Lada. 1995. "Intellectual concerns and scholarly priorities. A voice of an ethnographer." *Narodna umjetnost. Croatian Journal of Ethnology and Folklore Research* 32, no. 1: 79–90.

Čale Feldman, Lada et al. 1993. *Fear, Death and Resistance. An Ethnography of War: Croatia 1991–1992.* Zagreb: Institute of Ethnology and Folklore Research-Matrix croatica-X-Press.

Čapo Žmegač, Jasna 1994. "Plaidoyer za istraživanje (nacionalnoga) identiteta u hrvatskoj etnologiji." *Etnološka tribina* 17: 7–23.

———. 1996. "Les migrants forcés en Croatie 1991–1995." *Cultures & Sociétés. Cahier du CEMRIC* 7: 103–110.

———. 1999. "'We are Croats. It is not our goal to be set apart from our own people.' A Failed Attempt at Firmer Incorporation of Croatian Migrants." *Ethnologia Balkanica, Journal for Southeast European Anthropology* 3: 121–139.

———. 2000a. "Between the Communities of Origin And Settlement: Three Adjustment Strategies Of Croatian Migrants In the 1990s." In *Roots & rituals. The construction of ethnic identities,* ed. Ton Dekker, John Helsloot, and Carla Wijers. Amsterdam: Het Spinhuis.

———. 2000b. "From Local to National Community: Peasant Social Structure." In *Croatian Folk Culture at the Crossroads of Worlds and Eras,* ed. Zorica Vitez and Aleksandra Muraj. Zagreb: Klovićevi dvori.

———. 2001a. "'Either we will behead the ox, or we will be no more!': the Croats between traditionalism and modernity." In *Proceedings 21st Symposium of the ICTM study group on ethnochoreology 2000 Korčula,* ed. Elsie I. Dunin and Tvrtko Zebec. Zagreb: ICTM and Institute of Ethnology and Folklore Research.

———. 2001b. "Faire de l'ethnologie en Croatie dans les années quatre-vingt-dix." *Ethnologie française* XXXI, no. 1: 41–50.

———. 2002a. "Constructing difference, identifying the self. A case of Croatian repatriates from Serbia." In *MESS—Mediterranean Ethnological Summer School* 4, ed. Bojan Baskar and Irena Weber. Ljubljana: Faculty of Arts.

———. 2002b. *Srijemski Hrvati. Etnološka studija migracije, identifikacije i interakcije.* Zagreb: Durieux.

———. 2005. "Ethnically privileged migrants in their new homeland." *Journal of Refugee Studies* 18, no. 2: 199–215.

Čapo Žmegač, Jasna, Valentina Gulin Zrnić and Goran Pavel Šantek. 2006. "Ethnology of the proximate: the poetics and politics of contemporary fieldwork." In *Etnologija bliskoga. Poetika i politika suvremenih terenskih istraživanja,* ed. Jasna Čapo Žmegač et al. Zagreb: Institut za etnologiju i folkloristiku and Jesenski i Turk.

Černelić, Milana. 1994. "Ethnic Changes in Voivodina in 20th Century with Special Reference to the Position of the Croats Bunjevci." In *Ethnocultural Processes in Central Europe in 20th Century.* Bratislava: Philosophical Faculty.

Deklaracija. 1995. *Zov Srijema* I: 9.

Dimković, Berislav J. 1977. "Socijalni položaj starih seljaka u Vojvodini." *Sociologija sela* 55–56: 62–69.

Duijzings, Ger. 1995. "Egzodus iz Letnice—hrvatske izbjeglice s Kosova u zapadnoj Slavoniji. Kronika." *Narodna umjetnost. The Croatian Journal of Ethnology and Folklore Research* 32, no. 2: 129–152.

———. 2000. *Religion and the Politics of Identity in Kosovo*. London: Hurst & Company.

Elias, N. and J. L. Scotson. 1965. *The established and the outsiders. A sociological enquiry into community problems*. London: Frank Cass & co. Ltd.

Enciklopedija hrvatske povijesti i kulture. 1980. Zagreb: Školska knjiga,

Enciklopedija Leksikografskog zavoda, vol. 1. 1955. Zagreb: Leksikografski zavod,

Enciklopedija Leksikografskog zavoda, vol. 7. 1964. Zagreb: Leksikografski zavod,

Eriksen, Thomas Hylland. 1993. *Ethnicity & Nationalism. Anthropological Perspectives*. London-Boulder, Colorado: Pluto Press.

Forbes, H.D. 1997. *Ethnic conflict. Commerce, culture and the contact hypothesis*. New Haven-London: Yale University Press.

Frykman, Jonas. 1999. "Belonging in Europe. Modern Identities in Minds and Places." *Ethnologia Europaea* 29, no. 2: 13–24.

Frykman, Jonas, and Orvar Löfgren. 1987. *Culture builders. A historical anthropology of a middle-class life*. New Brunswick-London: Rutgers University Press.

Frykman, Jonas, and Nils Gilje. 2003. "Being There: an Introduction." In *Being There: New Perspectives on Phenomenology and the Analysis of Culture*, ed. Jonas Frykman and Nils Gilje. Lund: Nordic Academic Press.

Fulbrook, Mary. 1996. "Germany for the Germans? Citizenship and nationality in a divided nation." In *Citizenship, Nationality and Migration in Europe*, ed. David Cesarani and Mary Fulbrook. London-New York: Routledge.

Galenić, Senka. 1997. "Odosmo k'o ljudi marljivi, pošteni." B.A. Thesis, Faculty of Philosophy University of Zagreb.

Gavazzi, Milovan. 1939. *Godina dana hrvatskih narodnih običaja*, vol. 2. Zagreb: Matica hrvatska.

Geertz, Clifford. 1983. "'From the native's point of view': On the Nature of Anthropological Understanding." In *The Pleasures of Anthropology*, ed. Morris Freilich. New York: A Mentor Book.

Gerndt, Helge. 1988. "Zur kulturwissenschaftlichen Stereotypenforschung. In *Stereotypvorstellungen im Alltagsleben. Beiträge zum Themenkreis Fremdbilder—Selbstbilder—Identität*. Festschrift für Georg R. Schroubek zum 65. Geburtstag, ed. Helge Gerndt. München: Münchner Vereinigung für Volkskunde.

Ginsburg, Faye. 1992. "Quand les indigènes sont nos voisins." *L'Homme* XXXII, no. 1: 129–142.

Giordano, Christian. 1998. "'I can Describe Those I Don't Like Better than Those I Do.' *Verstehen* as a Methodological Principle in Anthropology." *Anthropological Journal on European Cultures* 7, no. 1: 27–41.

Grbić, Jadranka. 1994. *Identitet, jezik, razvoj.* Zagreb: Institut za etnologiju i folkloristiku.

———. 1996. "Bosanski pluralitet i hrvatski identitet: Prolegomena istraživanju." *Bosna franciscana* 6: 10–19.

———. 1997. "Searching for the familiar, facing the foreign . . . Dimensions of Identity of the Croats from Bosnia-Herzegovina." *Narodna umjetnost. The Croatian Journal of Ethnology and Folklore Research* 34, no. 1: 7–23.

———. 2002. "Jezik i govor kao komponente i faktori identiteta." In *Srijemski Hrvati. Etnološka studija migracije, identifikacije i interakcije,* Jasna Čapo Žmegač. Zagreb: Durieux.

Hammersley, Martyn, and Paul Atkinson. 1995. *Ethnography. Principles in practice.* London-New York: Routledge.

Handelman, Don. 1977. "The organization of ethnicity." *Ethnic Groups* 1: 187–200.

Heleniak, Timothy. 1997. "Mass Migration in Post-Soviet Space." *The World Bank* August 1997: 15–17.

Hirschon, Renée. 1989. *Heirs of the Greek catastrophe. The social life of Asia Minor Refugees in Piraeus.* Oxford: Clarendon Press.

Jackson, Anthony, ed. 1987. *Anthropology at Home.* London: Tavistock Publications.

Hrvatski leksikon. vol 1. 1996. Zagreb: Naklada Leksikon d.o.o.

Jordi, Jean-Jacques. 1995. *1962: l'arrivée des Pieds-Noirs.* Paris: Autrement.

Jurić, Mato: "Zakon o privremenom preuzimanju i upravljanju određenom imovinom." 1995. *Zov Srijema* 1, no. 4: 7.

Kaschuba, Wolfgang. 1996. "Les Allemands, des étrangers les uns pour les autres." In *L'Europe entre cultures et nations,* ed. Daniel Fabre. Paris: Editions de la Maison des sciences de l'homme.

Kaufmann, Jean-Claude. 1996. *L'entretien compréhensif.* Paris: Nathan.

Klekowski, Amanda. 1999. "Who Organizes? The Political Opportunity Structure of Co-Ethnic Migrant Mobilization: Post-Cold War Jewish Immigrants to Israel and German Immigrants to Germany." Paper presented at the conference *Diasporas and ethnic migrants in 20th century Europe,* Berlin, 20–23 May 1999.

Kolar-Dimitrijević, Mira, and Filip Potrebica. 1994. "Na slavonsko-srijemskom razmeđu 1918–1945. godine." In *Vukovar—vjekovni hrvatski grad na Dunavu.* Zagreb: "Dr. Feletar."

Laušić, Ante. 1993. "Uzroci i posljedice agrarne reforme i kolonizacije 1945–1948." In *Zbornik Slavonija-Srijem-Baranja-Bačka,* ed. Ante Sekulić. Zagreb: Matica hrvatska.

Lipiansky, Edmond Marc. 1998. "Comment se forme l'identité des groupes." In *L'identité. L'individu, le groupe, la société.* Auxerre: Editions Sciences humaines.

Loizos, Peter. 1981. *The heart grown bitter. A chronicle of Cypriot war refugees.* Cambridge: Cambridge University Press.

————. 1994. "Confessions of a Vampire Anthropologist." *Anthropological Journal on European Cultures* 3, no. 2: 39–53.

————. 1999. "Ottoman Half-lives: Long-term Perspectives on Particular Forced Migrations." *Journal of Refugee Studies* 12, no. 3: 237–263.

Lončarević, Juraj. 1997. "Tisak i izdavačka djelatnost o Hrvatima u Srijemu nakon Drugog svjetskog rata." *Zov Srijema* 3, no. 15: 19.

Mach, Zdzisław. 1993. "Migration, Ethnic Identity, and the Significance of Territory." In *Symbols, Conflict and Identity. Essays in Political Anthropology*, Zdzisław Mach. Albany: State University of New York Press.

Malić, Adolf. 1986. "Osnovne osobine suvremenog razvoja agrara u općini Virovitica." In *Virovitički zbornik 1234–1984*. Virovitica: HAZU.

Marcus, George E., and Michael M.J. Fischer. 1986. *Anthropology as Cultural Critique. An Experimental Moment in the Human Sciences*. Chicago-London: University of Chicago Press.

Markowitz, Fran. 1994. "Responding to Events from Afar: Soviet Jewish Refugees Reassess Their Identity." In *Reconstructing Lives, Recapturing Meaning. Refugee Identity, Gender, and Culture Change*, ed. Linda A. Camino and Ruth M. Krulfeld. Basel: Gordon and Breach Publishers.

Maticka, Marijan. 1990. *Agrarna reforma i kolonizacija u Hrvatskoj 1945–1948*. Zagreb: Školska knjiga-Stvarnost.

McDonald, Maryon. 1993. "The Construction of Difference: An Anthropological Approach to Stereotypes." In *Inside European Identities: Ethnography in Western Europe*, ed. Sharon Macdonald. Oxford: Berg.

Morokvašić, Mirjana. 1993. *Krieg, Flucht und Vertreibung im ehemaligen Jugoslawien*. Berlin: Humboldt-Universität.

Muraj, Aleksandra. 2002. "Ekonomska djelatnost srijemskih Hrvata (stanje iz godine 1996)." In *Srijemski Hrvati. Etnološka studija migracije, identifikacije i interakcije*, Jasna Čapo Žmegač. Zagreb: Durieux.

Münz, Rainer, and Rainer Ohliger. 1997. *Deutsche Minderheiten in Ostmittel- und Osteuropa, Aussiedler in Deutschland. Eine Analyse ethnisch privilegierter Migration*, Demographie aktuell 9. Berlin: Humboldt-Universität zu Berlin.

Narayan, Kirin. 1993. "How native is a 'native' anthropologist?" *American Anthropologist* 95, no. 3: 671–686.

Nijemci u Hrvatskoj jučer i danas. Zbornik. 1994. Zagreb: Njemačka narodnosna zajednica.

Okely, Judith. 1996. "Fieldwork in the Home Countries: Double vision and dismantled identity." In *Own or Other Culture*, Judith Okely. London-New York: Routledge.

Otto, Ton, and Henk Driessen. 2000. "Protean Perplexities: An Introduction." In *Perplexities of Identification. Anthropological Studies in Cultural Differentiation and the Use of Resources*, ed. Henk Driessen and Ton Otto. Aarhus: Aarhus University Press.

Phillips, Scott K. 1994. "Natives and Incomers: the symbolism of belonging in Muker parish, north Yorkshire." In *Time, family and community:*

perspectives on family and community, ed. Michael Drake. London: Blackwell.

Pieke, Frank N. 1995. "Witnessing the 1989 Chinese People's Movement." In *Fieldwork under Fire. Contemporary Studies of Violence and Survival*, ed. Carolyn Nordstrom and Antonius C.G.M. Robben. Berkeley-Los Angeles-London, University of California Press.

Popis stanovništva, domaćinstava, stanova i poljoprivrednih gazdinstava 31. mart. 1991. Prvi rezultati. 1991. Statistički bilten 206. Novi Sad: Pokrajinski zavod za statistiku.

Popis stanovništva 1991. Narodnosni sastav stanovništva Hrvatske po naseljima. 1992. Zagreb: Republički zavod za statistiku.

Povrzanović, Maja. 1992. "Kultura i strah: o ratnoj svakodnevici." *Dometi* 25, no. 3–4: 73–93.

———. 1993. "Ethnography of a war: Croatia 1991–92." *The Anthropology of East Europe Review* 11, no. 1–2: 138–148.

———. 1995. "Crossing the Borders: Croatian War Ethnographies." *Narodna umjetnost. Croatian Journal of Ethnology and Folklore Research* 32, no. 1: 91–106.

———. 1997. "Identities in War, Embodiments of Violence and Places of Belonging." *Ethnologia Europaea* 27, no. 2: 153–162.

———. 2000. "The imposed and the imagined as encountered by Croatian war ethnographers." *Current Anthropology* 41, no. 2: 151–162.

Povrzanović, Maja, and Renata Jambrešić Kirin. 1996. "Negotiating Identities? The Voices of Refugees between Experience and Representation." In *War, Exile, Everyday Life. Cultural Perspectives,* ed. Renata Jambrešić Kirin and Maja Povrzanović. Zagreb: Institute of Ethnology and Folklore Research.

Rabinow, Paul. 1977. *Reflections on Fieldwork in Morocco.* Berkeley-Los Angeles-London: University of California Press.

Raphaël, Freddy, and Geneviève Herberich-Marx. 1999. "L'Etranger." In *Netzwerk Volkskunde: Ideen und Wege,* Festgabe für Klaus Beitl zum siebzigsten Geburtstag, ed. Franz Grieshofer and Margot Schindler. Wien: Verein für Volkskunde.

Remennick, Larissa. 2002. "Transnational community in the making: Russian-Jewish immigrants of the 1990s in Israel." *Journal of Ethnic and Migration Studies* 28, no. 3: 515–530.

———. 2003. "From Russian to Hebrew via *HebRush:* Intergenerational Patterns of Language Use among Former Soviet Immigrants in Israel." *Journal of multilingual and multicultural development* 24, no. 5: 431–453.

Rihtman-Auguštin, Dunja. 1970. "Tradicionalna kultura i suvremene vrijednosti." *Kulturni radnik* XXIII, no. 3: 26–45.

———. 1984. *Struktura tradicijskog mišljenja.* Zagreb: Školska knjiga.

———, ed. 1991. *Simboli identiteta.* Zagreb: Hrvatsko etnološko društvo.

———. 1994. "Ethnology Between Ethnic and National Identification." *Studia Ethnologica Croatica* 6: 151–156.

————. 1996. "Junaci i klijenti. Skica za istraživanje mentaliteta." *Erasmus* 16: 54–61.

————. 1997. "Zašto i otkad se grozimo Balkana." *Erasmus* 19: 27–35.

————. 2000. *Ulice moga grada.* Beograd: Biblioteka XX vek.

————. 2004. "The Ethno-Anthropologist in his Native Field: to Observe or to Witness?" In *Ethnology, Myth and Politics: Anthropologizing Croatian Ethnology,* Dunja Rihtman-Auguštin. Aldershot: Ashgate.

Ritig-Beljak, Nives. 1996. "Croatian Exiles from Vojvodina: Between War Memories and War Experience." In *War, Exile, Everyday Life. Cultural Perspectives,* ed. Renata Jambrešić Kirin and Maja Povrzanović. Zagreb: Institute of Ethnology and Folklore Research.

Robben, Antonius C.G.M. 1995. "The Politics of Truth and Emotion among Victims and Perpetrators of Violence." In *Fieldwork under Fire. Contemporary Studies of Violence and Survival,* ed. Carolyn Nordstrom and Antonius C.G.M. Robben. Berkeley-Los Angeles-London: University of California Press.

Robben, Antonius C.G.M., and Carolyn Nordstrom. 1995. "Introduction. The Anthropology and Ethnography of Violence and Sociopolitical Conflict." In *Fieldwork under Fire. Contemporary Studies of Violence and Survival,* ed. Carolyn Nordstrom and Antonius C.G.M. Robben. Berkeley-Los Angeles-London: University of California Press.

Römhild, Regina. 1994. "Staying or Leaving? Experiences and Expectations of the German Minority in the Former Soviet Union." *Anthropological Journal on European Cultures* 3, no. 1: 107–121.

————. 1999. "Home-Made Cleavages. Ethnonational Discourse, Diasporization, and the Politics of Germanness." *Anthropological Journal on European Cultures* 8, no. 1: 99–120.

Scheper-Hughes, Nancy. 1995. "The Primacy of Ethical. Propositions for a Militant Anthropology." *Current Anthropology* 36, no. 3: 409–420.

Scherer, Anton, and Manfred Straka. 1998. *Kratka povijest podunavskih Nijemaca/ Abriss zur Geschichte der Donauschwaben.* Osijek-Zagreb-Split-Graz-Stuttgart: Pan liber and Leopold Stocker Verlag.

Schnapper, Dominique. 1976. "Tradition culturelle et appartenance sociale: émigrés italiens et migrants français dans la région parisienne." *Revue française de sociologie* XVII: 485–498.

Schuladen, Hans. 1994. "Wieviel Vielfalt ertragen wir? Zur Pluralität der multikulturellen Gesellschaft." *Zeitschrift für Volkskunde* 90, no. 1: 37–58.

Siebers, Hans. 2000. "Thinking Together What Falls Apart: Some Reflections on the Concept of Identity." In *Perplexities of Identification. Anthropological Studies in Cultural Differentiation and the Use of Resources,* ed. Henk Driessen and Ton Otto. Aarhus: Aarhus University Press.

Siegel, Dina. 1995. "Political Absorption. The Case of New Immigrants from the CIS in Israel." *Ethnologia Europaea* 25, no. 1: 45–54.

Simmel, Georg. 1984. "Digressions sur l'Etranger." In *L'Ecole de Chicago*, ed. Y. Grafmeyer and I. Joseph. Paris: Aubier.

Sivački, Jovan et al. 1986. "Longitudinalno istraživanje morbiditeta populacije ravničarskog mjesta Gradina." In *Virovitički zbornik 1234–1984*. Virovitica: HAZU.

Sklevicky, Lydia. 1991. "Profesija etnolog—analiza pokazatelja statusa profesije." In *Simboli identiteta (studije, eseji, građa)*, ed. Dunja Rihtman-Auguštin. Zagreb: Hrvatsko etnološko društvo.

Smith, Anthony. D. 1986. *The Ethnic Origins of Nations*. London: Basil Blackwell.

Soysal, Yasemin Nuhoglu. 1996. "Changing Citizenship in Europe. Remarks on postnational membership and the national state." In *Citizenship, Nationality and Migration in Europe*, ed. David Cesarani and Mary Fulbrook. London-New York: Routledge.

Statut Zajednice izbjeglih i prognanih Hrvata iz Vojvodine. 1991.

Stolcke, Verena. 1996. "Europe: nouvelles frontières, nouvelles rhétoriques de l'exclusion." In *L'Europe entre cultures et nations*, ed. Daniel Fabre. Paris: Editions de la Maison des sciences de l'homme.

Supek-Zupan, Olga. 1976. "Od teorije do prakse i nazad: mogućnosti marksističkog shvaćanja u etnologiji." *Narodna umjetnost* 13: 57–76.

Tyler, Stephen A. 1986. "Post-Modern Ethnography: From Document of the Occult to Occult Document." In *Writing Culture. The Poetics and Politics of Ethnography*, ed. James Clifford and George E. Marcus. Berkeley: University of California Press.

Valášková, Nada, Zdenek Uherek and Stanislav Brouček. 1997. *Aliens or One's Own People. Czech Immigrants from the Ukraine in the Czech Republic*. Prague: Institute of Ethnology.

van den Berghe, Pierre L. 1996. "Stereotype." In *Dictionary of Race and Ethnic Relations*, ed. Ellis Cashmore. London-New York: Routledge-Kegan Paul.

Verdery, Katherine. 1996. "Ethnicity, nationalism, and state-making. *Ethnic groups and boundaries:* past and future." In *The Anthropology of Ethnicity. Beyond "Ethnic Groups and Boundaries,"* ed. Hans Vermeulen and Cora Govers. Amsterdam: Het Spinhuis.

Vermeulen, Hans, and Cora Govers. 1996. "Introduction." In *The Anthropology of Ethnicity. Beyond "Ethnic Groups and Boundaries,"* ed. Hans Vermeulen and Cora Govers. Amsterdam: Het Spinhuis.

Webster's New World Dictionary. 1984. ed. David B. Guralnik. New York: Simon and Schuster.

Wolf, Eric. 1994. "Perilous Ideas. Race, Culture, People." *Current Anthropology* 35, no. 1: 1–12.

Yelenevskaya, Maria N., and Larisa Fialkova. 2002. "When Time and Space Are No Longer the Same: Stories about Immigration." *Studia Mythologica Slavica* 5: 207–230.

———. 2003. "From 'Muteness' to Eloquence: Immigrants' Narratives about Languages." *Language Awareness* 12, no. 1: 30–48.

————. 2004. "My Poor Cousin, My Feared Enemy: The Image of Arabs in Personal Narratives of Former Soviets in Israel." *Folklore* 115: 77–98.

Zebec, Tvrtko. 1998. "Dance Events as Political Rituals for Expression of Identities in Croatia in the 1990s." In *Music, Politics, and War. Views from Croatia,* ed. Svanibor Pettan. Zagreb: Institute of Ethnology and Folklore Research.

————. 2005. *Krčki tanci. Plesno-etnološka studija.* Zagreb-Rijeka: Institut za etnologiju i folkloristiku-Adamić.

Zonabend, Françoise. 1994. "De l'objet et de sa restitution en anthropologie." *Gradhiva* 16: 3–14.

Žanić, Ivo. 1998. *Prevarena povijest. Guslarska estrada, kult hajduka i rat u Hrvatskoj i Bosni i Hercegovini 1990–1995. godine.* Zagreb: Durieux.

Index